W9-CPJ-680

8/28/84

OSWEGO

EMPIRE STATE HISTORICAL PUBLICATIONS SERIES 56

OSWEGO

FROM BUCKSKIN TO BUSTLES

by

CHARLES M. SNYDER

ILLUSTRATED

IRA J. FRIEDMAN, INC.
Port Washington, N. Y.

EMPIRE STATE HISTORICAL PUBLICATIONS SERIES No. 56

CONTENTS

LIST OF ILLUSTRATIONS

INTRODUCTION

Scarcely anyone would dispute the primacy of the city in the United States in the seventh decade of the twentieth century. The Supreme Court's formula of one man one vote removes a last stronghold of rural America as census figures confirm the continuing pull toward megalopolis. But a century ago, more than eighty per cent of the American people lived on farms or in villages under 8,000, and the supremacy of the country-side was unchallenged. Traditionally, the historian has expressed understandable pride in New York's 800,000, Philadelphia's half-million, Baltimore's 212,000 and Boston's 177,000, the nation's four largest urban concentrations in 1860. But he has frequently overlooked the regional cities at the crossroads and along the waterways which were emerging as nerve centers of the hinterland.[1]

It was at these centers that country dwellers did their trading, gathered to hear the great (and not so great) men discuss public issues, bought books and papers, and kept in touch with the world outside. It was to these sources that they looked for guidance on political, economic and social issues.

Seen in this light, the lesser cities take on significance, and collectively embrace many of the major trends and developments which shaped the nation.

Some cities have more to offer than others. Obviously, those which depended upon a single commodity, Virginia City, Nevada, with its mountain of silver, or Scranton, Pennsylvania, and its veins of anthracite, have meaning for the history of mining, and Lynn and Gloucester, Massachusetts, for shoes and the fisheries, respectively. But they lack the breadth inherent in others which have mirrored the gamut of transitions. Pittsburgh, for example, was a rendezvous for thousands of pioneers en route to the West, and supplied them with necessities as varied as travel guides, hardware, livestock and flatboats. It was a regional center of Presbyterianism ,a stronghold of conservatism in politics as well as the "Birmingham of America." Cincinnati, St. Louis, Louisville and Cleveland were financial, political and intellectual centers for extensive rural dependencies. Not without claims among such urban satellites, also, is Oswego, New York.

In its infancy it was an outpost on the frontier of the British Empire, a fur trading center, and a pawn in the struggle of the French and English for possession of the North American continent. In the Revolutionary War it was an avenue for British and Loyalist forays against the Mohawk Valley—Washington's war-time granary. It was also the scene of an abortive snow march against Fort Ontario and a vantage point for the elusive Silas Town, who is said to have spied upon the luckless Colonel St. Leger, while enroute to bloody Oriskany.

During the post-Revolutionary generation it was an outlet for Salina salt bound for Great Lakes' ports to the west. And with the harnessing of the Oswego River and the construction of the Oswego Canal, it was a port of entry for western grain, and a milling center. Prospects were so exhilarating in the lush decade before 1837 that it became one of the nation's boom towns, property values soaring momentarily to astronomical figures. The resulting "bust" was both spectacular and painful.

Meanwhile, in the back-country, land speculators had

their brief hour of hopes and frustrations while frontiersmen enlarged the clearings and erected homesteads. In two
generations the country-side was filled, and farmers' sons
and daughters were moving to town.

By mid-nineteenth century Oswego had its first railroad
and was the home of Kingsford Starch, soon to be the largest industry of its kind in the United States. It afforded
jobs and homes (such as they were) for hundreds of Irish
immigrants and sizeable numbers of French-Canadians,
English and Germans. In a generation Catholicism surpassed a well-entrenched Protestantism in the city.

Oswego's palmy days as a crossroad for western grain,
Salina salt and eastern manufactures extended through the
Civil War era. But at its close it faced a rapidly changing,
and often frustrating, world. Trunk line railroads, mon-
opolizing the grain trade, by-passed it, and western sources
of salt and lower tolls on the Erie Canal terminated the salt
trade. Canadian timber temporarily offset the loss of grain,
and a network of local railroads compensated for lower
canal tonnage. But in time Canadian forests along the
Ontario lake shore were denuded, and the McKinley Tariff
shut out barley, the last of the grains to seek the harbor,
and ruined the local malting industry. Syracuse, athwart
the New York Central Railroad, attracted potential manufacturers, and the starch trust caught Kingsford in its web.
Then, with empty docks bearing witness to commercial decline, the manufacture of wood products and boilers and
the expansion of railroad shops again shored up the region's
economy at the turn of the century.

Oswego's development in the nineteenth century was a
challenge to leadership; and while it can claim neither a
President nor Governor, several of its leaders merit the attention of historians and have continuing interest for the
readers.[2]

George Scriba's dream of great cities upon his half-million acre patent, and his rude awakening under a crushing
burden of debt, warrants consideration. Notable, also, were

such early families as the Bunners and McWhorters, whose substantial investments in land and family connections with the Hudson Valley elite set them apart from their neighbors. A generation later shippers and millers shared the pinnacle of the social pyramid, filled the principal offices of the county and city, and dominated the Board of Trade.

By mid-century the area's most conspicuous success story was Gerrit Smith, the largest owner of its real estate. Though he was technically a non-resident, his influence was pervasive, and while the pursuit of wealth was always close to his heart, he also saw Oswego as a social laboratory for the regeneration of society. In this spirit he plied it with a succession of "causes" as they hatched from his fertile mind. A partial list would include temperance; abolitionism and the underground railroad; nondenominationalism, his panacea for religious bigotry; and Canadian reciprocity, a step in the removal of fetters to personal liberty. And while his advice was sometimes scorned, it was never ignored.

Edward Austin Sheldon made Oswego the "fountainhead" of the Object Method, a philosophy of education which discarded stultifying rote for a concept of learning adapted to the natural growth of the mind. In the process he revolutionized teacher education. Oswego was also the home of Dr. Mary Walker, pioneer female physician, Civil War surgeon, Medal of Honor winner, and stormy petrel of the Woman's Rights Movement.

Other Oswegonians found opportunities in politics. Entering the political arena in the Era of Good Feelings, the area's first leaders, whatever their earlier persuasions, were affiliated with Jeffersonian Republicanism. But Jackson's war upon the Bank of the United States and political Anti-Masonry restored the two party system; and when Anti-Masonry waned, Whigs and Democrats battled for supremacy.

The former provided DeWitt Clinton Littlejohn with an entree into politics; and he went on to twelve terms in the legislature and five terms as Speaker of the Assembly, and to a career which led him from the Whig Party to the Republican; and from the latter to Liberal Republicanism and the Democratic Party; and finally to a reconciliation with Republicanism. Meanwhile, he was a vital cog in the smooth-running machine of Thurlow Weed.

Combining a boundless optimism with a record of achievement and an almost matchless oratory, he became a local oracle. Calls for Littlejohn became proverbial at public forums, whether the issue was widening the Oswego Canal, raising a regiment in the Civil War, building a railroad, raising money for fire-stricken Chicago, constructing a Niagara Ship Canal or saving Canadian reciprocity. For forty years neither friend nor foe took his position lightly.

Area politicians engaged in the Hunker-Barnburner schism of the Democratic Party and participated in the demise of the Whigs and rise of Republicanism. During the Civil War, in turn, Republicans split into Radicals and Moderates, and shortly thereafter into Stalwards and Half-Breeds. Democrats, meanwhile, saw Free Soilism strip away their rural vote, but managed to retain a tenuous control over the city by enrolling the Irish and cultivating the patronage from Albany. An internecine struggle between the Cleveland and Hill factions added to their woes as the nineteenth century closed.

Thus, whether the criterion is political, social or economic, the history of Oswego reaches out to touch much of the history of America; and, when combined with other regional studies, offers an intimate picture of America at the grass roots, a view which may remain clouded when the focus is diffused across the entire nation.

OSWEGO

1

WHERE EMPIRES CLASHED
IN THE WILDERNESS

The cataclysmic upheavals on the earth's surface in the Pre-Cambrian eras have left scarcely a mark upon the face of the land in the Oswego Valley. Geologists theorize that Lake Ontario once flowed westward and drained into the Gulf of Mexico, and that hills rose many feet above their present crests.

But all this was ephemeral. During the Pleistocene epoch the temperature dropped below freezing, and the cold endured year after year. Giant glaciers formed and edged southward, their enormous weight shoving and gouging out everything which was loose in their paths. Eventually the cold abated, and the ice melted, but the cycle may have been repeated. In any event, only the last can be read with any certainty.

Inching southward from Labrador the ice mass dished out Lake Ontario to a depth of several hundred feet, pushing countless tons of stone and gravel before it. Farther south it dredged the Finger Lakes and shaped the drumlins. For a time as the ice receded, giant rivers flowed through the Finger Lakes into the Delaware and Susquehanna watersheds. Later a torrent cut its way eastward to the Mohawk Valley leaving the Jamesville gorge as evidence. Still later a huge basin, which geologists have labeled Lake Iroquois, enveloped Lake Ontario and the present lake plain. Finally the ice pack in the St. Lawrence Valley gave way, and an avalanche of ice and water poured out of Lake Iroquois carrying everything but the solid rock before it. Pinnacles left behind became the Thousand Islands of today.

As the water receded, the Oswego River took shape, bearing the overflow from Oneida Lake on the east and the Finger Lakes from Onondaga to Canandaigua on the west into the much reduced Lake Ontario. From the confluence of the Oneida and Seneca rivers at Three Rivers Point it flowed northward, falling just over one hundred feet in 24 miles before reaching the lake. Along its banks remained a potpourri of gravelly hills, rock-strewn low lands and shallow swamps.

In time vegetation crept back to the region. Forests of pine, hemlock and spruce rose upon the sandy soils, and hardwoods including oak, maple, elm and hickory covered the more fertile ground.

It would be interesting to know just when man first peered through the forest to view the swirling waters of the river and the great lake at its mouth. It is assumed that they came from the west, descendants of Orientals who had trekked across the causeway connecting Alaska with Siberia. Refuse from their campsites reveals that they used crude projectile points chipped from flint, and barbless fishhooks from bone. Apparently they lingered longest at their fishing camps, where archaeologists can trace basic changes in their culture: barbed fishhooks and pottery suggesting their growing sophistication.

The Oswego River Valley seems never to have had more than a sparse population. Perhaps it was too exposed to invite occupation. But well used campsites have been uncovered at Jack's Reef on the lower Seneca and at the foot of Oneida Lake, where Denman's Island at Brewerton has been particularly fruitful. Generations of Indians used it as a burial ground, and the soil is a storehouse of artifacts. Smaller bands of these primitive people also lived or camped along the shore of Lake Neahtawanta at Fulton and at several points on the Oswego River.

About the time Columbus reached America this archaic culture was superseded by the Iroquois. Until recent years archaeologists assumed that the Iroquois found their way into central New York from the West and North, and that they earned their right to occupy it by their prowess. But this hypothesis is now doubted.[1] It is possible that Iroquois culture simply emerged here through diffusion and gradual change. In any event the Five Nations, joined in a defensive alliance, were well established prior to the explorations of Hudson and Champlain in 1609.

Like their predecessors, the Iroquois preferred the interior to the more exposed shores of Lake Ontario, but held rather well defined hunting rights in the latter. The Onondaga had a priority to the forests and waters of the Oswego Valley, and for a time gave their name to the river. The Oneida had precedence in the Oneida Lake country, including its coveted outlet.

The first European to enter the Oswego area was Samuel de Champlain. In October 1615, six years after his famous volley against the Mohawks at Lake Champlain, he joined Canadian Indians at Montreal on a raid into Iroquois territory south of Lake Ontario. Traveling by canoe they entered Lake Ontario and followed its eastern margin to its southern shore. Leaving their boats, they proceeded on foot, where Champlain observed "a very pleasing and fine country. . . an infinite quantity of game, a great many vines and fine trees and a vast number of chestnuts, the fruit of which was yet in the shell."[2] Historians have disputed the location of this march, but agree that he crossed the Oneida River near the outlet of Oneida Lake. From this point Champlain was too busy to pay much attention to the *flora* and *fauna*. He assaulted a fortified village, only to learn that his warriors preferred ambush to exposure to arrows, spears and stones from the enemy's stockade. Disillusioned, and grievously wounded, the hapless leader withdrew his forces and endured a painful return to Canada.[3]

Thirty-nine years later, a second Frenchman, Father Simon LeMoyne, S. J., left brief observations of his passage through the area. En route to a goodwill call upon the Onondagas, he followed much the same route as his predecessor. His gracious hosts ferried him across the Oneida River in a canoe, and a husky brave carried him on his shoulders the last few yards, not permitting his robe to touch the water.

He visited the salt springs on the margin of Onondaga Lake, and seems to have been the first to comment upon the source of Syracuse's early growth and prosperity. The Indians, he noted, would not drink from the springs, believing that they were fouled by an evil spirit.

After a round of formalities the Onondagas provided him with canoe transportation down the Oswego River. He thus became the first European to witness its grandeur and feel the surge of its power.[4]

Having discovered the feasibility of the river route, subsequent French missionaries to the Onondagas made it their principal pipeline to Montreal, and on one occasion used it to flee precipitously from an alleged plot against their lives.[5]

As the rivalry of the English and French for possession of the interior of the continent and the fur trade intensified, the Ontario shore and the Oswego river pathway became increasingly strategic. In 1683 two of the truly great personalities in the history of France in America, Count de Frontenac and Sieur de la Salle, collaborated to build Fort Frontenac near present-day Kingston, Ontario, giving the French a strong tactical position on the lake. But the Indians continued to carry their furs to Albany, and resolving to chastise them, the governor of New France, A.J.L.de La Barre, led an expedition against the Onondagas. En route, his army was smitten by a plague, and he was forced to disembark at the mouth of the Salmon River, twenty miles east of Oswego. Short of food and medical supplies, the harassed commander dubbed the river's mouth *La Famine*, or Hungry Bay. He eventually returned without striking a blow.

The English-French competition for the fur trade was intensified about 1720 when Albany traders shifted their operations to the mouth of the Oswego River. There seems to be no record of the innovators, but they were doubtless convinced that the exchange must follow the source of supply as it edged westward. It called for courage. They were isolated in a wilderness 150 miles from the nearest settlements; the French saw them as trespassers, and the attitude of the Iroquois remained undetermined. But once the vanguard had initiated the traffic, the less adventuresome had little choice but to join the caravan or lose their share of the trade. They joined.

In 1726 a French official sailing to Niagara counted 100 Oswego-bound canoes loaded with peltry. If he had stopped at the little settlement he might have also seen several hundred traders, most of them Dutchmen, and a few women and children. Oswego's convenience contributed to the growth of the traffic, but a French observation undoubtedly touched the heart of the matter. Indians preferred French brandy to English rum, but they did their trading at Choeguen (Oswego) where bracelets, superior to the French stock, cost two beavers rather than ten.[6]

Traders assembled their wares at Albany in the spring, and delivered them to Schenectady, where they were transferred to bateaux for the water route to Oswego. A portage at Little Falls and another at the Great Carrying Place at Rome delivered them to the Oneida watershed, and finally to the Oswego River. They unloaded at the west side of the harbor at Oswego where early maps identify a row of tiny sheds and a narrow street. Beyond it, a second row of crude huts provided shelter for the Red Men while they carried on their bargaining.

John Bartram, the noted botanist, who was at Oswego in 1743, observed that the settlement consisted of about seventy log houses, "of which one-half are in a row near the river, the other half opposite to them. Between were two streets divided by a row of posts in the midst, where each Indian has his house to lay his goods, and where any trader may traffic with him. This is surely an excellent regulation for preventing the traders from imposing on the Indians, a practice they have been formerly too much guilty of."[7]

Though the social side of the trading seems not to have approximated the rendezvous of the uninhibited mountain men and Indians in the Rocky Mountains a century later, it was done leisurely, often pelt by pelt, according to the mood of the seller. And through it all, the rum flowed freely. As the first comers departed others arrived to take their places. Meanwhile, bateau-men completed the round trip with their precious cargoes of beaver and lesser pelts. The trade was minutely regulated by law. But codes formulated in New York were apt to be dead letters in the wilderness. Occasional visitors reported that interlopers on the river above the harbor and behind headlands on the lake waved rum jugs at thirsty Indians as they paddled toward Oswego, hoping to entice them to trade on the black market. A fine of twenty pounds awaited the offenders, but there were few convictions.

Indians charged repeatedly that unscrupulous traders watered the rum. Illustrative of such complaints is an incident described in Governor Cadwallader Colden's papers. A party of Indians purchased a cask of rum prior to leaving for their distant haunts. Knowing that it was their custom not to touch the drink while on their journey, the trader had filled the cask with water. En route, however, they met friends on their way to Oswego, and agreed to sample the rum. The first swallow revealed the deception.[8]

An Iroquois once referred to the trading post as "a trap, which when you intend to catch a prey you lay a bait on it, and so when the creature comes to eat the bait he is catched." Continuing, he declared, "You have told us that the more beaver and skins come to Oswego the cheaper the goods; but we can't perceive that, for we must pay now 3 beaver skins for a woman's petticoat."[9]

Another shrewd bargainer likened the exchange to a silver mine for the white traders, and asked for cheaper powder and lead, and for higher wages when they were employed upon the houses.[10]

The New York Assembly responded to Indian criticisms by requiring that the rum be examined and tasted weekly. It was a popular duty, but uncovered few offenders.

The fur trade gathered momentum to 1744, then slowed down for the duration of King George's War. It revived after 1748 to reach its peak just prior to the outbreak of the French and Indian War in 1755. Figures are incomplete, but in a single year during this decade, arrivals from the west included:

160 Patowatome with 140 packs
 88 Twightwee with 27 packs
200 Missisauga with 175 packs
 80 Menominee with 70 packs
 72 Michilimakinac with 63 packs
256 Chippewa with 224 packs.[11]

Traders returned again at the war's close in 1763, and the exchange continued to the outbreak of the Revolution; but the pace was slowing down. Oswego, like Albany a half-century earlier, was too far removed from the source of supply.

The opening of the fur trade at Oswego at once made it a focal point in the English-French struggle. To safeguard it, Governor William Burnet in the spring of 1727 dispatched carpenters and masons to erect a fortification. They chose the west bank of the river where it flowed into the lake, and constructed a rectangular stone redoubt sixty by thirty feet. It was manned by a detachment of twenty soldiers.

Obviously pleased with his handiwork, Burnet boasted that the fortification would "embolden our Five Nations, and will not easily be taken without great cannon, the wall being four foot thick of large good stone." He discounted the possibility of an assault with cannon, believing that the rapids of the St. Lawrence would deter such an undertaking. His prophecy proved sound for twenty-nine years, but no more. The fortification was designated Fort Oswego, but it was also referred to as Fort Burnet, Chouaguen, Pepperell and George.

Incensed at the affront, Governor Beauharnois declared it to be a violation of the Treaty of Utrecht, and ordered that the garrison be withdrawn and the blockhouse leveled within a fortnight.[12] Burnet refused, charging that the French had already violated the treaty by rebuilding Fort Niagara. And so the little fort remained unmolested.

In 1741 the New York Assembly provided for a stone enclosure flanked by towers at the corners. But funds were insufficient to complete the project, and when the work stopped only the western exposure had been reinforced. Even this was inferior. Bartram noted that the stone was "curious for its softness."[13] He carved his name in it with his knife.

Deciding to take the offensive in 1755, after they had permitted the French to stake out the Ohio Valley, the English dispatched General Edward Braddock to America as Commander-in-Chief. At a Council of War at Alexandria, Virginia, in April, Braddock revealed plans to head an expedition against Fort Duquesne at the forks of the Ohio and named Governor William Shirley of Massachusetts to command a second army against Fort Niagara, using Oswego as his rendezvous. William Johnson was chosen to lead a third movement upon the French forts on Lake Champlain along the route to Montreal.

Shirley set up headquarters at Albany and began to organize his forces. He appealed to the provinces for militia, and called upon Johnson to assist in recruiting warriors among the Six Nations. He also engaged ship carpenters, masons, sawyers and sutlers, purchased supplies and munitions, constructed bateaux, and hired boatmen to operate them. Oswego came alive overnight.

As workmen arrived they were set to work upon the construction of a new fort on the east side of the harbor to be named Fort Ontario. Others were employed in building a shipyard, the first such English facility on the Great Lakes. Shortly thereafter they laid the keel for the first English ship on the lakes. It was launched on June 28, and appropriately named the *Ontario*. The *Alert*, the *George*, and the *Oswego* followed.

Fort Ontario rose slowly from its base, a low elevation commanding the lake and river. It was a star-shaped stockade encircled by a dry moat. Inside were barracks for three hundred officers and men.

As the fort took shape, Shirley was beset by delays. The Iroquois proved difficult to recruit, and he could scarcely move upon Niagara without their guidance in the wilderness. He blamed Johnson for his predicament, and charged him with diverting men and material for his own campaign. Their differences eventually became a struggle for preferment, splitting the American military establishment into rival camps. It led to the dismissal and recall of Shirley, and endless charges and countercharges which historians continue to evaluate two hundred years later.[14]

At last on September 26 Shirley was ready to embark for Niagara. He crowded about six hundred men aboard the *Ontario*, and added ordnance and artillery to boot. The *Oswego* was prepared to follow with provisions. An additional four hundred men stood by to shove off in assorted bateaux. But before the encumbered ships could set their sails, a gale blew in from the lake. The storm continued day after day, battering the little vessels at the docks. After thirteen days the harbor-tossed soldiers were permitted to disembark and the Indians to return to their villages.

Failure, however, did not dim Shirley's hopes for future operations at Oswego, and he projected movements against Frontenac, Presqu'isle, Detroit, and Michilimackinac as well as Niagara for the following year. In anticipation of such an ambitious program, he retained the troops and laborers at Oswego and set them to work to complete Fort Ontario, restore Fort Oswego, and construct a stockade (Fort George) on the ridge west of Fort Oswego.

But Shirley's enthusiasm did not rub off upon the soldiers, who saw only monotony and privation. Desertions multiplied despite confinements and lashings, and on September 3 five were sentenced to death. They were robed in white and led before a firing squad, but at the last moment Shirley intervened and pardoned three. The two others were shot down in view of the entire encampment.

Neither severity nor clemency, however, provided a solution. Shirley's son Jack, a military aide, documented the strife and confusion. "Our Battoemen desert us in large numbers as do the soldiers who are dissatisfy'd at our being obliged to allow 'em no more than half a pound of bread and no Rum. We lost 21 of the latter last night . . . . We have now only 8 days bread, pork and beef enough, but no rum or peas . . . . We have many ill of fluxes and some of the dry bellyache."[15]

Shirley's ill-conceived retort to malcontents, that if they were dissatisfied with the rations they might eat stones, plummeted morale to a new low.

In October Shirley departed for Albany leaving Lieutenant Colonel James F. Mercer in command. It was an agonizing responsibility. Winter was approaching, his appeals to Rome and Albany remained unanswered, the barracks were unfinished, and the men huddled in the bark huts of the traders and lay at night on the ground. Many were unfit for duty; work on the fortifications languished.[16]

The continuing deterioration of the health of the men may be followed in Mercer's correspondence. "This garrison begins to be sorely afflicted with an inveterate and obstinate scurvy, the consequences of salt and unwholesome food," he noted in February.[17] "Our sole reliance is on you [Commandant at Rome]; exert yourself to save this garrison."[18]

Help came at last on March 20 when a convoy made a hazardous crossing from Rome, after sliding their bateaux across the ice on Oneida Lake. They were welcomed with "great joy."[19] Muster records indicate that in one company of fifty, thirty-nine died during the harrowing winter, and that eight companies lost more than thirty each.

With the coming of spring gaps in the ranks were filled and laborers recruited from points as distant as the New England coast. Fort Ontario was completed and work resumed on Fort George. But little could be done for the older Fort Oswego. Two cannons which had provided firing power were dismounted. "Firing them on rejoicing days," it was reported, "shook the wall so much that several stones fell out of the wall, for which they were obliged to remove them."[20]

But Oswego now faced a new menace. The French and their Indian allies operating out of Fort Frontenac and temporary bases along the east shore of Lake Ontario infiltrated the wilderness on three sides. Carpenters venturing into the woods for timber failed to return. Some were never seen again; the bodies of others were found where they had been felled by bullets or scalping knives. Work parties had to be protected by armed patrols.

A sense of foreboding soon gripped the settlement; it was as though they were besieged by an invisible foe. On Sunday, August 8, a chaplain preached from the text, "What man is he that liveth that shall not see death? Shall he deliver his soul from the hand of the grave?"[21] The occasion for this doleful sermon was the execution of two deserters: one before his regiment at Fort Ontario; the other, at Fort Oswego.

A momentary reprieve was the gallant action of Lieutenant Colonel John Bradstreet. After successfully delivering a convoy from Schenectady to Oswego he had scarcely entered the river on his return trip when he was ambushed by a party of French and Indians. He assembled his armed guard on a tiny island in his path (later named Battle Island) and pinned the French on the east bank while his bateau-men sought protection on the west side. After advancing several miles he fought off a second attack before proceeding down the Mohawk.

Bradstreet's escape did not disrupt the French encirclement. In fact, as he moved through the wilderness the

Marques de Montcalm, dynamic commander of the armies of New France, ferried an army southward along the eastern margin of the lake, and, before his movements were detected, disembarked just east of Oswego harbor.

A century later the celebrated proponent of naval expansion, Captain Alfred Mahan, cited the French superiority on the lake as evidence of the indispensability of sea power in war.[22]

When Mercer discovered his plight he could do little more than distribute men and arms to the three forts and await the assault. He had some 1100 troops at his disposal, also 120 seamen and 130 carpenters and sawyers. And, rather surprisingly at this zero hour, eighty women mingled with the throng gathering at Fort Oswego. Some were wives or servants, but most remain unidentified, and can only be labeled as camp-followers.

On August 11 and 12 the French dragged their cannon forward to the very shadow of Fort Ontario. The gravity of the situation was obvious; the stockade was vulnerable to cannon fire, and might become a prison rather than a defense.

Across the river at Fort Oswego, Mercer dug entrenchments on the river frontage of the post, and piled up fascines for batteries. Up on the hill the pigs were removed to Fort George (it had been serving as a pen) and earth was thrown up to strengthen the palisades.

On August 13, the third day of the siege, Mercer evacuated Fort Ontario and consolidated his forces on the west side of the river. With his ships now exposed to the French cannon, and no friendly haven to receive those fitted to sail, he bowed to the gloomy advice of his naval officer to hold the vessels in the harbor and to point their guns "into their holds to be ready to sink them and prevent their falling into the enemy's hands."[23]

By nightfall the French occupied Fort Ontario and the bluff commanding the river beyond, and at daylight on the 14th they unloosed a barrage upon Fort Oswego. The

English returned shot for shot for several hours. But Mercer's death from a bursting mortar, the infiltration of the woods adjacent to the fort by French and Indians, rendering Fort George untenable, and the plight of hundreds unable to enter the overcrowded blockhouse undermined the morale of the defenders.

In a hastily summoned council of war it was agreed that further resistance was hopeless. And thus before noon the battle was lost and the fleur-de-lis flew from the flag staff.

While the victors celebrated, many of the 1600 prisoners assuaged their despondency with rum. Less fortunate were the sober ones, who despaired of their lives through the long hours of the debauchery. "Our drunken soldiers," a witness recalled, "continued their noise and the Indians their struggles [to break in] and yelling [for scalps] until the operations of the liquor, together with the strong exercions [sic], began to dispose both parties to sleep, which about 12 o'clock took place, and to our great joy all was quiet."[24]

The next day the French leveled the forts. After the English officers had signed a parole not to serve again until exchanged by cartel, they were permitted to embark for Montreal in bateaux without guard. Other prisoners followed in the English ships which, after so many delays, at last plied the waters of the lake. Most of the personnel, including seamen and carpenters, were taken to France and incarcerated in prison camps there. One of the ship carpenters, for example, was accommodated in a donjon at Dinan; though he lived to return to his home in Newburyport, Massachusetts.[25]

On August 21, the demolition completed, Montcalm took his departure. At the river's mouth just beyond the smoking ruins Abbe Francois Picquet, Apostolic of Canada, erected a cross with the inscription, *"In hoc signo vincunt,"* and in the words of Francis Parkman, the nineteenth century historian of the French and English struggle, "Oswego reverted for a time to the bears, foxes, and wolves."[26]

News of Oswego's fall created a sensation in Albany and

London. In England men spoke of the loss of Oswego as being more serious than the fall of Port Mahon in the Minorcas, which had recently startled the nation. Officials left no stone unturned in their search for an explanation and a scapegoat, and even today historians disagree as they seek to fix the blame.[27]

If there was gloom in England and her colonies, there was joy on the St. Lawrence River and in France. Montcalm was the hero of the hour. Western Indians who had planned to meet General Shirley at Oswego, now turned to Montreal to set eyes on Montcalm. In the words of one of them, "We wanted to see this famous man who tramples the English under his feet. But you are a little man, my father. It is when we look into your eyes that we see the greatness of the pine tree and the fire of the eagle."[28]

King Louis XV broadcast his pleasure to the world by striking a commemorative medal upon which he recorded four French victories: Wesel in Germany, Port Mahon, St. Davids in India, and Oswego. The obverse face of the medal displays a profile of the be-wigged sovereign and the less than modest inscription: "Louis XV Ruler of the World 1758."[29] The reverse bears engravings to identify the four triumphs. Ironically, by the time Louis' silversmiths had executed their assignment, William Pitt had been called to the English Prime Ministry, and under his guidance the tide of the war was turning.

For two years, however, the ruined fortress was scarcely more than a memory. Even the river was sometimes called Onondaga. But it found its way back on the map in 1758 with an assist from Colonel Bradstreet.

For his efficiency in carrying supplies from Schenectady to Oswego, a role hardly calculated to furnish opportunities for heroics, Bradstreet had been appointed Aide-de-Camp to Lord Loudoun, who had replaced Shirley as the Commander-in-Chief in North America, and put in charge of quartermaster duties. But he preferred leadership on the battle field, and as early as December of 1757 volunteered to lead an expedition against Fort Frontenac, even offering to advance funds to get it underway.

Among the troops which he gathered at the newly constructed Fort Stanwix at Rome on August 11 were 1100 New York militiamen, companies from Massachusetts, New Jersey and Rhode Island, and a small contingent of British Regulars. There were also 270 bateau-men, and just forty-two Indians. The latter were Onondagas, led by Chief Red Head. No other Indians could be persuaded to join up, so low had the prestige of British arms fallen.

The expedition shoved off at Oswego on August 22 in a fleet of 123 bateaux and 95 whaleboats, and disembarked near Frontenac two days later. Failing to take the French garrison by surprise, Bradstreet mounted several cannon at an old breastwork south of the fort and opened fire at sunset; and then, while drawing the French to this position, quietly dragged the remaining cannon to a point just west of the fort. The next morning he had the defenders in a cross fire, and before the dew was dry he gained the victory.

In just four weeks Bradstreet was back at Fort Stanwix, a remarkable achievement. Here he paused to divide the spoils. His inventory tells a good deal about the goods used by the French to lure furs from the Indian. It included: 178 gold and silver laced hats, 400 pieces of ribbon, 445 pieces of gartering, 1978 woolen caps, 3690 men's shirts, 1064 women's and children's gowns and frocks, 270 bags of vermillion and 205 brass kettles. Bradstreet estimated that it was only a fourth of the quantity they had destroyed.[30]

The fall of Fort Frontenac was damaging to French defenses in the interior of America, and they soon abandoned Fort Duquesne at the forks of the Ohio. Of even greater consequence was its boost to English morale. General James Wolfe, to be immortalized for his stirring victory over Montcalm at Quebec a year later, spoke of Bradstreet as "an extraordinary man for expeditions . . . . Frontenac is a great stroke. An offensive, daring kind of war will awe the Indians and ruin the French."[31] Bradstreet had earned a promotion.

Oswego again was abandoned, but it sprang back to life the following year, when it became the rendezvous center for another assault upon the French line of fortifications. Three years after failing to reduce Fort Niagara, the English were prepared to try again.

In June of 1759 General Jeffrey Amherst, now Commander of British forces in America, dispatched an army of three thousand to Oswego, coordinating the movement with an even larger expedition against Quebec under General Wolfe. He named Brigadier General John Prideaux to lead the Niagara campaign, and appointed Sir William Johnson as his deputy.

Though the fabulous "Baron of the Mohawks" seems to have been Oswego's largest fur merchant, he had not visited the region personally until this time. Now his impressive arrival at the head of a thousand braves was a testimonial to his personal magnetism and Bradstreet's victory at Frontenac.

They paused at Oswego only to repack their gear before setting out upon the lake in bateaux and whaleboats. The water remained calm and they disembarked near Niagara on the fourth day. By a stroke of good fortune they had avoided French ships on the lake. At the investment of the fort Prideaux was killed, and Johnson assumed the command. He fought off a relief party en route to the fort from the west, and secured the surrender of the post.

Fearful that the French might occupy Oswego and nullify the entire campaign in a single counterstroke, Colonel Frederick Haldimand had remained behind with a force of 1000. Caution was justified. Chevalier de la Corne and Abbe Picquet swept across the lake and assaulted the camp, protected only by an improvised wall of pork and flour barrels. The attack might have been overpowering, since many of the defenders were in the woods cutting poles for a stockade. But, according to one version of the engagement, Picquet insisted upon first exhorting the French troops and giving them absolution.[32] The delay permitted the English to reach their arms and take positions behind the barrels. Whether the delay was decisive cannot be confirmed, but Haldimand eventually fought off the attack and the Niagara life line was not severed.

Johnson returned to Oswego early in August eager to carry the war to the St. Lawrence, but before he could formulate plans General Thomas Gage arrived as Prideaux's successor. The latter was more concerned with the rebuilding of Fort Ontario and the restoration of English power on the lake than in new campaigns, and the dispirited Johnson and his Indian guests returned to their firesides.

Gage accepted a pentagon plan for the new Fort Ontario, and set his carpenters to work, pausing only long enough to build temporary quarters for the garrison and the labor force. The construction languished through the winter, but quickened in the spring.

Meanwhile, Wolfe's triumph over Montcalm at Quebec in September of 1759 left only Montreal in the way of a complete victory. By the spring of 1760 Amherst planned the *coup de grace* in the form of a three-pronged assault: from Quebec by the St. Lawrence River; from Lake Champlain and the Richelieu River; and from Oswego and the upper St. Lawrence River. He directed the Oswego movement in person, and marshaled four thousand British Regulars and six thousand colonials. En route they were joined by Sir William Johnson with 1300 Iroquois confederates, and for a few weeks Oswego held what may have been the largest troop concentration assembled in America to that time.

During the rendezvous the last post was set in the stockade of Fort Ontario, and ship carpenters worked overtime. The drama attending the build-up is suggested by the launching of the sloop *Onondaga,* a name chosen to please Indian allies. A flag with an Onondaga warrior painted upon it was hoisted, a short address was delivered by General Amherst and translated for the Indians by Johnson, and rum was served to all. "The Indians were greatly delighted with the whole proceedings and promised to be fast friends."[33]

On August 10 the expedition moved out upon the lake with the *Onondaga* in the lead, and flying both the English and Indian ensigns. The row-galleys, whaleboats, bateaux and Indian canoes coasted behind. They reached the Thousand Islands without incident, but faced disaster in the rapids downstream. Amherst recorded that "the water boiled and churned in thousands of eddies and cross currents."[34] Entering the rushing water, the boats were swept pell-mell between the rocks, some capsizing and casting their occupants into the maelstrom. After a harrowing three hours the main body descended the rapids but not without loss of eighty-four lives and tons of gear.

The three expeditions converged according to plan, and on September 8, 1760, all of Canada fell into British hands.

Meanwhile, the second Fort Ontario was finished and occupied, and as peace returned to the wilderness, fur traders found their way back to their old haunts on the west bank of the Oswego River.

Undoubtedly the most colorful event during the decade which followed was the appearance of the renowned Ottawa Chieftain, Pontiac. Three years after crushing his "conspiracy" colonial diplomats persuaded him to come from the Ohio country to a conference at Oswego.

Preparations for the meeting were worthy of the Chief's fame. The conferees assembled on July 23, 1766 and were seated comfortably in the open air, shaded by a bower of greens. After the peace pipe had moved around the circle, Sir William Johnson in his finest oratory, "praised, chided, flattered, and cajoled. He told of their bad behavior, their promises, and of all the good they could hope to gain from their friendship with the English. He promised to be their friend and father if they were good children. He warned them against the French and the 'bad birds' who came with false stories to lead you astray."[35] During the proceedings the liquor flowed freely; the fragment of Johnson's bill to the Crown which survived the State Capitol fire of 1911 adds up to an astonishing sum for liquid refreshments. The conference ended on a note of friendship, and with his canoes well stocked with gifts, Pontiac took his departure on July 31.

One additional item provides a glimpse of the isolated outpost during these years. Annie MacVicar, who came to the settlement at the age of six, recalled fifty years later in her *Memoirs of an American Lady* that she and her mother were the "first females above the very lowest ranks who had ever penetrated so far into this remote wilderness." She also remembered a house on wheels, in which the Commandant, Major Duncan, moved about the base in comfort; she was reminded too of an active social life planned by Duncan to keep morale high during the long "Siberian like" winter. She found the summer particularly pleasant. The commandant's extensive gardens supplied tasty vegetables which brightened the plain fare. He also had a pen for poultry, hogs, and cattle. Unfortunately, little Annie moved back to the Hudson Valley the next year and the obscurity of the tiny settlement was ended only with the initial stirring of the American Revolution.

2

WAR AND PEACE AT THE MOUTH OF THE OSWEGO RIVER

It would not be inaccurate to say that the Revolutionary War on the Lake Ontario frontier began and ended at the mouth of the Oswego River. The conflict dates from an Indian council more than a year before the Declaration of Independence; it ended in an abortive winter march a few weeks after the drafting of the preliminary treaty of peace.

After Massachusetts patriots had precipitated the "shot heard round the world" at Concord bridge in April of 1775, it seemed inevitable that the clash of arms would resound throughout the Colonies, and Rebels and Tories—or to use designations preferred by Americans a century later, Patriots and Loyalists—began to take their places for the impending conflict. Oswego at once took on significance for Loyalists of the Mohawk Valley seeking to escape from their disaffected neighbors. Colonel Guy Johnson, nephew of Sir William, John Butler, a steward of the Johnsons, and Joseph Brant, the Mohawk Chieftain, reached Oswego in May, where they summoned the Iroquois.

Exhorting the hundreds who responded Johnson and Brant stressed the wealth of the English Sovereign and the contrasting poverty of the Americans, the security of the Indian under the protective care of the King, and the menace of the land-hungry colonials. It is interesting to speculate whether Sir William would have been a participant had he lived; and what difference his presence might have made.

Again, as in times past, the Indians preferred neutrality, but they were caught in a vise. Johnson obtained provisional support from all except the Oneidas and Tuscaroras, who had come under the influence of Samuel Kirkland, the Patriot missionary to the Oneidas. After a final distribution of gifts, including copper kettles said to have been in use a half-century later among the Senecas, the council disbanded, and most of the Indians returned to their villages. The Mohawks, however, followed Johnson and Brant to Montreal. Having committed themselves, they could scarcely risk reprisals in the Valley.

Johnson's departure appears to have left the fort unattended. With the British lifeline now joined to Montreal, Carleton Island in the St. Lawrence River, and Fort Niagara, Oswego was considered of little consequence. Nor did it figure in the strategy of the Patriots. Lacking means to challenge British supremacy on Lake Ontario, they were satisfied to occupy Fort Stanwix at the gateway to the Mohawk Valley. However, it occasionally emerged from the shadows to assume significance during the shifting currents of the war. Such was the case in the ill-fated British offensive of 1777.

Having discovered that New England was a hotbed of rebellion, British strategists decided to sever it from the more luke-warm Middle Atlantic and Southern Colonies along the Hudson River-Lake Champlain axis. To carry out the plan they formulated a three-pronged movement: the first to move southward from Montreal and Lake Champlain; the second to push up the Hudson Valley from New York; and the third to invest the Mohawk Valley from Oswego. The three were expected to converge near Albany.

Though the Oswego prong was to be the smallest, it was designed to strike at the heart of New York's rebeldom, and prevent Mohawk militiamen from joining Hudson Valley rebels in a bid to blunt the invasions from north and south.

Colonel Barry St. Leger assembled the first contingent of his army at Lachine on the St. Lawrence, and marched to Carleton Island, where ship carpenters had constructed bateaux for the expedition. Among the troops were several companies of English infantry, Hessian Chasseurs, Sir John Johnson's Royal Greens, made up of American Loyalists, Canadian provincial rangers, and several hundred Mississagues Indians from Canada—truly an international military body. The fleet of bateaux sailed up the lake, keeping within reach of the eastern shore. For a time St. Leger speculated on the possibility of making a surprise raid against Ft. Stanwix by marching overland from Mexico Point, on the southeastern margin of the lake; but he reconsidered and moved on to Oswego.

A persistent tradition in the Mexico area relates that Silas Town, a spy on the staff of General Washington, who had been assigned to watch St. Leger's movements, gazed out from the shore as the bateaux came in sight. When he noted that a landing was in process he hid in the bushes, where he witnessed a council of war. Learning of St. Leger's plans to continue to Oswego, and take the waterway to Fort Stanwix, he hastened through the wilderness and delivered the intelligence. Forewarned, the garrison was prepared for the assault.

No documentary evidence has been discovered to corroborate the tale, but it is known that a Silas Town lived in Mexico Point a quarter-century later, that he told the story, and was buried on the point of land where he claimed that he had watched and listened. It finally got into print as it came from the lips of elderly residents after the lapse of another sixty years.[1] In 1871 local residents raised funds to inscribe Town's achievement in stone, and erected an obelisk over his grave. On the side facing the lake it reads: "To the Memory of Silas Town, an Officer Under Washington, Died 1806." The site is appropriately, if not accurately, termed "Spy Island."

Awaiting St. Leger at Oswego were Daniel Claus, son-in-law of Sir William Johnson, Joseph Brant and Colonel John Butler with more than five hundred Iroquois warriors.

The expedition moved up the Oswego River on July 26 and paused at Three Rivers Point to permit Claus and Brant to confer with additional Indians who had gathered there. Most rejected their blandishments. Nevertheless, the recruits increased the Indians to eight hundred, and St. Leger's total force to almost two thousand.

St. Leger placed Fort Stanwix under siege on August 3, but lacking artillery he could not reduce it; and unwilling to endure a delay, he pushed ahead, leaving the fort in his rear. It proved to be a costly gamble.

Learning of the approach of the Mohawk Valley militia under General Nicholas Herkimer, St. Leger set an ambush along the narrow wilderness trail. The battle of Oriskany which followed on August 6 was one of the bloodiest of the war. It might have ended in a victory for St. Leger, but at a critical moment the garrison at Fort Stanwix sallied forth and destroyed the British baggage train. Unable to advance without it, St. Leger turned back, and brought his bedraggled force to Oswego. Ironically, several hundred of his soldiers were shuttled to General Burgoyne at Saratoga in time to become prisoners of war at his surrender. Meanwhile, the Indians disbanded, and quiet returned to the Oswego frontier.

A year later Colonel Peter Gansevoort at Fort Stanwix sent Lieutenant Thomas McClellan with a small detachment to Oswego to destroy the fort, hoping to discourage its use for raids into the Valley. They found only a woman with several small children and a fourteen year old boy at the stockade. Removing them to a shelter outside the compound, McClellan applied the torch and withdrew. The fate of the woman, her children and the teen-age boy remains undetermined.

The Tory and Indian raids of 1778 leading to massacres in the Wyoming Valley of Pennsylvania and Cherry Valley, New York, were based at Niagara, not Oswego, and the retaliatory expedition of General Sullivan did not touch Oswego. But in 1780 Sir John Johnson and Colonel

John Butler made Oswego their rendezvous for a raid upon
the Mohawk Valley. At the head of about five hundred
troops on October 1, they moved up the Oswego River
to Onondaga Lake, proceeded overland to Schoharie Creek,
and thence to the Mohawk and up that Valley, burning
homes and barns, mills, and granaries. Circling back to
their boats on Onondaga Lake they returned to Oswego four
weeks after their departure. Tory losses were light, but along
their path lay the smoking ruins of thirteen grist mills, un-
counted sawmills, one thousand houses and barns, and six
hundred thousand bushels of grain. Generations of Mohawk
Valley residents looked upon Tories as devils incarnate.

A year later Major John Ross assembled a similar
raiding party at Oswego. They skirted the southern fringe of
the Mohawk Valley until they reached Duanesburgh near
Schenectady. They then wheeled back through Johnstown,
burning and pillaging as they went. But finding Colonel
Marinus Willett, Commander of the militia of the Valley, in
pursuit, Ross abandoned the Oswego route to seek refuge in
a forced march northward to Carleton Island, only pausing
at West Canada Creek to skirmish with his pursuers. Later,
advancing Patriots discovered the body of Walter Butler,
the notorious "renegade," where he had fallen. Few victories afforded as much satisfaction to the long-suffering
frontiersmen.

In the spring of 1782 the British reoccupied Oswego, lest
it be lost by default. They restored the fort, and while it was
not as imposing as its predecessors, it housed a small garrison, and re-emphasized its strategic position as a base for
raids against the Valley.

The sounds of the hammer and saw were not interrupted
by military activities in 1782, but its restoration was not lost
on General Washington, who resolved to destroy it by a
sneak attack under Colonel Willett.

During the winter lull at Newburgh, Washington participated in a surprising amount of the minutiae including
the procuring of woolen hose and vests, woolen caps, mit-

tens, Indian moccasins, and snow shoes. He advised that the marchers carry a few tools, "axes, saws, augers and a gouge," to fashion ladders, which would be needed to scale the wall, rather than be burdened with them en route. He discussed the procurement of horses and sleighs and the need for "picked men of tried fidelity," and guides who would be trustworthy.[2] One of his last bits of advice to Willett from Newburgh was an admonition to abandon the assault if the attackers were discovered prematurely.

> From having recourse to the almanack, I am led to wish that the night for the attack may not be delayed beyond the 12th [of February]; as I find the setting of the moon (even at that time) approaches so near daylight that the intervening space is short and consequently must be very critical . . . Let me caution you, therefore, against being too exact in your [allowance] of time for your last movement—reflect that you can always waste time, but never recover it. Halts, or snow marching will accomplish the first; but nothing can effect the latter. Consequently in such an enterprise as yours, want of time will be a certain defeat.[3]

On the morning of February 8, 1783, Willett marched out of Fort Herkimer with five hundred heavily clad New York and Rhode Island militia, their provisions, blankets and other gear piled on 120 sleighs. After four days and three nights on the trail they reached Oneida Lake, and fearful lest they be discovered, Willett ordered a march through the night across the length of the lake. By morning they were at the foot of the lake after a tramp of thirty miles.

They rested here briefly to unload the sleighs and serve rations, but then moved forward, walking on the ice of the Oneida and Oswego rivers. By mid-afternoon they were at the falls of the Oswego where they halted to construct scaling ladders.

After dark they resumed their weary march; and about eleven o'clock, fearing discovery if they remained on the river, they entered the woods on the east bank, guided by three Oneida Indians. About two a.m. they halted, but instead of the fort there was only the Stygian forest. They advanced again only to stumble into a thicket where the snow was deep and walking exceedingly difficult.

As the day dawned they climbed a ridge, later known as Oak Hill, and from this elevation looked down upon the elusive post. Smoke curled from its chimneys.

Their situation requires little elaboration; unable to carry out the surprise attack and unable to endure another day and night in the woods, they could only turn their backs to the fort and resume the long hike. Exhausted and frost-bitten—they had been forty-eight hours without sleep—their plight was indeed pitiful. As Willett explained to Governor Clinton:

> In the situation we were then in, our hope gave way to despondency, and the spirits of the troops which had hitherto been supported by the pleasing prospect of success, now sunk under the severity of their fatigue . . . In this mortified and cruelly buffeted situation, we had nothing further to do but return, which considering the amazing fatigued state of the troops and that a number of them were badly frosted, was performed in as good order as could be expected. One of the Rhode Island regiment and one of our state soldiers by leaving their ranks and lying down was killed by the cold.[4]

In the words of Willet's son "Such was the gloomy end of an enterprise which at ten o'clock at night, presented so fair a prospect of success."[5]

They staggered to their sleighs at the foot of Oneida Lake, and finally reached the warmth of Fort Stanwix, where 130 required hospitalization. And though the harrowing experience needed no exaggeration, the story of their suffering grew with the telling. An application for a pension some years later noted that "many perished miserably and were left in the snow where they fell."[6] And an early Oswego newspaper multiplied the personnel to fifteen hundred and the number frozen to fifty.[7]

Incidentally, Washington accepted the failure philosophically. In his report to Congress he expressed gratitude to the officers and soldiers for their "spirit, activity and patience. . . . Nothing that depended upon Col. Willett to give efficacy to it was wanting."[8]

As indicated above, Willett's march was the closing chapter of the war in the Lake Ontario area. A short time before he and his men undertook their desperate mission, English and American diplomats agreed to a truce to end hostilities, and in April the word reached the Mohawk country.

New York officials at once determined to relay the news to Major Ross at Fort Ontario, lest he should launch additional forays upon the Valley. They selected as message-bearer Captain Alexander Thompson, a veteran of Willett's march, who had recuperated from frost bite.

Details of his journey are supplied by Jeptha Simms, a none-too-accurate historian of the New York frontier. According to his version of the expedition, Thompson set out from Fort Herkimer on April 19 under a flag of truce with an Indian guide, a flag-man and a musketeer. Proceeding to Fort Stanwix and across the portage to Oneida Lake, they reached their destination without incident. At Oswego, Ross took the precaution of having Thompson blindfolded before allowing him to enter the fortification. But he accepted the dispatch as authentic, and permitted him to return as he came, after repeating the ritual of the blind-folding.[9] Thus the last expedition to Oswego was a mission of peace.

With the boundary line between Canada and the United States drawn through the center of Lake Ontario, Oswego was now on American soil. Yet the British garrison remained in the little fort month after month, and year after year. It would require the pressure of the pioneer and Jay's Treaty to remove the last Redcoat.

* * * * *

The war's close brought little immediate change at the mouth of the Oswego River. For the moment it was too remote to feel the stir of the restless frontiersman; and the British at Fort Ontario seemed determined to turn back the clock, and ignore the terms of the treaty of peace. A garrison of about thirty troops not only guarded Fort Ontario but stopped travelers who sought to pass, regulated trade, and collected customs.

With Americans resentful, and the British anxious to safeguard their lucrative fur trade and obtain justice for Loyalists, friction was inevitable. Unlike the absolute monarch, who could do no wrong, Captain Schoedde, the commandant, could do nothing right. The vigorous prosecution of his duties invited retaliation from his American neighbors, and their neglect brought down the wrath of English officialdom in Canada.

His attempts to handle desertion bear out this anomaly. Learning that several deserters were harbored at Fulton eleven miles up the river, he dispatched an armed patrol under the command of Ensign Holland to apprehend them. But when Holland and his men entered a house they were surrounded and disarmed by a gang of frontiersmen. According to Schoedde's report, "Holland was insulted with gross language, and a subscription of three dollars was made and offered to his men in his presence if they would desert."[10]

Apparently the offer was refused, but after Holland and his men were released they were warned that if they returned on a similar mission they would be arraigned and taken downstate for trial. Schoedde estimated that as many as eighteen to twenty Americans had participated in the fracas.

A short time later the advantage seems to have been reversed. The story is told by descendants of John Van Buren, who moved to Fulton in February of 1796, that when British soldiers at Van Valkenburgh's tavern cheered for King George, John responded with three cheers for President Washington; and for his patriotism was "obliged to take to his horse."[11]

Schoedde insisted that he had been civil to the Americans in the area, "but you can hardly form any judgment what kind of people they are in general. They are the scum of the states." His views disagree with local traditions regarding the character of the pioneers. In Churchill's *Landmarks of Oswego County,* Daniel Masters was recorded as being the first permanent resident of the Town of Volney, a blacksmith who built the first log cabin at the Upper Falls, and fashioned spearheads for fishermen for a silver dollar each.[12] He was also identified as a constable and pathmaster. Schoedde's evaluation was a cryptic, "Pilot to all the smugglers; a violent man." He referred to one Haskill as an "infamous character, who tried to get [his] men to desert and harbored those who did." [13] Haskill receives no mention from local historians.

Of particular interest in this connection is "Major" Lawrence Van Valkenburgh, mentioned elsewhere as a founder of Fulton. Somehow, Van Valkenburgh managed to hold the respect of both Schoedde and his American neighbors. Schoedde took him and his family into the fort during the winter of 1794-1795, where they were undoubtedly more comfortable than in their cabin in Fulton, and referred to him as the "only decent man among them." He also claimed that "he is entirely in my interest. He has on different occasions used persuasion with deserters to return, hitherto ineffectually; and now I will try whether pecuniary advantage will persuade him greater exertions."[14]

There is no report that Van Valkenburg accepted British money for his services, but had Schoedde's letter fallen into American hands, his life might have been jeopardized.

Incidentally Van Valkenburgh's residence in the fort ended suddenly and dramatically in the spring. According to a local tradition preserved in Johnson's *History of Oswego County,* a Lieutenant Hamilton and Schoedde's youthful wife became lovers during Schoedde's absence on a hunting trip. Learning of it he "came back raving with fury. Lt. Hamilton was secreted to save his life, while the other officers and soldiers restrained and guarded the captain. At night Lt. Hamilton came and tapped at Major Van Valkenburgh's window begging him to protect Mrs. Schoedde from her husband's wrath. He then embarked in an open boat and made his way to Kingston, Canada."[15] According to the same source, the affair ended tragically. Mrs. Schoedde deserted her husband, and found a passage to Schenectady. Captain Schoedde followed Hamilton to Montreal, where they fought a duel. Both were wounded, Hamilton fatally.

But a wife's infidelity and the desertion of soldiers were not the only problems at the little citadel. When surveyors of the Scriba patent approached the fort to run their survey at the mouth of the river, they were halted and ordered to leave. They improvised their lines as well as they could from a safe distance in the woods. Agents of the French Castorland Company, who sought permission to pass the fort en route to their lands east of the lake, were forced to leave a hostage to guarantee their good behavior.

British officials also stopped General Moses Cleveland with some twenty surveyors en route to the Western Reserve for the Connecticut Land Company. Pretending that they accepted the commandant's order to turn back, they withdrew, but that night they paddled past the fort and into the lake before the surprised garrison could stop them.

If a justification for the British behavior were needed, it might be noted that the fort was virtually defenseless; and the commandant could never be sure that an innocent-appearing party of travelers was not the advance guard for an armed force. The situation seemed particularly perilous after General Wayne's victory over the Indians at Fallen Timbers in Ohio, when there were repeated rumors of Yankee aggression.

The cat-and-mouse attitude of the British backfired at least once. When a report spread on the frontier that the notorious Loyalist, Guy Johnson, had purchased an order of supplies at Albany and planned to transport them to Upper Canada by way of the Mohawk-Oswego watercourse, a band of frontiersmen (Schoedde called them Banditti), anxious to injure their old foe, gathered at Three Rivers Point, seized the cargo, and disappeared into the forest. Tempers flared on both sides of the border, but public opinion frowned on the illegal act, and the local constabulary helped to round up the loot.

Actually more travelers were permitted to go on their way at Fort Ontario than were detained. British records indicate that 1,064 settlers traveling to new homes in Canada passed through Oswego between April 15, 1795 and October 15, 1795.[16] But the exaction of tariff payments by a foreign government on American soil remained an irritant.

Jay's Treaty at last provided for the delivery of the fort to the United States; and while its critics back east might castigate it for its omissions, Oswego frontiersmen gave it their unqualified blessing.

Arrangements for the transfer were entrusted to Captain James Bruff who set out from Schenectady on June 23, 1796, with an entourage of one hundred troops and a few civilians, including a local Congressman, Henry Glen, and his son. They reached Oswego falls on July 11, and camped there awaiting "T" day on July 15.

According to Glen's diary, the British, having put everything in order, departed for Kingston on the afternoon of the 14th. He counted four women and thirty men on the boats as they embarked; the latter being members of the First Battalion of the Sixtieth (or Royal American) Regiment of Foot, commanded by Captain Clark.

The American force descended the river the following morning and made preparations for the formal occupation of the post. When the last detail had been completed the colors of the United States were hoisted, and the "wind being high made the colors show well . . . There were fifteen guns fired and then three cheers given by all in the garrison. The number inside I compute, officers, soldiers, battoemen and spectators, about 130 persons. After the cheers were given, I stepped up with my son, Mr. Clench followed, and gave Capt. Bruff and other officers joy on the occasion."[17]

Glen's diary is in conflict with local tradition, which assumes that the British troops remained at the fort until the transfer on the 15th.

In the spirit of this tradition a local historian wrote of the British standing at attention as their flag was slowly lowered and the stars and stripes raised to the top of the staff. To the salute by the cannon he added a rendition of "Yankee Doodle" by a drum corps, presumably American! He also described the mingling of the officers and men, their felicitous greetings and their utmost courtesy.[18]

On the centennial of the transfer Charles H. Grant, a native of Oswego, and nationally famous for his seascapes, added his brush to the local version. On his canvas hanging in the City Hall of Oswego, American troops stand at attention as the colors are raised. Cannoners have just touched off the initial gun, and the smoke rises above the ramparts. Off to the right a detachment of Redcoats marches away in perfect cadence.

Surely, this local version depicts a more colorful transfer than Glen's meager resume. But in the absence of other evidence the latter must take precedence.

If the departure of the English removed the principal obstacle to the settlement of Oswego, the expansion of the salt industry at Salina provided the incentive for its growth.

In the decades following the Revolution salt was in short supply in America. In addition to its use as a condiment, housewives consumed thousands of bushels annually to preserve meat and fish, eggs and fruits. It was a handy item in every home, and indispensable on the farm. Salt was imported along the seaboard, but its bulk and weight made its cost prohibitive in the interior.

Hence, when it was extracted in commercial quantities from the salt springs at Salina, where the state had reserved land on the banks of Onondaga Lake for its development, it was in demand from the Mohawk on the east to the St. Lawrence on the north and across the widening arc of the frontier on the west. It is said that Asa Danforth and Colonel Comfort Tyler were the first to produce salt at

Salina, boiling their initial batch in 1788 in a five-pail kettle. James Geddes and John Danforth were soon producing larger quantities. And thus the village of Salina was founded, and coopers and bateau-men joined the infant community to find a livelihood in barreling and transporting the product.

The Onondaga Lake outlet and the Seneca and Oswego rivers offered the one feasible route for its distribution north and west, and Oswego was the logical jumping off place for both. Its strategic location for the salt trade was not unobserved by Captain Schoedde, who was trying to keep the cork on the bottle. In the spring of 1794 he apprehended boatmen with a cargo of salt valued at sixty pounds, and confiscated it. Reflecting on this and similar incidents, he observed that Americans could scarcely be blamed for coveting the post. Salt production was increasing to many thousands of bushels annually, and "with this place in their hands, they would soon supply the whole country."[19]

Its strategic situation was not lost either upon enterprising Americans; and once the cork had been removed, they began to collect at the harbor. In fact, without exception, the early arrivals were boatmen and forwarders, tavern keepers and laborers, who came in search of profits from the trade.

Boatmen picked up the salt on the margins of Onondaga Lake. It was ordinarily packed in white oak barrels, heavily hooped to withstand the weight and pressure. A variety of boats were used to transport it. The most common at the outset was the pole boat, which measured from twenty to thirty feet and had a four or five foot beam. It was guided down stream by oars or poles, but going up stream required heavy labor; and six or eight miles against a swift current might consume an entire day.

The keel boat was also used in the trade. Longer and broader than the pole boat, it was strengthened and made more maneuverable by a stout keel about four inches square. It was commonly fitted with a mast, holding a square main and top sail.

The Duke de la Rochefoucauld-Liancourt recorded the
laborious passage of a keel boat up stream from Oswego.
They covered but two miles the first day, and but ten the
second. "The navigation of the river Oswego is extremely
troublesome," he noted, "as there is but very seldom sufficient water, even for pushing the vessel along." The crew
was forced to get into the water, and spend three-fourths of
the day there, lifting and pushing. "In five or six places the
strength of a single ship's company was not sufficient and
the men of both vessels were obliged to join for that purpose."[20]

At Oswego a motley row of sheds and cabins rose on the
west bank of the river to provide storage for the salt and
housing for the laborers. Keel boats and a few schooners
were soon operating on the lake. Portages were established
at Lewiston and Queenstown below Niagara Falls, and
within a decade of Fort Ontario's transfer the salt trade
reached Lake Erie and the interior of Ohio and Pennsylvania. Production statistics at Salina suggest the effects of
the transfer upon the industry. In 1797, the year after the
British withdrawal, production jumped from a few thousand to twenty-five thousand bushels. The next year it rose
to sixty thousand, and by 1820 Oswego was recognized as
the leading distribution center for the salt industry.[21]

Secondary to salt at the start, but of increasing importance, was the transfer of general merchandise at the
harbor. Pioneer communities needed endless quantities of
domestic and European goods. The construction of locks at
Little Falls and Rome by the Western Inland Lock Navigation Company in 1794 opened keel boat navigation without
breaking cargo from Schenectady to Oswego falls. It cheap-
ened costs at Oswego and stimulated activity at its waterfront.

The harbor, of course, was the center of the trade. In its
original state it was simply a channel protected from the
lake by an eight-foot bar and a sand spit along the west
bank. A pilot needed favorable winds and experience to
navigate it. The west side was soon studded with wharves,

and in time several drydocks were cut into the bank for boat building. There was no bridge across the stream until 1822; just a ferry for occasional traffic at the foot of Taurus [Seneca] Street.

The first settler at Oswego is said to have been Neil McMullen, a Scotsman from Kingston, New York. He arrived by keel boat, bringing boards for a framed house. He converted the small building into a tavern, and also furnished stores for the American garrison at the fort. He was soon disillusioned with life on the frontier, and returned to the East and lived in Schenectady.

A second early arrival was Captain Edward O'Connor, who had led a company in Colonel Willett's ill-fated expedition against Fort Ontario. Apparently, he did not hesitate to take a second look at Oswego, but it might be noted that after building a log cabin, he removed his family to Salina during the first winter. O'Connor was one of the village's first school teachers, conducting classes in a log cabin. A third new-comer, Captain August Ford, sailed the first salt ship stationed at the harbor, and in a reminiscence noted the problems of sailing upon an uncharted waterway:

> I arrived at Oswego on July 7, 1797 [and] took charge of the first vessel on the American side of the lake. I was entirely ignorant of the lake, having no chart, or the distance from one point to another. No pilot was to be found and I began navigation on the lake with barred harbors and many dangerous shoals. I began keeping a journal. I made soundings and kept the hand lead in constant use, and examined the shoals, taking bearings and the distance from the mainland. I not only sounded both sides of the lake but through the middle, the whole work occupying twelve years.[22]

Navigational charts bear witness to this early skipper's leadline in the guise of *Ford Shoals* a few miles west of Oswego harbor.

Peter Sharpe and William Vaughan came about 1798. Sharpe built a tavern at the waterfront where he accommodated boatmen and travelers. Vaughan in partnership with Sharpe purchased a small schooner and engaged in the salt trade. He later commanded ships on the lake in the War of 1812.

Daniel Burt and his sons, J. Bradner and Joel, settled here at the turn of the century. They purchased several military lots and other property on the margins of the settlement, and through the years held many local offices.

One of the region's most prominent early figures was Matthew McNair. Born in Paisley, Scotland, he had set out to seek his fortune in the New World with a pedlar's pack. He was a merchant, shipbuilder, forwarder and contractor for a half-century in the city of his adoption. He built one of the first ships in Oswego, the *Linda,* fifty tons, in 1804. Prior to this date lake vessels appear to have been purchased in Canada.

Another well known family was founded by Daniel Hugunin. He and his twelve children exhibited a strength of character, individuality, and longevity which exerted a formative influence. Mention, too, should be made of Thomas H. Wentworth, who came to the village from Connecticut by way of St. John's, New Brunswick in 1806, and entered the forwarding business. His business associations, education and hospitality made his home an intellectual center, and a stopping place for visitors en route to or from Canada. He was a gifted artist and an early abolitionist.

Undoubtedly the community's outstanding citizen during the first half-century was Alvin Bronson, who came from New Haven, Connecticut, in 1810, when twenty-seven. Though his formal education was limited, he had a broad experience as a storekeeper, merchant, and coastal shipper. When disaster at sea and the Embargo Act combined to ruin his business, he and his partner agreed to transfer to an inland port. His decision to settle in Oswego was to be significant for both Bronson and Oswego.

Forty years after settling in Oswego, Bronson recalled his passage down the Oswego waterway:

> The road by which I approached the lake, at the breaking point of winter, was so impracticable that I was compelled

to abandon it for an Indian canoe at Three Rivers Point,
and allow my ship carpenters to lead my pack horses to the
Falls. I had been accustomed to the rude Atlantic, with a
good ship under me, but here was a novelty; I found myself
in a cockle shell, deeply laden with iron and carpenters'
tools, plunging down the rapids of the Oswego river upon a
winter flood, with a strip of birch bark only between me and
strangulation. I appealed to John, my Indian conductor, for
his opinion of the safety of our voyage, who replied somewhat slyly, there was not much danger, though if he touched
a rock he might lose the iron and the Yankee; but my
aboriginal navigator, with his cool head, quick eye, and
strong arm, soon restored me to confidence and ease.[23]

In 1797 the state took cognizance of the stirrings at
Oswego. The Legislature directed the Surveyor-General to
lay out one hundred acres on the west side beginning at the
river's mouth. The spot should be "known and called forever thereafter by the name of Oswego." The ubiquitous
Benjamin Wright made the survey, and in the vernacular of
the twentieth century, he "thought big." Blocks were 200 by
396 feet, and lots 66 by 200; streets were 100 feet wide (a
waste of land for more than a century, but a blessing in the
twentieth century). Those running parallel to the river
were designated numerically, and those extending at right
angles were named after the signs of the Zodiac: there was
Cancer (Bridge) Street, also Lyra, Aries, Taurus and
Gemini, and others equally celestial. Unfortunately the village fathers renamed them later, giving them designations
related to the geography of New York. Three blocks, later
reduced to two, were reserved for a public square, and three
others for civic uses. One was to hold an academy, another
a prison, and a third the court house. All were subsequently
released for other purposes. Land at the northern extremity
was set aside for a cemetery, but it was to prove too stony,
and was moved in 1827 to the south side of the village. The
original survey also marked out a fish market, and a block
of parsonages. Neither turned out as planned.

The heart of the early village was the waterfront, which
was situated several blocks north of the present business

section. Progress in the village is suggested by the erection of a customs office in 1803, and the appointment of a postmaster in 1806.

Alexander Wilson, a distinguished ornithologist, who hiked from Philadelphia through the back-country to Niagara by way of Oswego in 1804, recorded his impressions of the journey in a poem titled "The Foresters." [24] The stanzas relating to Oswego serve to summarize its appearance and activities at this time;

> Mark yon bleak hill [on the right] where rolling billows break
> Just where the river joins the spacious lake,
> High on its brow, deserted and forlorn,
> Its bastions levelled and its buildings torn,
> Stands Fort Oswego [Ontario]; there all the winds that blow
> Howl to the restless surge that groans below.
>
>   *   *   *   *
>
> Those straggling huts that on the left appear
> Where boats and ships their crowded masts uprear
> Where fence, or field, or cultured garden green,
> Or the blessed plough, or spade were never seen,
> Is old Oswego; once renowned in trade,
> Where numerous tribes their annual visits paid.
> From distant winds, the beaver's rich retreat,
> For one whole moon, they trudged with weary feet,
> Piled their rich furs within the crowded store,
> Replaced their packs, and plodded back for more.
>
> But time and war have banished all their trains
> And nought but potash, salt, and rum remains.
> The boisterous boatman, drunk but twice a day,
> Begs to the landlord; but forgets to pay;
> Pledges his salt, a cask for every quart,
> Pleased thus for poison with his pay to part.
> From morn to night here noise and riot reign,
> From night to morn, 'tis noise and roar again.

Village life at the beginning was confined to the west bank of the river, and for a decade only the fort broke the sweep of the forest on the opposite shore. Then in 1807 Dr. Deodatus Clarke cut out a second clearing a mile east of the river, connected only by a serpentine path with the harbor. An equally primitive track continued eastward from his lot for two miles to the clearing of Major Jehiel Stone at Scriba Corners.

The Clarkes became intellectual leaders in the primitive community. A son, Edwin, practiced law and for many years served as village clerk. He was also one of the area's earliest historians, and, along with others in the family, an active abolitionist and station keeper on the Underground Railroad.

The growth of the village was slowed momentarily by the Embargo Act of 1807. It seemed ridiculous to Oswegonians that a European war should halt the friendly and profitable relations with Canada. The law was first ignored; then frequently evaded. When the collector of the port attempted to crack down he was threatened by irate boatmen; and for some years after the law's repeal he was involved in suits alleging his interference with domestic trade. The smaller coves along the lake shore were soon rendezvous for smugglers, and while Federalism rebounded, Jeffersonians observed a discreet silence.

Though destructive of commerce, the war scare stimulated activity in the harbor when a delegation of naval officers and workmen appeared with orders to construct a 16-gun brig, the *Oneida*. Surprisingly, among the small circle of officers no less than three were at the threshold of distinguished careers: Lieutenant Melancthon Taylor Woolsey would win renown as a commander in the War of 1812; Henry Eckford would become a noted naval architect; and James Fenimore Cooper would be one of the nation's pre-eminent novelists.

Students of Oswego's history are indebted to Cooper for a brief account of his impressions: He found a frontier village of about thirty houses on the west side and a solitary cabin and the ruins of Fort Ontario, now abandoned, on the east bank. The presence of the officers and a work gang of ship carpenters, riggers and blacksmiths created quite a commotion and taxed living quarters. It also brought hard money into the community, most transactions having been reckoned heretofore in salt.

The inhabitants, Cooper related, "consisted of four or five traders who were mostly ship owners, the masters and people of the vessels, boatmen who brought the salt down the river, a few merchants and a quarter educated personage who called himself a doctor."[25]

The naval officers rented a house, formerly used as a tavern, and set up housekeeping. They were soon joined by a small detachment of army personnel. Lieutenant Woolsey, who presided over the table, was a witty, resourceful conversationalist, and the officers had a convivial mess featuring such specialties as salmon, venison, goose and duck.

They joined in the social life of the village, entertaining with suppers and parties. The launching of the *Oneida* was celebrated with a frontier ball. Women were scarce, but boats and carts were sent out to gather them, and they were not unwilling. When a delicate question of etiquette arose regarding the order in the dances, Woolsey had a ready answer, "All ladies, sir, provided with shoes and stockings, are to be led to the head of the Virginia Reel; ladies with shoes and without stockings are considered in the second rank, ladies without shoes or stockings you will lead, gentlemen, to the foot of the country-dance." Unfortunately there are no additional details, but considering the prestige of the young officers, it would seem likely that most of the females came dressed in their finest attire, and that there would have been few who were relegated to the "foot of the country-dance."[26]

More significant than Cooper's reminiscences of Oswego were his reflections upon the earlier history of the region— reflections which later provided the setting and theme for his widely read novel, *The Pathfinder*.

Two years after Cooper's residence in the village, another distinguished visitor jotted down his impressions. DeWitt Clinton, serving on the Canal Commission, stopped briefly while exploring a route for the proposed Erie Canal. The houses, he noted, "are huddled together in a confused manner. There are at present fourteen (framed) houses, six log houses, six warehouses, and five stores, and five wharves covered with barrels of salt at which were four square-rigged vessels. A post office, custom-house, three physicians, no church or lawyer . . . There was a brig on the stocks. There belong here eleven vessels, from eighty-two to fifteen tons, the whole tonnage amounting to 413 . . . In 1807, 17,078 barrels of salt were shipped from this place . . . Two thirds of the salt that is exported from Oswego is consumed on the Ohio . . . There is no fur trade."

"Extending between three and four hundred yards up the river are to be observed the remains of old Dutch trading houses. The stone foundations yet remain even with the ground . . . There was another tier of houses in the rear, forming an oblong square."[27]

The future governor thus saw Oswego in transition. The physical remains of the once-thriving fur trade were slowly disintegrating, and across the river the old fort lay in ruins. But elsewhere was the bustle and clatter of a rising commercial emporium.

3

GEORGE SCRIBA'S
DREAM AND NIGHTMARE

While the American Revolution would inevitably bring significant changes to the Oswego country, its immediate effects were scarcely perceptible. The forest extended eastward to Rome and beyond, broken only at the river's mouth, where trees had been felled for the construction of barracks and stockades, and at the portages, where crude traces marked the points of transfer. The Oneida and Onondaga Indians still frequented their favorite fishing sites on the streams and tended their weirs at the mouth of Oneida Lake.

But the frontier's tranquility was deceptive. During the war the Sullivan Expedition had played havoc with Iroquois villages in the Finger Lakes region, and at the advent of peace the once mighty Confederation was but a shadow of its former self. But even if the Iroquois had remained intact, the land hunger gnawing at thousands of New Englanders would have pushed them aside.

For almost thirty years events had conbined to discourage the Yankee invasion of New York. The French and Indian War, Pontiac's Conspiracy, Imperial protection of the fur trade, and the coming of the Revolution had in turn been deterrents. The uncertainty attending the Massachusetts—New York dispute over the title to lands in upstate New York was also a temporary brake against the Yankee tide. But this obstacle was overcome at the Hartford Conference of 1786, where Massachusetts obtained first sale of the land west of Seneca Lake, but yielded political jurisdiction to New York.

As New England burst at the seams New York prepared to receive the horde. Between 1784 and 1790 Governor Clinton held a series of conferences with the various Iroquois tribes, and secured the cession of their claims, excepting the reservations. In 1791 Herkimer County was cut away from Montgomery to incorporate the area from the Mohawk River to Seneca Lake. Two years later Onondaga County was set off from Herkimer, so as to include the towns of present-day Oswego County west of the Oswego River. In 1798 Oneida County was carved from Herkimer, including what would later be Oneida, Jefferson and Lewis counties, and the part of Oswego east of the Oswego River. Mexico, "mother of towns," was also created with boundaries stretching from Oneida County across Oswego County and south to encompass Onondaga and Cortland counties. Thus a pioneer, migrating to the Oswego Valley at the turn of the century, would have had as an address: Town of Mexico, and either Oneida or Onondaga County, depending upon his choice of the east or west bank of the river.

Meanwhile, in recognition of its debt to the service men of the late war, the state set aside 1,500,000 acres as a military tract. It was a rectangular area extending from the Oswego and Oneida rivers on the east, to Seneca Lake on the west, and the southern tier of counties on the south, and including the present counties of Onondaga, Cayuga, Seneca and Cortland, and portions of Oswego, Wayne, Schuyler and Tompkins. It was sub-divivided into twenty-eight townships approximately six miles square, and each township, in turn, into 600 acre lots or homesteads. The townships were numbered and named by personnel in the land office, who displayed their erudition by bestowing classical names to twenty-five of the twenty-eight. Oswego County, when it was incorporated in 1816, included Lysander (number 1) and Hannibal (number 2), while Onondaga contained such old world designations as Cicero, Fabius and Camillus; Cortland contained Solon and Virgil; and Cayuga encompassed Cato and Brutus.

In the distribution a private was given six hundred acres, five hundred from the state and one hundred additional from the United States. Officers received multiples of six hundred acres; a major general, for example, was entitled to 6,600 acres and a captain 1,800. Two lots in each township were reserved for the support of schools and the gospel. A fifty acre corner in each lot was surveyed separately, and if the recipient paid a six dollar fee for the costs of the survey within two years, he retained the fifty acres. If he did not the Surveyor-General sold it to the highest bidder. Thus, the expression "survey-fifty," which turns up on deeds in this region.

A six-hundred-acre lot in the fertile Finger Lakes section might appear to be a veritable paradise to an "old soldier." But unfortunately, there were several flaws. Settlement was required within seven years. The lands were distant from populated areas, and roads to many sections were virtually non-existent. Times were hard during this "Critical Period." Many ex-soldiers, in fact a vast majority of them, inquired what a lot would bring, and then accepted the market value, about eight dollars for a six hundred acre lot. To make the situation worse, the certificates of ownership were some-times forged and the unscrupulous sold the same lots to two or more unwary purchasers. Soon the conflicting claims and uncertain titles gave the tract a bad name, and prospective buyers looked elsewhere. Few of the original holders settled and retained their lots long enough (and it required only a decade in more favored locations) to see the eight dollars for six hundred acres appreciate to three or five dollars per acre.

Having satisfied its obligation to its soldiers, New York sold off millions of acres of land to the highest bidders. The resulting scramble has been aptly phrased a saturnalia of land speculation.

In the Cooperstown area Judge William Cooper, father

of the novelist, James Fenimore Cooper, carved out a princely tract; a few miles west of his domain Peter Smith opened a land office in present-day Madison County. At nearby Cazenovia Dutch investors were among the first on the scene. Beyond the Preemption Line along the west shore of Seneca Lake, Massachusetts speculators Oliver Phelps and Nathaniel Gorham, held title to some 6,000,000 acres. But most of it soon slipped through their fingers, and Robert Morris, James and William Wadsworth, William Pulteney and his partners, and the Holland Associates became the largest operators there.

Alexander Macomb, a New York fur merchant and associate of John Jacob Astor, obtained title to more than 3,000,000 acres in the North Country, a region bounded by the St. Lawrence River on the north and Lake Ontario on the west; and he, in turn, deeded the southern portion of the tract, a part of which was later incorporated into Oswego County, to William Constable. The latter hastily turned over four thousand acres to Thomas Douglas, Earl of Selkirk.[1]

Other famous names involved in Oswego's "wild lands" were John Laurance, John B. Church and Alexander Hamilton. Each was prominent in politics and business and related by blood and marriage to the socially elite of New York and the Hudson Valley. None settled in Oswego, but daughters of Laurance and Church, with their husbands, removed there to manage investments.

Through foreclosure Laurance obtained one of the seventy-five thousand acre shares of the Scriba patent, the land lying principally in the towns of Volney, Scriba and Richland. He shared the tract with Church and Hamilton, who were brothers-in-law, having married daughters of General Philip Schuyler. The most valuable acquisition was the Hamilton Gore, a wedge shaped tract extending eastward from the harbor at Oswego; land with great potential in the event that Oswego blossomed as a port.

Like other speculators, however, they could not afford to

sit back and wait for profits. Hamilton's involvement in the speculation became a part of the tragedy which ended his life. The investment, which was completed only a few months before his duel with Aaron Burr, over-extended his credit and left him financially embarrassed. In fact, he delayed the rendezvous with his political adversary while he grappled with his accounts, seeking security for his wife and seven children. He failed, and it required Gouverneur Morris' last minute drive to raise funds among the lamented Hamilton's friends to save his widow from foreclosure.

Speculators won and lost. The Wadsworth brothers amassed fortunes. Peter Smith left substantial legacies to his sons Gerrit and Peter Skenandoah, and Dutch investors, who could afford to wait for a half-century, won modest returns. But Phelps and Gorham turned back most of their acres to Massachusetts, unable to meet the payments, and Robert Morris, the "financier of the American Revolution," ended his speculations in a debtors' prison.

Lesser figures with smaller holdings often fared better than their more prominent contemporaries. The experience of George Casper Schroeppel is a case in point. A native of Nuremberg and a partner of Scriba in New York, he purchased 20,000 acres in Township 24 of the Scriba Patent on the north Bank of the Oneida River. He settled there with his French bride, whom he had courted on the long voyage from Europe, and built a pillared mansion at Orchard Rifts. In addition to the Town of Schroeppel, the villages of Hinmansville and Pennellville, named for the husbands of Schroeppel's two daughters, attest to the prominence of the family in the area.

Other place names in Oswego County which recall early promoters include the Town of Parish (David Parish, a Philadelphia merchant), the Van Buren tract in Oswego (President Martin Van Buren), the Henderson tract in Palermo (William Henderson, an associate of Scriba), L'Hommedieu's Location in the Town of Hastings (Ezra L'Hommedieu), the Village of Phoenix (Alexander Phoenix), the Town of Boylston (Thomas Boylston of

Boston); also Pierrepont Manor just across the Jefferson County line (Hezekiah B. Pierrepont).

Oswego's greatest landlord was George Ludwig Christian Scriba. Born in 1752 in Hesse-Cassel, Germany, of middle class parentage, he went to Amsterdam when a young man to enter upon a business career. He found employment in a banking house for a time, and then joined the stream of emigration to America, and settled in St. Eustatius, a tiny Dutch island in the West Indies. The time was propitious. The American Revolution had begun, and merchants on the island opened a lucrative trade with the newborn republic. Tradition has it that Scriba prospered there, and when he migrated to the mainland he brought his profits with him in Dutch guilders packed in kegs. His short stay in the West Indies — less than two years — would make this story doubtful!.

The wayfarer was now ready to sink his roots, and become an American citizen. He married Sarah Dundas. And after her death a few years later, he wed her sister Maria Dundas Starman, widow of a business partner. Of this union a son, Frederick William, was born.

No contemporary appears to have left a detailed description of Scriba, but a portrait reveals an aristocratic bearing, a long nose, full lips, firm chin, and an over-all delicacy suggesting the dreamer rather than the man of action. There is sartorial elegance in the style and cut of his clothes.[2]

Scriba engaged in banking and insurance, was a founder of the Bank of New York, and a director of the Mutual Assurance Company. His office at number eight Wall Street was a landmark among the business community, and his substantial home at seventeen Queen Street testified to his success.

But "business-as-usual" seems to have lost its appeal, and he turned from Manhattan to face the more intoxicating prospects of the West. He invested in canals, possibly from his knowledge of their worth in the Low Countries, and in

time became a director of the New York Western and
Northern Canal Company and the Western Inland Lock
Navigation Company. The latter was designed to construct
locks on the Mohawk River, and thereby open transportation to Lake Ontario at Oswego and to the Finger Lakes by
way of the Seneca River. Then he prepared for the plunge
which was to alter his life from that moment forward. In
1791 the Land Commissioners had signed a contract with
John and Nicholas Roosevelt for the sale of a vast tract of
land in present-day Oswego and Oneida counties—some
540,000 acres at three shillings and one penny per acre.
The Roosevelts promised to pay one-sixth of the purchase
price in six months, a half of the remainder in one year, and
the balance in two years. Within a few months the buyers
had second thoughts about their "bargain" and peddled it to
the eager Scriba who accepted the terms of the original contract, and in addition agreed to cancel loans totaling 5000
pounds which he had extended to the sellers.

The transfer was accepted by the state on December 12,
1794 and entered in the Secretary of State's records in
book eighteen of Patents, page 155. Many years later
Scriba's copy was presented by his descendants to the
Oswego County Historical Society. Inscribed on heavy
parchment, it bears the signature of Governor George Clinton, and a massive seal of the State of New York.

Scriba and several partners bought the tract sight unseen.
It began at a certain marked beech tree on the northeast
bank of Canada Creek (several miles west of Fort Stanwix), and extended west-north-west to Lake Ontario at the
mouth of Salmon River at Port Ontario. It bordered the
lake to the mouth of the Oswego River, followed the east
bank of that river to Three Rivers Point, and continued
along the Oneida River to Oneida Lake, and up the lake to
the mouth of Wood Creek at present day Sylvan Beach.
Finally, it followed Wood Creek to Canada Creek. Within
this rough quadrilateral were a variety of smaller tracts,
which were already spoken for, and therefore excluded
from the patent. Ezra L'Hommedieu, for example, had

seven thousand acres, and the Oneida Indians retained half-mile strips along Fish Creek; also the state reserved a square mile of land at the mouth of the Oswego River, where Fort Ontario, still flying the British flag and garrisoned by His Majesty's troops, defied Federal and State authority. These exceptions reduced the 540,000 acres to 499,135.

Beyond the monetary consideration the state reserved all gold and silver mines, a limitation of no consequence thus far, and five acres out of each one hundred for highways. It also required that within seven years one family be settled on the tract for every 640 acres. Should the buyer fail to carry out this stipulation the grant would "cease, determine and become void." Difficulties and delays in opening the "wild lands" of Central and Western New York induced the state to ease this requirement, and subsequently drop it altogether.

Scriba's focus, however, was on the development of his wilderness paradise, not its limitations. He engaged Benjamin Wright of Rome to survey it, and lay it out in survey towns. Already an experienced surveyor at twenty-three, Wright later won renown for his work on the Erie Canal, and is remembered by canal enthusiasts as the "Father of American Engineering." With twenty-two assistants, including Benjamin Winch, who later surveyed the Pulaski area and became one of its first citizens, Wright set up a base line extending from Fort Ontario to Fort Stanwix, and drew town boundaries parallel or perpendicular to the base. When he had finished, the Scriba Patent was divided into twenty-four towns, sixteen of which were eventually to fall into Oswego County, and the remaining eight into Oneida County. Many of the town names reflect Scriba's teutonic origins, and contrast with the classical names emanating from the land office in Albany. In the eastern extremity of the tract were Fulda, Munden, Embden and Edam, all subsequently renamed. Elsewhere, the present Amboy was Middleburg, Constantia, Rotterdam. West Monroe was Delft, Hastings was Breda, and Palermo, Metz. There were also Brugen, Fredericksburg, Alkmaer, Strasburgh and Erlang. Unrelated to Scriba's early life were Mexico, Vera Cruz, Richland and Bloomfield.

With the survey completed the partners divided the tract into individual plots. As the principal investor Scriba received Mexico and seven thousand acres in Rotterdam, a combination which gave him access to both Lake Ontario and Oneida Lake. The remainder was divided into six equal parts of 75,000 acres each, and the titles determined by lot. Scriba's draw entitled him to Solingen (Annsville, Oneida County), Georgia (western Schroeppel and southern Volney), Strasburgh (Parish), and a part of Fredericksburg (Volney). The draw gave him more than his share of river frontage and correspondingly less of the more isolated back country. There was a good deal of buying and selling among the speculators before they offered the land to *bona fide* settlers, but Scriba preferred to gamble upon the long range development rather than the quick dollar. In fact, his absorption in his patent soon overshadowed everything else. Long before Andrew Carnegie, he put all of his eggs in one basket, but with quite different results. Scriba had bargained for a lordly domain, but beyond its location on a map and a few details provided by the survey, it was *terra incognita,* and its owner, a babe in the woods.

Possibly the first details of his purchase came unsolicited from Francis Adrian Van der Kemp, an aristocratic Dutch ex-patriate, whose enthusiasm for the frontier led him to explore the patent, with the hope of finding a setting for a manorial estate.

He found the prospects exhilarating and envisioned a lively trade with Canada, and mills and docks and commercial fisheries.

> I do not hesitate to make you this frank and honest confession, that I have not yet encountered in this State an equal extensive tract of land on which I would prefer to end my course, if joined by a few respectable families in the vicinity of a tolerable settlement, of which, if my wealth was equal to its acquisition, I should, in preference to all which I have yet seen, desire to secure its possession.[3]

If proof of Van der Kemp's sincerity were required, it might be found in his subsequent decision to purchase one thousand acres from Scriba several miles east of Rotterdam in 1793. Here, on a clearing overlooking the lake, he built "Kempwick", consisting of a rather substantial log house and barns and stables. The following year he settled down with his wife, two children, and several servants, and for a time served as a justice of the peace. But illness and loneliness made life unbearable for his wife, and after two years he reluctantly moved back to Oldenbarneveld, fourteen miles north of Utica, where there were neighbors, including several old friends from the Netherlands.

Scriba's early endeavors to promote the sale of his lands centered upon Rotterdam, which he planned as his principal land office. It could accommodate the small boats sailing on Oneida Lake, and was accessible to his tract on the lake shore. It was also the logical starting place for a road into the interior to open Strasburgh (Parish) and Mexico, and in the more distant future to provide overland transportation to Lake Ontario. He began the construction of dams on Scriba (Bruce) Creek to supply power for grist and saw mills and a store building to meet the needs of settlers and transients.

In retrospect, it would appear that Scriba's venture was doomed to failure. His initial investment appears to have exhausted his liquid capital, and he had to borrow to meet subsequent payments. Land values after deductions for interest, roads, taxes and development did not appreciate rapidly enough to carry the load. Scriba discovered that settlers seldom arrived with substantial sums in hand. They sought "easy payment plans" and extensions when due dates came around. It was a buyer's market, and many pioneers drove on to see the Genesee country, already heralded for its fertility. Few came back.

But Scriba fought a good fight, though it was occasionally marked by more grit and determination than good judgment. As an absentee owner he was dependent upon agents, and competent men were difficult to find and retain.

And even the most competent agents could not avoid pit-
falls incumbent in the situation. They were endeavoring to
sell and lease lands inadequately surveyed, to erect business
properties, mills, dams and houses with insufficient materials, to feed, house and maintain labor forces many miles
from labor markets, to collect payments from impoverished
frontiersmen, and make decisions with uncertain and inadequate lines of communication. A host of problems defied
ready-made solutions.

Scriba's first agent seems to have been John Jacob
Werth. His tenure was brief; his relations with Scriba reaching an impasse in less than a year. Scriba directed Werth to
cease operations at once, and, to remove all doubt as to his
intentions, ordered him to leave the mill unfinished, the
store building untouched, and the land unsold, for he could
not suffer further misuse of his property.[4]

The proprietor's relations with John Meyer, on the other
hand, were friendly, though the problems remained vexa-
tious. In October 1796, Meyer reported that sales at the
store were slow. He had but fifty pounds in cash and would
require an additional sum to buy meat. He would also have
to find three hundred pounds to pay Judge White at Whites-
town for wheat and provisions. Ten houses remained unfinished for want of boards. The cost of clearing land had
been excessive; the cows were dried up for want of a little
corn, and there was not a hog fit to kill. Also, winter was
approaching.[5]

A month later a sawmill was in operation but required
frequent repairs. The carpenters wished to pay their hands,
but he had refused to settle with them until the houses were
finished according to agreement. His own house was unfinished, and he complained that he had to live and work in
the kitchen with a dozen of people, white and black.[6]

By the end of the year the situation had deteriorated. He
had driven ten of the oxen to Gilbert's (at the head of
Oneida Lake), and he would have to send the ten others
also, for he had no feed for them. Gilbert was supplying

flour, pork and some dry goods, but he might have to seek corn in Westmoreland (thirty miles distant). He had an order on the store for one thousand pounds, and did not know how to pay it. Cash was short, and the snow was deep.[7]

Late in February Meyer found time to think of spring and the replenishment of the store. He anticipated a demand for seemingly prodigious quantities of liquors, also cloth, thread, combs, hair powder, two dozens of black castor hats for ladies, also knives, locks, razors, spectacles, almanacs, and even a chest of violins, imported if possible, and not the cheapest.[8] It is obvious that Meyer's harassments had not destroyed his optimism. But before the year was out he was gone and Scriba was trying to break in a successor.

While Scriba struggled to found Rotterdam he did not lose sight of his major objective—the sale of land throughout his patent. He appraised the lots, putting a higher price tag on mill sites, waterfront areas, and those easily accessible by water or overland transportation. The reputed qualities of the soil also figured in the asking price.

Though he varied his offers from time to time and place to place, the following terms were typical. In Volney he advertised lots at three dollars per acre with credit for six years, interest-free for one year, and legal interest annually thereafter. The buyer was obligated also to make a downpayment or "consideration money" of fifty dollars, and cultivate four acres within twelve months of the purchase date. By paying a higher price per acre the purchaser might extend his payments over a ten year period.

He offered other lots for lease. In Constantia, for example, a twenty acre lot might be leased for fourteen years. No payments were required for three years; then for eleven years the lessee was expected to pay two dollars annually for every ten acres. He was also required to build a house, clear fields, and plant fifty apple trees. At the expiration of the lease the proprietor might regain possession on terms agreeable to both parties; or if they did not agree, for a sum fixed by "two disinterested persons."

He was not unwilling to provide special inducements to attract craftsmen to his patent. In Mexico and Volney he extended loans of two hundred dollars each to millers to expedite the erection of grist mills. Milling grain with a mortar and pestle or a stump mill, though it may seem romantic in the twentieth century, was shunned by the frontiersman, and the convenience of a grist mill was a solid attraction. Scriba also offered a limited number of lots free of charge to mechanics and tradesmen who would settle on the tract, build houses with chimneys, and apply their skills. He proffered land for road construction, but found few takers.

To promote the growth of towns he agreed to bequests of land for education and religion. At Camden he authorized his agent to set aside fifty acres for a school and meeting house; he made a similar grant to the residents of Vera Cruz.

In addition to extending liberal terms, Scriba accepted a variety of goods and services in lieu of money. From one debtor he received eighty-five bushels of wheat, an item in short supply; from others, a fat ox and a fat hog, some fat cattle, and steers.

For many he simply extended additional credit when interest and principal remained unpaid. Evictions were costly, and sources of ill will. He sometimes threatened, then reconsidered, hoping that the ensuing months would yield the elusive revenue. They seldom did.

Scriba's most ambitious, and possibly most illusory project was his promotion of the "City" of Vera Cruz, a plan which Elizabeth Simpson, Town Historian of Mexico, termed "George Scriba's Dream."[9]

If a traveler today drives fifteen miles eastward from Oswego toward the Thousand Islands he passes through the hamlet of Texas. A cursory glance reveals about a dozen houses, several taverns, an antique shop, a small bridge

across Salmon Creek and a state marker noting the proximity of "Spy Island." The modern visitor might observe
also that the stream becomes sluggish below the bridge as it
flows toward Lake Ontario a half-mile distant, and that it
accommodates a variety of small crafts moored behind rows
of cottages lining its banks.

A traveler visiting the same spot one hundred fifty years
earlier would have observed a younger village with a bridge
and mill sites, little more. But it was then called Vera Cruz.
Neither traveler would have seen what George Scriba envisioned there.

As he scanned his maps he reflected upon the paths of
commerce from the West: from Lake Erie by way of the
Niagara River and the Lewiston portage to Lake Ontario,
and down the Lake to either Oswego or Montreal. The latter afforded the shortest route to tidewater, but two long
rapids on the St. Lawrence River were formidable barriers
to its expansion. Oswego, at the outset, suffered from the
obvious disadvantage of being controlled by the British;
and even with that obstacle removed, merchandise had to
be portaged around the falls of the Oswego River, and
moved elsewhere against the strong currents of the Oswego
and Oneida rivers before reaching Oneida Lake and the
portage at Rome. He became convinced that a route across
his tract was more feasible than either the Montreal or
Oswego outlet. The mouth of the Salmon Creek, he ration-
alized, would provide a harbor for the transfer of goods to
Rotterdam on Oneida Lake but twenty-two miles away.
Furthermore, Salmon Creek on the north and Bruce Creek
on the south might be converted into a canal by overcoming
a slight elevation.

The traffic, he believed, would nourish and sustain two
major cities: Vera Cruz on Lake Ontario, and Rotterdam
on Oneida Lake. His efforts to found the latter have been
noted; they appear modest when compared with Vera Cruz.
A map of 1796 contains fifty-seven numbered city blocks,
and General Washington Avenue, a broad thoroughfare
measuring 120 feet. There is a public square, also named to

honor the Father of the Republic. Footnotes call for two additional parks, Adams and Hamilton, further evidence of the proprietor's Federalism. The map also designates a dam and bridge, a sawmill and gristmill, and docks. Fifty acres were available for the support of a church and school.

To attract settlers to his remote "metropolis" Scriba offered twenty-four lots rent-free for twelve years to the first takers who would erect frame houses and clear their lots and half of the width of the adjacent street, and set up "straight and lawful fences."[10] There appear to have been no acceptances.

By 1798 a small cluster of families had gathered at Vera Cruz, but that fall an epidemic of fever carried away two members of the infant settlement and incapacitated most of the others. The arrival of Captain Christian Geerman and his wife appeared to be a good omen. Geerman built a sloop and shuttled between Vera Cruz and Kingston, exchanging potash for Canadian merchandise and cash. But tragedy followed.

Sally Smith Davis recalled the incident more than seventy years later at the age of ninety-six:

> The great calamity came upon us in the fall of 1799. Captain Geerman who lived near the lake built a small sloop or had one that he ran to Canada for goods and provisions for the settlers. The last trip was late in the fall. He had only one young lad with him, Welcome Spencer, 16 years old. They were driven on shore on their way home and both lives and vessel were lost not far from the Galloup Islands. We did not hear from them for three weeks until it was reported that a light was seen on Stony Island. It was feared that Captain Geerman was cast away on that Island and he and young Spencer might be there starving to death. Sylvester Spencer, father of Welcome, Nathaniel Rood, Chipman Wheadon, Miles Doolittle and Green Clark started from Mexico Point to rescue these men, if they could be found.
> After a long and fruitless search among the islands and about the lake shore they gave up all hopes and on their return home off against Stony Point there came up a blow that capsized their boat and they all found a watery grave. For days and days nothing was heard from them. After about three weeks one day Captain Hamilton came along to

our house with a hat in his hand. I asked him if he had heard anything from the men. "Yes," said he, "they are all drowned; this is Mr. Wheadon's hat. The boat was seen from the shore when it upset. One man was seen to hang onto the boat for some time after it upset, supposed to be Wheadon as he was a very smart and active man."

These five men were lost and the two that were lost on the schooner making seven in all out of 12 which was all there was in the country at that time. Those left were Phineas Davis, Capt. Hamilton, Calvin Tiffany, Jonathan Parkhurst and Benjamin Winch. The reason why our men did not go; we were all sick with ague and fever except Tiffany and he had to stay to take care of the sick. The loss of these men was a terrible blow, what few was left in town were completely discouraged and part of them left the place. Some lots that had been taken up and improved were left to grow up to bushes.[11]

This picture of desolation was corroborated by a visitor. "Everything is stripped and dismantled, and every nail that could be pulled is drawn and [as] a finishing stroke they are now taking the bricks from the chimney, piles of which are placed on the creek ready for freight as soon as winter will permit."[12]

For a time Jefferson's unpopular embargo seems to have re-invigorated the hamlet. Smuggling offered unusual profits to the successful, and the collector at Oswego complained that residents at the eastern end of the lake paid no attention to the law, and continued to trade with Montreal. The revival of Vera Cruz encouraged Scriba to try again to convert it into a great port. A handbill which he published at this time sets forth its advantageous situation, its commodious harbor, its proximity to timber for ship building, its location on the Utica-New York trade axis, its mill sites, fisheries, and access to stone and clay for construction and earthenware manufacture.[13] But a few months after publishing this glowing prospectus the War of 1812 exposed the lake shore to British depredations. Sackets Harbor on one side and Oswego on the other were subsequently invaded, and the British fleet brought trade to a stand-still. Migration into the area halted, and even reversed itself. Vera Cruz ceased to grow and became ghost-like. And thus ended Scriba's dream of a metropolis on Lake Ontario, of Washton Avenue, and of Adams and Hamilton parks. Thus ended too his vision of El Dorado on the American frontier.

Scriba's personal misfortunes present no climax comparable to his dream city. It is simply a repetition of mounting costs, a growing burden of debts, and a final reckoning.

When rumors first circulated that he was mortgaging his lands, he was quick to deny them, charging that they were deliberately planted to injure him and discourage settlement.

The hard-pressed landlord eventually closed his office in New York and removed to Rotterdam, where his agent had constructed a substantial residence for him. The salt-box style homestead still stands today on the north side of the highway in Constantia, and is occupied by Scriba's descendants.

In 1811 he gave a mortgage to a Baltimore creditor on twelve thousand acres of the patent, and in 1818 mortgaged a larger tract to David Parish. About this time, also, he executed a trust deed to other creditors, leaving him little more than his home. Parish later foreclosed the mortgage, and purchased the land for twelve and one half cents per acre.

At seventy, the land baron was simply an aging resident of Rotterdam, a spectator of the growing tide of settlement which in another forty years was to fill the rural towns of his patent to overflowing.

He died at eighty-three, and was buried in the shaded Episcopal churchyard in Rotterdam. His gravestone, a simple marble slab engraved with a sprig of weeping willow, stands next to that of his sister and reads;

SACRED
To The Memory of
GEORGE SCRIBA
who
Departed this life
August 11th 1836
in the 84th year

4

PIONEERS:
THE WAY THEY REMEMBERED IT

The tangled and sometimes frenzied dealings of the land speculators should not overshadow the more substantial though more obscure contributions of the pioneer.

New England was the seed bed for the peopling of the Oswego area with liberal transplanting, also, from the Hudson and Mohawk valleys. New England was bursting out all over, but was most explosive in the interior counties of Massachusetts and Connecticut. Most of the Pioneers were farm and village people in search of more and better land. They were of all ages, excepting the elderly. Parents of grown children were well represented, though the accent was upon youth.

They were not a cross section of the settled region left behind, but clusters or colonies from particular areas. If first reports were favorable, relatives and neighbors caught the enthusiasm, and were apt to pack up and follow. Good reports spread. The tardy might also profit from the experience of those who had gone before them. Knowledge of the land, costs, and routes broke down inhibitions. Hence, without formal planning, it was not uncommon to find nuclei of kinsmen and former acquaintances in the budding communities. Bridgewater in Madison County, for example, though only a generation older than Oswego, supplied the latter with a disproportionate share of its leading families. Pawlett, Vermont, did the same for Pulaski.

61

Earliest settlers came by way of the Mohawk Valley and the Oswego waterway; there was no other generally accessible route. Scriba and other speculators, of course, fostered road building and the improvement of water routes. In addition to the road from Rotterdam to Vera Cruz, Scriba offered inducements to construct a highway from Vera Cruz to Oswego, and from Rotterdam to Fredericksburg (Fulton). He sought also to join Rotterdam with Camden and the Black River, and to deepen Wood Creek to facilitate transportation across the Rome portage. The importance of roads in populating the region is suggested in Redfield's rapid growth. One of the least populous towns in Oswego County today, it ranked first in 1798. It was not that its soil was rich; it was not. But Redfield was on the road between Rome and the North Country and accessible by ox team.

By the 1790's boatmen might be employed at the Rome portage if the traveler had patience to wait for the service. A bateau could negotiate Wood Creek if the water was high. Upon reaching Oneida Lake the way was open for a quick descent unless western head winds slowed the process. An experienced pilot reduced the risk at the rifts on the Oneida and Oswego rivers.

Arriving at a prearranged rendezvous, the newcomer might be greeted by friends or relatives, or possibly the land agent, and given temporary shelter. Or he might find lodging in a tavern, usually a bare cabin with an extra room. Sometimes he camped in the woods while he erected a crude shelter. Fortunate indeed were those who found helping hands to ease the burdens of settlement or who obtained boards, sawed at a local mill, for construction. Fortunate, too, were dependents who could wait behind, while the husband or father journeyed to the new homesite, cleared a few acres of land, and erected a primitive cabin. Only a few, however, could afford such a comfortable approach to the frontier.

The first arrivals in what would later become Oswego County were Oliver Stevens, his wife and three children.

Natives of Caanan, Connecticut, they migrated to Brewerton at the outlet of Oneida Lake in 1789. There is a tradition that two of his brothers had served in Bradstreet's expedition against Fort Frontenac, and had been impressed with the spot. There is logic in the story; otherwise Stevens' decision to occupy a clearing some twenty miles beyond the frontier line would appear foolhardy. They settled without the formality of purchasing the land near the ruins of an old fort.

While the Stevenses may not have been in a mood to appreciate it, the site had several advantages. It was on the line of communications between Rome and Oswego, and at a fording place below the outlet of Oneida Lake. Here more than a century earlier Champlain had crossed the river with his Indian allies on his campaign against the Iroquois, and around them were camp-sites where the Oneidas still gathered during the fishing seasons.

Stevens built his cabin of sufficient size to accommodate travelers and a small store. He traded with the Indians, bartering rum, ammunition and provisions for furs and ginseng, and his house became a stopping place for bateaumen and more casual passers-by. He used the enclosed area of the old fort for a pig pen, where, a son recalled years later, the hogs uprooted a variety of utensils, tools and and nails. Stevens and his neighbors, as they arrived, used the bricks from the fort for chimneys and fireplaces. He planted a garden and several plots of corn; and sometimes had surpluses to sell.

About a year after their arrival a fourth child, a son, was born without the presence of a physician or midwife. He was sickly, and died when two. According to a family legend, lacking boards for a coffin, Stevens broke up an old chest which they brought from Connecticut and fashioned one. They buried him on a sand knoll near the house.

About a year after the arrival of the Stevens family other settlers came to Brewerton, and property lines were staked out. Finding that he could not buy the land he had occupied, Stevens began to pay rent. In 1794 with Indian wars in Ohio, and a threat of hostilities in New York, Stevens secured permission to erect a blockhouse at state expense for the protection of the settlement. Built of hewn logs it stood two stories high with the second protruding over the first. Stevens used the blockhouse as a home and tavern for a number of years. It later served as a barn and cider mill, and was finally removed in 1849 to make way for a hotel on the main street of Brewerton. A locust pin, used to tie the timbers, was salvaged from the old structure, and is on display at the sight of the fort.

Possibly because Stevens was a gracious host and could tell a good story, or because of his natural fortitude and resourcefulness, anecdotes relating to his exploits have been handed down from generation to generation. The best remembered among them concerns a trip from Brewerton in search of Pulaski. In March 1793 he decided to walk to the latter to attend a town meeting in the newly created town of Mexico.[1] He set out in the morning on the twenty-four mile trip with a gun and a sack of provisions. There was no road, and he relied upon the sun and his woodcraft for guidance. By evening a pack of wolves was at his heels. He shot one but failed to scare off the others. He lighted a fire and skinned the carcass, while its companions snapped and snarled a short distance away. He finally threw burning brands among them and scattered them. In his moments of terror the doughty frontiersman did not forget that the pelt bore a bounty of forty dollars.[2]

Completely lost, he passed a second night in the woods, and on the following morning stumbled upon the clearing at Fort Ontario— twenty-four miles from Pulaski. He was cordially received by the English soldiers and given a night's lodging. The next day, it was the fourth, he found his way back to his home, the none too savory wolf pelt hanging from his shoulder.

A less-likely tale relates that the Stevenses were interrupted at dinner one day by a Frenchman who approached their cabin shouting for help. The dripping figure stammered in a dialect reminiscent of his Gallic origins that a bear had swum to their boat, and throwing his forepaws over the gunwale, had cast him and his companion into the water. Stevens seized his loaded musket and hastened to the river bank. Emerging from the water unharmed but thoroughly confused was the second Frenchman, and beyond him, majestically floating down the river, was a boat occupied by a solitary bear seated on its haunches and presumably enjoying the unusual experience.[3]

Perhaps the second family to reach the Oswego frontier after the Revolution was the least typical of the pioneers, though a goodly number of their countrymen settled in the North Country. The Des Vatines, husband, wife, and two small children, occupied a tiny island near the western shore of Oneida Lake in 1791, a place which has been identified as Frenchman's Island from that day to this. Both their early years and their later ones are shrouded in mystery, but it was reported that they had emigrated from France after being disinherited. Disillusioned further by business losses in America, they salvaged their remaining pittance and headed for the wilderness. A library, and silver on their table, were mementoes of their former affluence. Life was harsh, and they survived the first winter by living with the Oneida Indians, but Des Vatines eventually built a cabin and cleared several acres on the island. He planted vegetables, fruit trees and flowers. In fact the little garden spot amidst the raw frontier was soon known near and far, and it was inevitably incorporated into the diaries and reminiscences of travelers.

One visitor noted, "Although we found him busily gathering potatoes and onions, yet both his physiognomy and demeanor marked him as a man of some distinction."[4] As for Madame Des Vatines, she was said to have had grace and charm, and though she labored in the field, and baked and sewed, her hands were delicate and well formed.

They gave up their home on the island after several years, and lived for a time in Rotterdam on a lot supplied by Scriba. Then they seem to have had another vicissitude.

It was reported that Madame Des Vatines' father had a change of heart and invited her to return and share his estate. Whatever explanation, the Des Vatines departed, never to return. Years later their little island became a favorite resort, linked by steamboat service with ports across the lake.

Shortly after the coming of Stevens and Des Vatines. "Major" Lawrence Van Valkenburg turned up at Oswego falls, having acquired title to military lot seventy-five on the west side of the river. He was accompanied by his wife, two sons and a sixteen year old daughter-in-law. Natives of the Hudson River Valley, they were the first of what would be a substantial element of "Yorkers" in the community.

Conflicting claims for his military tract induced Van Valkenburgh to cross the river, and thus he also became the founder of Fulton, or Fredericksburg, as it was called during the early years. Here he settled just below the lower rift and built a house, which served also as a tavern. It was a framed structure with log compartments at both ends. The middle section became the social center of the community, where parties, dances and town meetings were held. A century ago an elder resident recalled attending her first dance here, the music furnished by the melodious voice of a Negress, a slave of Peter Sharpe.

The initial years, however, were difficult, and the family abandoned their cabin during the first winter and found refuge in Fort Ontario. Though he could neither read nor write, Van Valkenburgh had a good business sense. He became Scriba's land agent, and also operated a sawmill on Black Creek.

Three years after the Van Valkenburghs settled in the new country they were joined by former acquaintances from the Hudson Valley. John Van Buren, a cousin of Martin Van Buren, migrated to the Oswego Valley with his wife and four sons. The Van Burens were river men: they rafted logs, boated, and later canalled. They also became tavern keepers. Two fine brick homes facing the river, one a former tavern, the other a columned neo-classical structure, and a neglected cemetery nearby continue to be identified with the family, and a goodly number of descendants bear the family name.

One of the first pioneers to settle in the Military tract west of Oswego was Asa Rice. A native of Connecticut and a veteran of the Revolutionary War he had assisted in placing the great chain across the Hudson River at West Point and had fought in the Battle of Saratoga. Later he traded his rocky farm for a bounty lot, and in September 1797 set out with his wife and eight children for the land of promise.

At the Phoenix rift on the Oswego River, their boat ran upon a rock and sank, and though uninjured, their plight was pitiful. Everything but the clothes on their backs was soaked, and they huddled through a night in an unoccupied cabin. Several days later they secured another boat, salvaged some of their belongings, and proceeded to Oswego. They sailed out of the harbor and along the shore to the west, and landed at Three Mile Creek (Fruit Valley). The boatmen left them there promising to return in three weeks with provisions for winter. It was October 2.

Many years later one of the sons recalled their privations during the first winter in the wilderness:

> There they were in the woods without a friend or neighbor, with only a pillow case partly full of flour, very little or no meat or other provisions. They were longer on the road than was expected so that their provisions were nearly exhausted.
>
> However, the weather was fine and the mother with the girls spread their beds, bedding and clothing on the shore to dry, while the father put up a tent seven feet by nine, which they had borrowed.
>
> Before night there came a terrible storm of wind, thunder and rain. The next day the father and two eldest boys aged eleven and fourteen years, set to work to build a house seven by nine feet of such poles as they could carry over which they spread the tent for a roof. It had no floor, window or door.
>
> Provisions soon became scarce, and the father tried his skill in fishing, but only caught one; and that was a salmon. It was a poor time of the year to fish; he, however, robbed

an eagle of one, but these did not last long. He then went to Oswego to buy provisions of the soldiers, but there were none to be had. He finally succeeded in obtaining a barrel of flour that had lain in the water six days and was covered with blue mold. It was brought home but was so injured that it would not rise, so they had to bake it without, but when baked and eaten it would rise in their stomachs and could not be kept down. Their stomachs were not strong enough to contain it. The children would eat it, then go out and vomit it up; it was so hard that it had to be cut up with an axe.

It was six weeks before the winter provisions came. In the meantime, the mother and youngest child; then about three years old, were taken sick, so they could not leave their beds. After lingering awhile, the child died from starvation. The mother lingered until spring then recovered. After six weeks, the men returned with the winter provisions, but having no mother's care, the children suffered nearly as much from eating to excess as they had done from starva- ion.

The boatmen helped build a log house, sixteen by eight- een, and covered it with basswood bark. After it was fin- ished, they gathered together in the evening, and with the wine in their glasses they named the place Union Village [Fruit Valley]. The next day the boatmen left and took with them two of the families, who lived where the city [Oswego] now stands, so there was only one left. During the winter the boys (for the father was a feeble man) cleared four acres, ready for a spring crop . . . The father also split basswood logs and laid the flat side up for a floor, and made some other improvements for domestic comfort, their floor previously having been the ground carpeted with hemlock boughs.

Thus the family survived the first winter. The second was somewhat easier, and by the third, new settlers came in and they began to see better times; still they had no meetings, schools, mills, or conveniences of grinding, sawing or man- ufacturing of any kind.[5]

More than a century and a half after the Rices stepped ashore at Three Mile Creek descendants live on a part of the original lot, and a tiny family burying ground with headstones for Asa and his wife Elizabeth remains on the bank of the creek.

By the turn of the century the extension of roads into the

interior facilitated overland transportation, and emigrants from New England and down-state began to reach the frontier on horseback or in country wagons or sleighs depending upon the season.

George Washington Wheeler traveled by horseback to the town of Mexico from Templeton, Massachusetts, to take a look at the land. From his pocket diary it is possible to reconstruct his impressions. He suffered nothing worse than dirty and noisy taverns until he reached Camden, but on the Camden Woods road enroute to Mexico, "an exceedingly bad road," it began to rain "like a torrent. I put on my great coat pretty fast. It did not rain more than half an hour, but O how sick I was! I could not ride out of a walk, and where there were not sloughs there were hillocks and roots and log bridges without covering or gravelling. Is it possible said I for me to think of moving a family thro' here?"[6] . . But he ultimately reached Mexico and found two adjacent lots, one for himself and the other for his parents. He made down payments on them, and returned to Templeton. The following year he and his father spent the summer clearing the land preparatory to settlement. George did not live to enjoy his home site, but after waiting until the birth of his son, his sorrowing parents and widow came on as planned.

Sally Smith Davis made the trip from Connecticut in a sled in February 1799. Years later she recalled:

> We were about three weeks on the journey. We had one ox-sled with two yoke of oxen. Our load consisted of two beds and bedding with some few things to keep the house with and provisions enough to last for some time. We had a cover for our sled made of sheets sewed together, made fast to hoops bent over the sled . . . We crossed the Hudson River at Albany on a scow and came along on our journey past the Little Falls where we stayed over night . . . From Rome we came to Rotterdam where there was a grist mill and a sawmill built by Mr. Scriba . . . It began to snow and came so deep that it made it hard getting along. We started the 22nd in the morning when the snow was about two feet deep and yet snowing and after a hard day's work wallowing through the snow made about three miles. . . . The 23rd we started again and now had only three miles to go to get

through. The snow was near three feet deep . . . yet with great exertions we did succeed in getting through to our journey's end.[7]

Time did not dim the memory of a nine-year-old girl who rode in a wagon to her new home in the Oswego country:

> The journey was attended with great danger, being exposed to robbers by day and beasts by night. The settlements were few and far between, much of the track lying through a dense wilderness and our only guide a line of marked trees. Often the men went in advance of the wagons with an ax in hand to clear a track for the train to pass and at night they stood on picket duty to guard the train from starving wolves . . . We pushed onward [from Camden] and when night came we tied our horses and cattle to the trees near Kasoag, built our fires, and laid ourselves down to rest; but the wolves were so numerous that the horses took fright, broke loose and ran back to Camden, where they were caught by a Mr. Tuttle and cared for till the men found them in the morning.
>
> At the close of the second day we came in sight of a log hut occupied by Thomas Nutting which we hailed with joy. Mr. Nutting, though a stranger, received us joyfully and entertained us sumptuously with the fat of the land. We were fourteen days on our journey, cooking our meals on the way.[8]

Sally Smith Davis also recalled her first impressions upon reaching the frontier:

> There was a log hut built by Nathaniel Rood, called a "duty house." Scriba had proposed that, if a man would build a house and clear three acres of land on a lot, he could live on the lot as long as he might wish by paying the interest on what he would have to pay for the lot. One or two had built on those conditions, but got sick of the terms and left. This house was a mere shanty built of poles, not one over six or eight inches in diameter. On our arrival at the house we found the snow about as deep inside as it was outside. The men went to work, cleared out the snow, procured wood, and built a great rousing fire, while Mrs. Tiffany with her little babe Rufus and myself sat in the sled. We went into the house. Mrs. Tiffany after looking around burst into a flood of tears, and said: "Is this our home?" I told her this was no time for shedding tears, that we must have the things from the sled and get a good cup of tea and she would feel better, which was done and Mrs. Tiffany, sure

enough, began to cheer up. I did not blame her for feeling
bad on account of her having a little babe to take care of.[9]

The newly arrived, of course, were sources of information for later comers. One such bit of advice has survived in
the town of Mexico. Polly Wheeler, sister of George Washington Wheeler, mentioned above, offered a variety of sug-
gestions to her brother and his family:

> We can have a good fire and bread and meat and sauce
> [awaiting you] if we have our healths. You must get dollars
> and cents in York bills. Pistereens [Massachusetts curren-
> cy] won't fetch but 18 cents here. I pakt our earthen ware,
> glass, etc., among my clothing—all came safe, not one thing
> broke . . . It would be well to fetch what butter you have as
> we have but one cow, also a few pounds of hops if you can
> get them. My father wants you should get a little foul mea-
> dow grass seed if you can, if it is not more than half a pint.
> We want you to fetch your shoe-making tools, also a jointer
> foreplane and a small augur or bitt that will do to tap trees
> and bour [sic] bed-steads with, likewise a little leather.
>
> I must advise you to come in September, be sure. One
> reason is that the great rains are apt to come in October
> which would be bad for you overhead and underfoot. Your
> father says you must set out the fore part of September if
> possible, Ma'am says you must make it possible. It will be
> well to have your wagon of the Dutch fashion, if you could
> conveniently.[10]

After several delays, one occasioned by the birth of a
son, the recipients of the above mentioned advice, Edmund
and Caty Brown Wheeler, finally got underway. Besides
the furnishings, provisions, and three children, the last
corner of the wagon held a keg of rum, having been considered less expendable than a large brass kettle, which was
left behind.

Once the tide of settlement had set in, newcomers encountered fewer problems. There were more traveled roads
and neighbors to assist in house and barn raisings; and occasionally there was spare labor for hire. They might borrow items in short supply, and if a saw mill or grist mill
were operating in the vicinity, they could enjoy their convenience and save many hours of heavy labor. A store in the
neighborhood was an invaluable asset. It was not only a

source of countless necessities, but also a market for "black salts," which the pioneer rendered from his hard wood ashes, one of the few sources of cash in the early years.

Life was crude; labor, long and arduous, but the work was rewarding and there was the satisfaction of achievement.

Each fall, if his health was sound, the farmer could look out upon a broader clearing, often lined with stones he had hauled from his fields. He also beheld the multiplication of his stock and the larger sheds and barns to house it. His wife might find similar enjoyment in improving the home: a brick or stone chimney, safer and more efficient than clay over logs; glass in the windows and an extra room added to the house. It is surprising to note how rapidly the log cabins were abandoned and replaced by framed houses. A generation after the initial settlements the log cabin was out of style, and after two generations it rarely appeared on the census returns.

5

THE WAR OF 1812 AND A
STRAND OF CABLE

There were few "War Hawks" in Oswego in 1812. Armed conflict on Lake Ontario might prove more destructive than the Embargo, and there was no echo to the spread-eagle oratory of Congressman Peter Porter of Niagara Falls, who was prepared to invade Canada to avenge British insults on the high seas.

When war was declared on June 18, Oswegonians accepted it reluctantly. But if they lacked enthusiasm, they did not obstruct it, despite close ties with Neo-Federalist New England. Perhaps their vulnerability to attack spelled the difference in attitude.

Actually, Oswego was not as strategic as in times past. Its harbor had proved too shallow to accommodate ships of the line, and the navy had moved its shipyards to Sackets Harbor. It will be recalled that the *Oneida* had been constructed at Oswego, but once it had been armed, it could not re-enter the harbor. Nor was Fort Ontario the military objective it had been in earlier wars. Long neglected, it was scarcely a shadow of its former strength.

Gradually, however, the village assumed significance as a supply depot. Munitions, hardware, cannon, anchors, and cables, and other naval stores, destined for Sackets, were forwarded to Oswego for delivery by water.

To discourage these expeditions, the British patrolled the

water between Oswego and Sackets, but their narrow margin of naval superiority hampered the operation. Thus an assault upon the depot itself might be the most effective means of halting construction at Sackets. In retrospect, it is surprising that they did not resort to the tactic with greater dispatch.

Otherwise, times were slack at Oswego. The navy purchased the commercial vessels, and converted them into warships. Townsend and Bronson sold their *Charles and Ann,* which was armed and renamed the *Governor Tompkins,* for the state's war governor. Matthew McNair's schooner *Julia* was also added to the Federal flotilla.

To handle the war materials for Sackets, Alvin Bronson was appointed Military Store Keeper, and later Naval Storekeeper also. McNair was named Commissary of Subsistence. Both owned warehouses, and were logical choices to administer the Oswego-Sackets "pipeline."

Meanwhile, the war on Lake Ontario became a contest of shipbuilding. Both navies had little to recommend them at the outset, but once the war was a reality, the race was on. The British at Kingston and the Americans at Sackets turned out ships with astonishing speed, considering their isolation from salt water and centers of population. Oft-times the tide of battle depended upon the completion of a single ship, and naval supremacy fluctuated from month to month. The *Madison,* flagship of the United States fleet, was built in forty-five days! It should be noted that without canals on either the Niagara or St. Lawrence rivers, the lake was landlocked; ships could not be recruited from either the Atlantic or the other Great Lakes. Both contestants named top-flight commanders to direct operations. The youthful Sir James Lucas Yeo was a veteran of campaigns in the West Indies, and Commodore Isaac Chauncey had performed brilliantly on the *Constitution* in the Mediterranean in the victory at Tripoli. Both commanders, however, proved reluctant to directly challenge the other, and there was more shadow boxing than fighting. The British twice menaced Sackets, but failed to destroy the American fleet, and the latter on one occasion bottled up the enemy at Kingston, but withdrew when ice threatened to lock them in the harbor. And so for two years Oswego remained untouched.

In the spring of 1814, however, Yeo shifted his strategy to bypass Sackets and strike the Oswego supply depot. Sir James sailed out of Kingston on May 4 with his flagship, *Princess Charlotte,* 1200 tons and forty-two guns, and five reconverted lake schooners, the *Montreal, Niagara, Charwell, Magnet* and *Star.* The fleet had 222 guns and about one thousand sailors. Its landing force, commanded by Lt. General Sir George Gordon Drummond, was composed of two companies of DeWatterville's infantry, one company of the celebrated Glengary regiment, a battalion of Royal Marines, two hundred blue-jackets armed with pikes, and detachments from the Royal Newfoundland and the King's Eighth and Tenth regiments, more than one thousand in all. The expedition approached its objective as the sun rose on May 5.

At Oswego, meanwhile, where rumors of an impending attack had circulated, last ditch preparations were under way. Bronson halted the supply trains at Oswego falls, dispatched some stores to Niagara and Sackets, and ordered that others be buried in the woods. Major General Jacob Brown "The Quaker Soldier," enroute overland from Sackets to Niagara detached Lt. Colonel George E. Mitchell at Batavia, and sent him back to Oswego with three hundred men. After a forced march they arrived just five days ahead of the British.

They found the stockade rotted and the cannon encrusted with rust. But they mounted five of the guns on the old breastworks, and set the place in order. At the sight of the enemy they scuttled the *Growler,* a brig recently recaptured from the British with its cargo of seven guns awaiting shipment to Sackets, and consolidated its crew with the defenders of the fort.

The fleet approached the shore and launched landing crafts. But when they came within range of the cannon, they were repulsed, and before they could reform a storm interrupted further operations. The British ships put out into the lake, but returned the next morning. This time they unleashed their heavier guns upon the fort, and sent their landing parties ashore. The red-hot balls from the ramparts set several of the ships ablaze, but failed to halt the landing parties, and the invaders were soon scaling the walls.

Finding that his position was hopeless, Mitchell abandoned the fort, and retreated until he reached Oswego falls, felling trees enroute to delay the British advance. The attacking force swarmed into the citadel, where a British Lieutenant scaled the flag pole, tore down the Stars and Stripes, and attached the British colors. Drummond made no attempt to follow Mitchell, and thus failed to obtain the stores at the falls. But he burned the barracks, and left the fortifications in ruins. Yeo raised the *Growler,* and the *Syren,* a schooner belonging to Bronson, which had also been scuttled in the harbor. He emptied McNair's warehouse, but the total, excepting the much coveted ships, fell below expectations.

More than a half-century later Bronson recalled the attempts of the British to locate additional spoils. When they identified him as Store Keeper they took him before Yeo for interrogation. "Now sir, I want you to tell me all about the public stores: what have been sent to Sackett's Harbor and Niagara, if any; what have been detained at the posts in the rear; and what, if any, are concealed in the vicinity. If you will give me full and correct information on these points, you can remain here; if not, you will be taken a prisoner to Quebec."

"Well, Sir James," replied Bronson, "my books and papers have been sent away for safety; I do not think I could give you this information if I would, and I am sure it would be inconsistent with my duty for me to do so if I could."

"I have nothing to do with your duty," retorted the exasperated officer; "all I have to say is, if you give the information I want, correctly, you can stay; if not, you go to Quebec."

"Very well, sir," responded the faithful storekeeper, "that settles it; I will go to Quebec."[1]

Four others were also taken as prisoners: Abraham D. Hugunin, William Squires, Eli Stevens and Carlos Colton.[2] Colton was a boy of fourteen, and a clerk from Bronson. The wily captors, attempting to extract from him what they had failed to get from his employer, plied him with questions.

"Come now," they said, "Mr. Bronson has owned up all about the public stores, and you may as well do so too and save going to Quebec."

But Colton refused to divulge the secrets and his interrogators soon abandoned the deception.[3]

At daylight the next morning the invaders departed with their prisoners, but they set them ashore a few weeks later at Sackets and permitted them to find their way home.

Bronson's geniality, meanwhile, had won the admiration of the British officers, and as he departed from the man-of-war, he was asked whether he would accept a memento of his experience. He suggested the chair on which he had been lowered to the tender. He kept it during his life, and his descendants presented it to the local historical society.

Cemetary records provide the following information regarding the casualties at the fort:

> In the battle there were nineteen of the enemy and six Americans slain. Among the latter, Lt. Blaney, U.S.A., a Sergeant named Wright, and four privates. The enemy had two officers killed, one of them Capt. Haltaway of the Marines. Their remains were taken away, but the bodies of the seventeen privates were left on the field.
>
> During their stay the British collected the dead of both parties and put them into two piles in a natural hollow of earth and covered them slightly with turf torn up for that purpose. The battleground and the place of burial was about sixty rods east of Fort Ontario. After the enemy had retreated, these mounds were overhauled and the bodies of the Americans taken out, enclosed in coffins, and interred with Martial ceremonies on a rise of ground about eighty rods southeast of Fort Ontario. Lt. Blaney, however, was buried in the west village cemetery. Seven soldiers wounded in the

battle subsequently died and were buried with their com-
rades.[4]

While Mitchell was placing the redoubt in readiness,
townspeople were scrambling to get out of the way. Hasty
preparations were made to evacuate women and children
and such personal effects as they could carry. One housewife took a long looking glass (they were rare on the
frontier) to the woods expecting to hide it there. But it slipped from the wagon and was shattered. Her son recalled
that he had gone with his mother and sister to an out of the
way cabin beyond Unionville (Fruit Valley), and had spent
the night packed in with other refugees. The next morning
they walked to the lake at Three Mile Point, where they saw
the fleet and heard the gunfire. After another night in the
cabin they ventured back to their home. A cannon ball had
pierced one of their chambers; another had wrecked the
Hugunin's chimney; a third had crashed through Bronson's
warehouse.

With several accomplices the boy crawled over the ruins
of the fort. They observed blood stains on the rocks, and
saw a trench where the dead were partially buried. "Here a
hand, there a foot and again other parts of the bodies were
exposed."[5]

Shippers also suffered losses in the assault. T.S. Morgan,
a forwarder, advised a client that he had suffered the fate of
others; some of his salt having been taken away, and the
remainder thrown into the river and destroyed. "I cannot
ascertain that there is any of it remaining. Teams could not
be provided to carry it into the woods, and boats could not
get out of the river."[6]

The resourcefulness of one witness to the battle is suggested by his investment in cannon balls, and his tidy profit
from a quick turn-over:

> An immense number of cannon balls were fired into the
> woods by the British vessels, and the very next day all of the
> boys and some of the men who had not left the vicinity were
> at work picking up these relics of the battle. They were not
> sought as relics, however. Dr. Deodatus Clarke, then resid-
> ing on a farm just inside the present eastern city line, know-

ing that cannon balls were in good demand, offered to pay for all the eighteen-pound, twenty-four pound and thirty-two pound balls that could be brought him. What he picked up himself and what he bought amounted to nearly five tons. Besides these there were some still larger, and some twelve-pounders that he would not buy. He readily sold his 'pile' to Judge Forman at Onondaga Hollow, the contractor for furnishing the government, as these balls were much better than those which that gentleman could cast in his forge.[7]

Physicians had to be resourceful as well as skillful to find a livelihood on the frontier!

A tiny diary, kept by a young man living three miles from the fort, confirms the value of the cannon balls:

Thursday [May] 5: An alarm at Oswego, turned out and went down. The British shipping lay off. Sent out their gun boats and fired upon the fort and village. Did not land this day.

Friday [May] 6: This morning the British fleet stood in at 12 o'clock commenced a very heavy cannonading upon the fort and fired upon the village, put out their boats and landed below the fort. Marched up and carried the fort about three o'clock. Our troops retreated up the river.

Saturday [May] 7: This morning went to Oswego and the British had burnt the barracks and plundered the place and evacuated the place.

Monday [May] 9: Went to Oswego, dug cannon balls 42.

Tuesday [May] 10: Digging cannon balls on the state lot.

Thursday [May] 12: Went to Oswego, dug cannon balls 12.

Friday [May] 13: Went with horses and Waggon, gathered cannon balls.

Thursday [July] 21: Had father's horses and waggon to draw cannon balls to Oswego which I sold to Dr. Clarke.[8]

Captain Melanchton Woolsey, who was in Oswego to sail the *Growler* to Sackets, had accompanied Mitchell on his retreat to Oswego Falls. Having lost his vessel he was now perplexed to find a means of transporting the naval stores. He finally proposed to take them quietly along the shore in open boats to the mouth of Stony Creek about ten miles south of Sackets, and portage them across the peninsula to Henderson Harbor adjacent to Sackets. This would circumvent Yeo's blockaders. Chauncey accepted the plan, and agreed to provide military protection from Stony Creek.

The stores including twenty-two long 32-pounders, ten 24-pounders, three 42-pound carronades and twelve large cables were loaded on nineteen boats. The main cable for the *Superior,* a war-ship nearing completion at Sackets, measured twenty-two inches in circumference, and weighed 9,600 pounds.

Guarded by 130 riflemen, under the command of Major Daniel Appling, the flotilla left Oswego at dusk on May 28. The rowers toiled through the misty night, and, notwithstanding their heavy freight, reached the mouth of the Salmon River at dawn. A tally revealed that one boat was missing; and suspecting that it had been intercepted by the British patrol, Woolsey hastily dispatched a messenger overland to Sackets asking for reinforcements. He also de cided to shorten his hazardous voyage by disembarking at Sandy Creek, seven miles short of his objective. At the mouth of the Salmon River he was strengthened by a force of 150 Oneida Indians. The warriors, "stripped and painted for battle, each arrayed in only a breech-cloth and a crest of feathers, and armed with rifle, tomahawk and scalping-knife, strode proudly along the sandy shore, abreast of the flotilla."[9]

They reached the shelter of Big Sandy Creek at noon, and proceeded a mile up the south branch of the stream. While they unloaded their cargo, Appling sent runners to guide the reinforcements from Sackets, and to arouse militiamen who might be found in the scattered clearings. Later in the day a company of cavalry and one of infantry arrived.

Woolsey judged correctly that they had been discovered, and that they had no choice but to dig in and fight. Appling placed the riflemen and Indians in the woods on both sides of the creek, and sent a small detachment of militia forward to make a token resistance of the enemy's landing.

The following morning the British squadron stood off the inlet and sent landing parties into the creek. The Regulars and Indians hidden in the bush opened fire at short range, hurling the British back toward their boats. The engagement lasted but ten minutes before the British commander tendered his surrender. Included was the entire landing force of 175; also several boats and six pieces of artillery. The American loss was a single rifleman killed and an Indian wounded.

The supplies had been saved, but they were still eighteen miles from their destination. However, Woolsey was not without resources. He scoured the vicinity for wagons and oxcarts, and in a few days had everything on its way except the great cable. The officers of the line met, and proposed that it be carried by man-power, excusing only the major from the onerous burden. Reports differ somewhat on the details. One story is that half of the cable was coiled on an oxcart and the remainder carried on the shoulders of the men. Another is that all of it was borne on the shoulders of one hundred men, arranged according to stature, and walking Indian file. They used plaited grass mats to protect their skin from the rough cordage. Volunteers relieved the marchers periodically without forcing a halt.

At the end of the first day they were at Ellis Village; they reached Smithville on the second. On the third the trail was smoother, but weary and shoulder-sore, they were forced to slacken their pace. Nevertheless, they trudged into Sackets that evening, where they were met by soldiers and sailors, who took the cable from their shoulders. Fifers and drummers now led the cheering procession, and brought it to the docks.

The cable was quickly attached to the anchor of the *Superior*, and the launching was consummated on schedule.

A Sandy Creek historian has found the names of eighteen of the marchers; she continues to seek others. In 1928 a boulder commemorating the battle of Sandy Creek was unveiled, and several years later cable trail-markers were set up along the route.

The ineffectual naval war continued on the lake until navigation closed in the fall. Chauncey and Yeo never came to grips, and both lost stature for their alleged ineptitude. No further action touched the Oswego Valley.

The war, of course, slowed the growth of the area. Few settlers arrived during these years, and most of the families, who could do so, left for the interior at the time of the invasion in 1814. The salt trade came to a virtual standstill, though some boatmen found employment moving military stores. The community's lukewarm attitude toward the war discouraged recruitments, but some Oswegonians joined companies organized in the interior. The war also delayed the surveying of the military reservation extending for one mile square beyond the fort, thereby discouraging land sales on the east side. Then, when the survey was completed in 1815, its discrepancies continued to plague land transactions there.

But the village rebounded quickly at the war's end. Ships taken earlier by the navy were resold at auction, and shippers such as Bronson and McNair were soon back in business. Immigration increased, the salt trade revived, and construction boomed. In 1816 the creation of Oswego County unified the area. In 1817 the first newspaper in the county was published, and two years later the *Oswego Palladium* went to press; it is still rolling today. The bridging of the river was a stimulus to the east side, which had lagged because of its isolation. Even bigger things were anticipated.

6

THE OSWEGO CANAL

The Oswego Canal was much more than the sum of its parts—a thirty-eight mile extension of the Erie Canal. It was at once a cord binding East and West, providing a means to transport manufactures westward and raw materials eastward and a passage-way to the West for thousands of Europeans and Americans. It also served as an international waterway between the United States and Upper Canada, delivering Canadian timber and grain in exchange for American and European manufactures. It was a means of freeing Americans along the Lake Ontario frontier from a Canadian outlet for their produce; yet in stimulating Canadian - American trade it tended to make Americans and Canadians interdependent and, in the long run, to reconcile traditional enmities, the legacy of two wars.

Finally, the canal was a leavening agent in the lives of Oswegonians, bringing them closer to the world outside, and broadening their intellectual horizons. In short, its influence in shaping the area can scarcely be over emphasized.

When DeWitt Clinton and his farsighted associates first speculated upon a waterway to join the Hudson Valley to the Great Lakes, two plans were considered. The first was the Oswego route. It would involve the enlargement and extension of improvements made on the Mohawk River by the

Western Inland Lock Navigation Company, locks around the falls of the Oswego River, and a canal on the Niagara River to bypass Niagara Falls. The second proposal was a canal crossing the state from the Hudson River to Lake Erie. It would follow the Mohawk River and Lake Ontario plain to Lockport, where it would climb the escarpment to find its outlet in the harbor of Buffalo. Proponents of the Oswego route argued that it was cheaper than its rival, and that it was the "natural" course, since it utilized two hundred miles of natural lake and river navigation. They also alleged that it could be built more quickly, and that the costs of operation would be lower.

In 1808 James Geddes was authorized to survey two possible routes to connect Lake Ontario with the Mohawk River: one by way of the Oswego River; the other through the Scriba tract between Lake Ontario and Oneida Lake. His report was an endorsement of the former, including a terminal basin in Oswego harbor.

If action had been taken at once, the Oswego line might have won out, but the War of 1812 delayed a decision, and at its close the rapid opening of the western counties along the proposed Erie route swung the pendulum in its favor. Advocates maintained that the overland waterway would serve the entire state, not just the northern and eastern fringe; also that there would be no need to break cargo except at the Buffalo terminal. They argued that it would obviate improvements on the Canadian border which might encourage western trade to pass down the St. Lawrence River to Montreal.

Oswego's most widely circulated answer came from the pen of one Samuel Bellamy Beach, a local druggist, lawyer, politician and pamphleteer, who had once attended Yale College. Using the pseudonym "Peter Ploughshare" he published a thirty page paper-back titled *Anti-Canal Considerations against Continuing the Great Canal West of the Seneca; Addressed to the Members-elect of the Legislature of the State of New York; Facts Are Stubborn Things*. He ridiculed the digging of a ditch alongside the commodious and natural Lake Ontario route, using a homely illustration in verse to make his point:

> The man, who constructing a hole in the wall to
>   admit his two cats, the one great, t'other small.
> When a great hole was made for great puss to pass through,
>   he a little hole cut for his little cat, too.[1]

In the contest at Albany, Oswego was handicapped by a lack of representation in the legislature. The two sides of the river remained in different counties until 1816, and no legislator representing either lived in the river valley. One Oswego landholder whose aid was expected in the State Senate was neutralized by a conflict of interest. Former President Van Buren recalled in his *Autobiography,* that an amendment had been prepared to the Erie authorization bill, which would have incorporated the Oswego branch. It placed the crafty Kinderhook Senator upon the horns of a dilemma. He favored the amendment, but since its success would undoubtedly increase the value of the "Van Buren tract" in the western part of the village of Oswego, and since this speculation was well known to his colleagues, he felt that he could not support it. He voted against it, and thus contributed to its defeat. Needless to say, it did not increase his political stock in the Valley.

As every school child in New York State knows, DeWitt Clinton's long fight for the Erie Canal was crowned with success, and celebrated with pomp and circumstance. But no shouting or cannon fire broke the silence of the Oswego area.

Instead of resorting to self-pity, however, leaders simply shifted their strategy. Their goal now was to add the Oswego Canal to the "Erie system" at the village of Syracuse. Such a canal, they affirmed, would feed the commerce of Lake Ontario and the Oswego-Oneida-Seneca waterways, including the salt trade at Salina, into the main line, and be a source of profit to the Oswego area and the state at large.

Beyond its appeal to logic the Oswego route was strengthened by developments in Albany. The two banks of the river were joined to create Oswego County in 1816. Four years later a resident of the village of Oswego was elected to the Assembly, and in 1822 it furnished a member, also, to the State Senate. It comes as no surprise to note that the Assemblyman was T.S. Morgan, and the Senator, his business partner, Alvin Bronson. Both, of course, were ardent advocates of the canal in Albany.

In the gubernatorial election of 1820 the county gave Tomkins, identified with the anti-Erie Canal faction, 455 votes and but 311 to Clinton, who nevertheless won a re-election.

The timing of the drive proved propitious. Appropriations were sought annually by the Clintonians to continue construction of the Erie, but opposition mounted with the growing cost, and the Erie men needed assistance wherever they could find it. In 1817 they had accepted the Champlain Canal to win support in that sector; now more help was required. They found Oswego ready to reconsider; but the price was the Oswego Canal.

In 1819 the Canal Commissioners recommended that a lateral canal be extended from Syracuse to the Salina salt works. In reality, this sidecut, slightly over a mile in length, was the beginning of the Oswego Canal. A year later the legislature appropriated $25,000 for a survey of the Oswego River. Two plans emerged: the first calling for a series of dams to permit slack water navigation and a short canal around the Oswego falls, and the second, for a dug-canal paralleling the river. Neither was adopted at once, but the legislature authorized the cutting of a canal from Salina to Onondaga Lake to provide a link between the Erie Canal and the Seneca and Oswego rivers.

In 1823 the legislature instructed the Canal Commission to make a scientific investigation of the route, and two years later it accepted the latter's report and its estimate of $227,568.33, and voted the first appropriation for construction.

With success in sight area residents were jolted by a proposal to reconsider, introduced, to be sure, by a Buffalo Assemblyman. Though he had retired from the Senate, Bronson hurried to Albany to lobby against it. Years later he recalled that the first person he met at the capitol was Aaron Burr, who had sacrificed his public career twenty years earlier in his duel with Hamilton. He was now finding a meager living as an attorney.

"Ah," exclaimed the veteran, as he met the Oswego merchant, "so you have come to look after your canal?."

"Yes sir, that is my main object."

"Well, now Mr. Bronson, I am disposed to be on your side; I am in favor of the Oswego Canal too."

"Well Colonel," said Bronson, "I believe that all sensible men are on our side."

"Ah, my young friend," replied the disappointed and cynical politician, "if you have none but the sensible men, there is a vast majority against you."[2]
But apparently there were "non-sensible" men supporting Oswego, for the Buffalo maneuver failed, and the work was begun in 1826.

The cornerstone of the first lock was laid at Fulton on the 4th of July, just fifty years after the signing of the Declaration of Independence, with impressive Masonic ceremonies. Judge David P. Brewster of Oswego delivered the principal address, and Peter Schenck of Fulton read the Declaration of Independence. Fortunately, the accidental explosion of an eighteen-pound cannon had no serious consequences.

Unlike the Erie Canal, which remained within its own banks, the Oswego Canal utilized the river wherever there was a sufficient depth of water unobstructed by rapids. The towpath was built on the east bank of the river, except in a few locations, where it was set in the middle of the stream to be near deep water. Where slack water river navigation was not feasible, a separate canal was dug.

In all, there were 19.7 miles of independent canal and 18.56 miles of slack-water navigation. Its structures of tim-

ber and stone included twenty-two towpath and other
bridges, seven culverts, one aqueduct across Waterhouse
Creek near Fulton, and two waste weirs. Eight dams controlled the flow of the river. There were sixteen locks of
stone masonry and one of stone and timber, having a total
lift of 155 feet. The canal at its opening had a minimum
depth of four feet, and a width at the surface of forty feet;
locks were ninety feet long and fifteen feet wide—dimensions similar to the Erie.

The canal cut away from the Erie Canal at Syracuse
(East Erie and Oswego streets,) and was lowered by locks
one, two, and three (32 feet) to Salina. Lock four was a
sidecut at Salina. It proceeded along the east bank of Onondaga Lake to Liverpool, a section which was later oblit-
erated by the Onondaga Parkway. It then followed the
outlet of the lake, and after passing through Mud Lock (9
feet, 7 inches), moved down the Seneca River. It entered
the Oswego River at Three Rivers Point, but again left the
stream at Phoenix. At Hinmansville lock six (7 feet) carried it back into the river; lock seven (5 feet, 8 inches) at
Moresman's took it out again briefly to circumvent a dam.

It left the river at Fulton, where locks eight, nine, ten and
eleven (39 feet) guided it around the falls. It returned to
the river-bed below Fulton, but again skirted it at Battle
Island at lock twelve (11 feet), and remained in its own
banks past Seneca Hill (lock thirteen, 5 feet, 6 inches). It
entered the river below Seneca Hill, and continued in the
stream until it reached the High Dam above Oswego. Locks
fourteen, fifteen, sixteen, seventeen and eighteen then lowered it to the harbor (45 feet) at East Bridge Street.

At Oswego the canal utilized a dam built by the state in
1824, and an hydraulic canal constructed by the Oswego
Canal Company in 1825. Later this arrangement proved
unsatisfactory, and the two canals were separated.

The completion date had been set for the spring of 1828,
but an epidemic of malignant fever in 1827 greatly reduced
the labor supply. The lock contractor died a victim of this

disease and other contractors could not fulfill their obligations. The fever abated during the winter but returned the
following summer. Wet weather, too, slowed the work and
the consummation of the project was delayed until December, hardly an auspicious time for canalling in upper New
York. Traffic finally moved through the waterway on April
28, 1829. The entire work cost $525,115, twice the original
estimate.

The canal was designed to accommodate boats or packets carrying about forty tons. The packets were light, blunt
and narrow, their characteristics determined by the size of
the locks and the low elevation of the bridges—limitations
by no means eliminating opportunities for variation in detail. They were drawn by horses or mules, usually driven in
tandem. Passengers in fair weather rode on the upper deck
above the cabins, sheltered from the sun's rays in mid-
summer by a resplendent awning or a more humble umbrella.

The arrival and departure of the packets at Oswego were
occasions of great interest attended by curious onlookers.
Churchill, in his *Landmarks of Oswego County* recalled the
excitement of these moments.

> The bugle notes which announced its approach were the
> signal for a gathering at the landing place 'to see the packet
> come in,' while the horses which towed it made a spurt for
> the finish.[3]

The same writer viewed the canal as a way of life:

> Sons followed fathers and children grew up along the
> canal, cradled in their mother's arms, while she watched the
> steering, the family wash waving on lines overhead, with
> many acquaintances to be met nightly at the groceries, 'the
> five-mile grocery,' or some other name, canal bestowed, that
> made a landmark and a stage of the voyage. There were
> gatherings of canal folk, dances to the music of accordion
> and fiddle, and at sun-up sleepy-eyed youngsters harnessed
> canal nags to resume the plodding along the towpaths. A
> leisurely life, paced to the gait of the horses or mules, with
> breaks or high water to be accepted philosophically, even as
> the frequent altercations over crossed and snagged tow-lines
> brought spice to the day's proceedings.[4]

It has been frequently repeated that in any Oswego assemblage prior to the turn of the last century, a shout of "Low Bridge" would have caused at least one-half of those present to lower their heads to escape the ever-threatening menace from above.

While the canal's impact was greatest on Oswego, it affected the lives of people along its entire length. Fulton, with its four locks, became a canal town. It supplied labor and services for construction and maintenance, and the produce of its farms was exchanged at the wharves for the manufactures of the East. John Van Buren in Volney, not only operated a tavern on the bank of the canal, but had stables for canal animals, a blacksmith shop, and a store stocked with merchandise for canallers. His role was duplicated by other enterprisers at Liverpool, Phoenix, Hinmansville, Seneca Hill and Oswego.

The history of the canal during the two decades after 1828 reflected the economic well-being of the nation with variations due to conditions more local in character. For two years the volume of the traffic was moderate, and by no means up to the predictions of its promoters. A typical week's traffic in 1830 (week of May 19-26) included:

Packet arrivals at Oswego:
> Packets with passengers 6, with merchandise 13, with salt 4, miscellaneous 2—Total 25.

Departures:
> Packets with passengers 7, with flour 6, with merchandise 7, whiskey 1, with stoves 1, with rope 1, with hogs 1—Total 23.[5]

Toll collections at the outset were insufficient to avoid criticism in the Buffalo press that the Oswego Canal was operating at a loss. The charge, of course, was resented in Oswego, as was the practice of grouping the Oswego Canal with other lateral canals in making financial reports with the inevitable tendency to underscore the profits of the main line and the losses of the laterals.

Oswego's spokesmen were ever ready to answer their

critics. The *Oswego Palladium* compiled a list of assets which must have tested its ingenuity. The canal, it alleged, augmented the Erie Canal revenues; it promoted the salt industry at Salina, and also supplied the wood used for fuel at Salina toll-free; it also enhanced land values in Oswego and along its route, and thereby increased tax returns. Such "indirect" benefits, the newspaper insisted, took the canal out of the "red" and put it in the "black."[6]

But better times were just around the corner. In 1830 the Welland Canal, connecting lakes Ontario and Erie on the Canadian side of the Niagara River, was completed, making the Queenstown and Lewiston portages obsolete. Ships could now pass from Oswego to Cleveland and Detroit without breaking cargo. It opened the western grain trade to Oswego and stimulated the milling industry; in fact it made it one of the "boom towns" of that era.

Oswegonians had impatiently awaited its completion, and on August 4, 1830, the arrival of the schooner *Erie* from Cleveland brought demonstrable proof that the lakes were joined. As the *Erie* entered the harbor it was greeted by the ringing of bells, a salute of twenty-four guns, a display of flags in the harbor and village, and the cheers and congratulations of the citizenry. An editorial in the *Palladium* captured the spirit of this joyous moment.

> Thus this great event, the offspring with us of so many hopes and fears, and expectations and disappointments, has at length taken place, and with exulting hearts we hail the harbinger of the commerce of Erie. Another triumph of human ingenuity and wisdom is achieved. The hitherto insurmountable barrier of the Niagara is overcome and the waters of Erie may now mingle with those of Ontario, bearing upon their bosoms the bounties of civilization and the gifts of the arts. If there be a spot on the western waters, which more than any other, is to reap the commercial harvest of which the Welland Canal is to be the parent, that spot is Oswego. To the 600 miles of coast to which we had access, 1000 more are now added, comprising the most western counties of New York, the county of Erie in Pennsylvania, the shores of Ohio, Michigan and Upper Canada—the abodes of a large and enterprising population,

stimulated by the wants, and actively engaged in administer-
ing to the supplies of civilized life. It is needless to speculate, for imagination cannot compass the extent of that
commerce which will inhabit the bosom of the northern
lakes, when the regions of the far west shall yield their
spoil.[7]

At four o'clock in the afternoon citizens gathered at the
Welland House to honor the crew of the *Erie*. Their toasts
reflect both the pride of achievement—so obvious that
glorious day—and the almost boundless optimism of the
era:

Oswego—Nature has done her duty, art hers; may her citizens do theirs.

The schooner *Erie*—The first to tell us that Erie is ours;
Huron is ours; Michigan, Superior and all are ours.

The schooner *Erie*—Like the Dove from the Ark, a messenger on the winds; but unlike the Dove, she proclaims
that the waters are flowing not ebbing.

Oswego—May she realize all the benefits from the Welland
Canal which her enemies predicted.[8]

The hopes expressed at the Welland House were vin-
dicated in the years which followed. Canal and lake commerce, shipbuilding and milling flourished, and Oswego's
population expanded. The community barely felt the business panic occasioned by President Jackson's war with the
Bank of the United States in 1833; and 1835 was a year of
record-breaking activity. Between 1830 and 1836 tolls on
the canal increased from $3,673 to $53,677 and boat arrivals rose from 546 to 2,004.

By 1835 eleven lake steamboats made scheduled runs up
and down Lake Ontario weekly. Two packets departed
daily for Syracuse; two others arrived from Syracuse. Inaugurated that year, also, was a daily packet to Utica. To
quote a current user of this accommodation:

The traveler from Utica to Rochester taking this route,

may spend a few hours in our village [Oswego], take a steamboat and arrive at Rochester some hours sooner and with lighter fare than he could take the canal direct from Utica to Rochester. So from Rochester east, the traveler can reach our village in six or seven hours after leaving that city, and by the packets from this place he will reach Utica in twenty-two hours more and at less expense than by taking the canal direct from Rochester to Utica.[9]

Both packets on this line, the *Niagara* and the *St. Lawrence,* were built in Oswego boat yards, and were "fitted up in a style not inferior to any packets upon the Erie Canal." As the *Palladium* jovially expressed it, "A sharp competition is now carried on between these lines of boats, and in consequence, fare is so reduced that a man can hardly afford to remain at home."[10]

The panic of 1837 curtailed canal traffic, but it began to revive as early as 1839. In fact, that year tonnage more than doubled the volume of the five branch canals, the Chemung, Seneca, Cayuga, Chenango and Crooked Lake (Keuka), and was about one-fourth that of the Erie. Freight and passengers increased sharply in the decade of the 1840's, a decade which might be termed the golden age of the canal.

Contributing both to the volume and service of the canal was the construction of the Oneida Lake Canal sidecut in 1835, and subsequent marine activity on Oneida Lake and Oneida River. When the Erie Canal was dug from Rome to Oneida and Syracuse the old lock of the Western Inland Lock Navigation Company at Rome, which had conveyed bateaux from the Mohawk River to Oneida Lake, was abandoned. Wood Creek, Oneida Lake and Oneida River residents were thereby cut off from the main line of travel, and relegated to a backwater. Like people in many other sections of the state, they at once sought a connection with the much-traveled Erie, and got it in 1835 when the Oneida Lake Canal Company built a five mile canal from the Erie at Higginsville to Oneida Lake near the mouth of Wood Creek. The side-cut had seven wooden locks, a fall of fifty-six feet, and dimensions similar to the Erie Canal. Timber products from the shores of Oneida Lake could now move eastward into the Erie system. But one obstacle remained; the tolls charged by the Oneida Lake Canal were higher than those on the Erie. Local residents now petitioned that it be purchased by the state. Again they were successful. The state absorbed it in 1841 and reduced the tolls.

It was at this point that Oswego's promoters got into the act. If steamboats were put into operation on Oneida Lake, and if navigation on the Oneida River were improved, traffic on the Erie might be tapped at the junction of the Oneida Lake Canal and towed down the lake and river to the Oswego Canal at Three Rivers Point. This would shorten the distance from Albany to Oswego, cut the time in transport by two days, and funnel additional traffic at Oswego.

With an assist from New York City capitalists, Oswego merchants organized the Oneida Lake and River Steamboat Company in 1838. For a few years it simply operated a small steamboat on the lake, towing barges to the entrance of the side-cut canal. Later, however, it built locks at the rifts of the Oneida River and established a regular towing service east and west between the side-cut and the Oswego Canal.

The firm kept four steamboats in operation, the *Oneida, Onondaga, Oswego* and *Madison*. It also maintained navigational aids, docks and warehouses. Tows of twenty or twenty-five barges not only presented a colorful sight, but testified to the popularity of the service. With the savings in time and the advantages given to the oft' jaded animals, which were permitted to rest through the forty-five mile tow, to recommend it, the business prospered. At its peak more than 3000 barges a year, yielding $60,000 in tolls in 1850, turned out of the Erie at Higginsville and headed toward Oswego. Between 1847 and 1861 the company had receipts of $186,799.

How many barges were induced to pass up the longer haul from Higginsville to Buffalo in favor of the Oneida

Lake-Oswego route remains undetermined, but it was sizeable, and contributed substantially to Oswego's growth and prosperity.[11]

While the traffic on the Oswego canal remained heavy in the 1850's and 1860's its days were numbered. The passenger trade became more competitive as railroad connections were completed between Albany and Buffalo. A local news item illustrates this threat. It reported that a hand bill which had been circulated among passengers on trains between Utica and Syracuse hinted that Ontario Lake travel was perilous. "As soon as the dangers of navigation are overcome," it read, "a packet will leave Syracuse for Oswego on the arrival of the cars." The paper complained that this was "one of the many devices which persons interested in the western lines take to deceive passengers inclined to take the Oswego route." In truth, it insisted, "no more safe, expeditious, agreeable or cheap route exists than the Oswego route for travellers between Syracuse and Rochester or Buffalo. The packets are handsomely and conveniently furnished, and are commanded by officers, who will give every attention to the comfort of the traveller; and the steamboats upon this route are second to none upon our waters for speed, safety and spacious accommodations, or in the urbanity of their commanders."[12]

But even more destructive to passenger service than the Syracuse-Buffalo railway or misleading handbills was the advent of a railroad in the Oswego Valley in 1848. Overnight, travel time between Syracuse and Oswego was cut from eight to two hours. Packet service was never the same again.

Meanwhile, enlargements and improvements were lavished upon the Erie, and the Oswego Canal struggled to retain an equality. Buffalo argued that an enlarged Erie would be adequate for all traffic moving east and west. It also charged that the Oswego route, by using 200 miles of lake navigation for which the state received not a cent, was actually withholding substantial sums from the treasury. Oswego responded that a "more selfish set of mortals never infested the earth than are the Buffalonians. They would lie to monopolize not only all the travel between the East and West, but the trade likewise."[13] Spokesmen also contended that only Oswego prevented the entire traffic passing through the Welland Canal from going down the St. Lawrence River to Montreal.

Erie proponents dealt Oswego a blow by blocking improvements and repairs on the Oneida Lake Canal. Without them the wooden locks not only deteriorated, but became inadequate to handle the newer crafts built for the enlarged Erie. The canal's traffic fell off, and Oswego shared its misfortune.

Particularly grievous to Oswego was the granting of rebates upon salt tolls on the Erie but denying them to the Oswego line. The salt trade was regarded as rightfully belonging to Oswego, for it had always gravitated to it. The trade had become "blended and interwoven with the manufacture of flour at Oswego, the purchase and transport of nearly all the wood used in the manufacture of salt at Geddes, Syracuse, Salina and Liverpool, the lumber for vats, salt works and other village purposes as well as barrels for the salt."[14] The stated purpose of the rebates was to reduce the cost of salt in the West, and thereby stimulate sales there. But the *Oswego Palladium* insisted that it was a flagrant discrimination enacted "to gratify the cupidity of Buffalo." The rebate was not repealed, and Oswego's salt trade declined after 1858, though it matched the volume of Buffalo's trade until 1863; a tribute to the ingenuity of Oswego's forwarders.

More serious to the canal than the salt rebate was the general policy of reducing tolls. This action in the long run was required by competition from the railroads, but its immediate effect was to jeopardize Oswego's share of the western trade. Since tolls on the Welland Canal were not reduced, shippers were inclined to keep their barges on the main line.

The old canal lived on into the twentieth century, but grass crept across the towpath, and if the horns sounded, few heeded their call.

7

BOOM TIMES AND
MOUNTAINS OF STARCH

After years of uncertainty and disappointment attending the Embargo, the War of 1812, and the Erie Canal, Oswego's good fortunes came with a rush in the 1820's and 1830's, converting it into one of the "boom towns" of the era.

The first portent of better times was a wing dam at the head of the Oswego rift, which was built in 1824 by the state as a first step in the utilization of the stream. Power sites on the river were numerous and easy to identify, but the magnitude of harnessing them at first repelled millers who contemplated it. Andrus and Hiram Gilbert, for example, had come to Fulton from Oneida County in 1819 with plans to build a mill. They viewed the falls, then turned their backs on it, and chose instead a location on Six Mile Creek, where they built a grist mill, and founded the village of Gilberts Mills or Gilbertsville. A few years later, after dams and race-ways had controlled the falls, the Gilberts returned to Fulton to grind their grist.

Now, with a dam waiting to be tapped at Oswego, business men headed by William Dolloway and Rudolph Bunner hastened to exploit it. They organized the Oswego Canal Company, or Hydraulic Canal as it was identified for many years, and obtained a charter permitting them to use surplus water not needed by the state. They dug a channel one and one-fourth miles in length along the east bank of the river to Seneca Street. With an average elevation of sixteen feet above the stream, it provided a continuous line of excellent mill sites. Power users on its lower course fronted the harbor, and had the additional advantage of being able to transfer freight directly from the lake to canal without portage.

Another timely, though inadequate, contribution to the port's future was the erection of the first break-wall for the harbor. Reflecting the solicitude of John Quincy Adams' administration in Washington for internal improvements, Congress voted the sum of $50,000 in 1826 to enclose the mouth of the river. Jetties were extended 230 feet into the lake from each bank, and then turned at right angles toward the channel, leaving an opening of 250 feet. Subsequent appropriations added a mole beyond the west pier, and a stone lighthouse on the west pier, the latter replacing an older one on the bluff at the fort. The improvements eased passage into the harbor, but they were not stout enough to contain gale winds, and time and time again piers were ripped away and ships were beaten at their moorings.

An unexpected boon to the port's development stemmed from an auction in 1827. In July of that year two young men joined a throng at the waterfront to witness the sale of state land adjacent to Fort Ontario. One was Gerrit Smith, thirty year old capitalist from Peterboro, New York. Eight years earlier, his father had deeded thousands of acres of land to him—properties so scattered that it required several years to complete an inventory. In return the recent graduate of Hamilton College had agreed to pay $125,000 in installments and annuities to his sister and brother, a sobering responsibility for the untried but not unwilling recipient. But the value of his holdings permitted him to operate on a broad stage, and to obtain credit to enlarge and develop them. In the panic year of 1837 it provided the collateral to borrow $300,000 at a time when he was hard pressed and might otherwise been forced into insolvency.

The second young man was John B. Edwards, a twenty-five year old canal worker. Edwards grew up in Lyons, Wayne County, in the pathway of the Erie Canal. He worked first as a laborer on the Erie Canal, then as a sub-contractor, and finally as a superintendent at the age of twenty. In 1824 the self-taught engineer came to Oswego to direct the construction of the Hydraulic Canal. When he had finished, he engaged in construction work around the harbor; hence his interest in the auction.

When the last bid was made Smith had purchased the property for $14,000 and staked a share of his future upon the growth of Oswego. Several years later he bought controlling interest in the Hydraulic Canal, thereby enlarging and diversifying his property.

Though they may have rubbed elbows at the auction, Smith and Edwards had not met formally. Thirty-eight years later Edwards recalled, "I saw you there; you was [sic] a brilliant looking young man. You foresaw that land on the east side of the river was about as valuable as the west side, notwithstanding it sold about 3 times as much on the west."[1]

Smith's venture in Oswego real estate could have scarcely been timed better. The Oswego Canal was already under construction, and was opened the following year. He was thus on the ground floor for the anticipated business spurt, with much of his property near the canal and harbor.

Three years after his initial purchase of land and just a few weeks before the opening of the Welland Canal, he entered upon another venture, which proved to be profitable both to himself and the community, a marine basin, or as it was usually termed, the Cove Property. The cove area was a stagnant pool in low water and a channel or "gut" in high water along the east side of the harbor at the foot of Schuyler Street. In combination with David S. Jones, a New York financier who purchased a half interest, Smith converted the waste land into a docking area for the transfer of lake and canal cargoes. Its significance was recognized in a local editorial titled "Village Improvement."

> The [Cove] lot, which has lately been acquired from the
> state by our energetic corporation, is now in progress of
> rapid improvement . . . and this hitherto sink of filth and
> source of contagion is now becoming rapidly renovated. A
> channel sufficiently large for any of the lake vessels is now
> almost completed through it, and instead of a pool of
> standing water, a portion of the pure water of the river
> will be conducted through it, on which, we understand,
> it is the intention of the enterprising lessor, to erect a dry
> dock, wharves, and other conveniences for business.[2]

The developement of the cove, however, brought home to
the owner the disadvantages of absenteeism. At the outset
responsibility for the project was undertaken by Peter
Skenandoah, Smith's eccentric brother, who had settled in
Oswego. Giving little heed to his instructions, Peter Skenandoah entered into contracts which Gerrit disapproved and
eventually cancelled at a considerable loss.

It was at this juncture that Smith turned to Edwards, who
appears to have been recommended by Henry Fitzhugh, a
leading Oswego shipper, and brother of Smith's wife, Ann
Carroll Fitzhugh Smith. Smith hired Edwards as his land
agent, and made him reponsible for the completion of the
cove. The relationship lasted for forty years, and until the
day that Smith died; and Edwards continued to manage the
Smith estate in Oswego for another twenty years. It was an
opportunity for the unlettered Edwards to grow under the
tutelage of one of the most remarkable personalities of that
era. Each week he read one, two or more letters from Smith
devoted chiefly to Oswego property, but interspersed with
his views on religion, abolition, temperance, philanthropy
and politics. Smith also supplied him with copies of his
speeches and tracts, which he ground out in seemingly inexhaustible numbers and varieties. It amounted to a correspondence course in many interesting, though sometimes
tedious and obstruse, lessons. These letters have been lost,
but Edward's letters to his employer supply us with a yard-
stick to measure his progress.

His spelling, for example, at first consisted largely of
phonetics, and he seldom commented on anything except

business. But as time went on his spelling improved and his written vocabulary expanded; and as the business relationship broadened and deepened into a close personal friendship, he frequently referred to family matters, and of more general interest, community activities, including local politics, church news, population trends, fires, storms and epidemics; in fact few major occurrences were not recorded. He also touched on state and national issues, particularly those in which Smith happened to be engaged.

Edwards' views, it might be noted, usually coincided with those of his employer, and were formulated under the latter's influence. Smith stimulated Edwards' interest in abolition, the Underground Railroad, and the Liberty Party; in temperance and in nondenominationalism in religion. He also fostered in him a skepticism for the major political parties and politics generally. Some men would have undoubtedly resented Smith's tendency to preach and moralize; others would have become mere "rubber stamps." But Edwards' personality enabled him to transform causes emanating from Smith into convictions and a way of life; and contemporaries respected him for his strength of character, and not simply as a mouthpiece of Smith.

Edwards completed the cove and found lesees for it. No detailed drawing of the property as it appeared in 1833 has been found, but it is known to have had a rectangular basin connected to the river by two channels. One section accommodated sloops, and the other, smaller crafts. It was lined with wharves and warehouses on three sides and a drydock on the fourth.

As lake and canal shipping expanded the cove became the principal transfer point in the harbor. It attracted business to the east side, and fostered a rapid expansion there. In a few years it matched the west in both business and population.

When Edwards was not engaged on the Cove Property he attended to the maintenance of the Hydraulic Canal, which was soon serving a host of users. He also found time to lease, sell and buy real estate. He occasionally traveled across New York and into neighboring states to assess lands which Smith had marked for speculation.

Perhaps his most persistent chore was the rental of the Fitzhugh House, one of Oswego's largest hotels. Ordinarily this would have been just another property, but a hotel of Gerrit Smith's was a temperance house. Edwards learned that proprietors of temperance hotels were few in number, and that one who could pay his rent was a rare breed.

In his promotion of residential sections Edwards served both the affluent and the humble Irish immigrant. His correspondence is replete with entries representing quarterly or monthly payments of ten dollars, five dollars and sums as small as one dollar. For Irish and other humble clients he divided sixty-foot lots into two—thirty feet in width. Many of these narrow lots remain unaltered today; and a surprising number of the modest story and a half houses, built at this time are still in use. Edwards advised Smith that the Irish met their obligations just as regularly as other buyers, and that two half-lots brought in as much revenue as a whole one!

One of Edwards' most frustrating duties was his role as trouble shooter for the Hydraulic Canal. Lacking efficient means to regulate the flow of water, the canal was subject to extremes: flooding and draught. In 1831 it was the former. A freshet burst through the wall of the wing dam and poured into the canal. Before it could be tapped the torrent carried away a huge section of the outer wall, and several months were required to restore it. Five years later there was another flood, and the need for another major restoration. In between these untoward events the problem was low water.

At the outset the Hydraulic Canal had a virtual monopoly on the water, but after the building of the Oswego Canal, it had to limit its consumption when water was needed for the locks. Worse, it soon had to share it also with a user on the west side when in 1832 Richard L. DeZeng, a

local engineer, with funds supplied by Abraham Varick, a
Utica financier, dug a waterway along the west bank. The
Varick Canal, as it was called, was in most respects a re-
plica of the Hydraulic Canal, but extended only half its
length and did not reach down to the harbor.

There was sufficient water to supply both canals when
the river was high, but low water spelled trouble for all
concerned. Mills were forced to curtail operations, and the
two suppliers vied to draw more than their shares of the
coveted liquid. On one such occasion, DeZeng removed
boards from the dam on the west side, narrowly avoiding
being swept over the spillway; Edwards put them back; and
DeZeng sued him for trespassing. Meanwhile, dissatisfied
users turned to the courts for protection, and the suppliers
prosecuted consumers for manipulating the flow from their
flumes. Rising water usually quenched such litigation until
another dry spell came around.

By 1836 the principal users of water power were the millers of grain. Such operations on the Oswego River prior to
the opening of the Oswego and Welland Canals had been
limited to local grain supplies. But these waterways opened
the fields of Ohio and Michigan to Oswego. Almost overnight the grain traffic was second only to salt, and in a few
years it surpassed it. In 1830 there were two flour mills in
Oswego. By 1836 the milling fraternity included Henry
Fitzhugh, Bronson and Morgan, C.J. and C.R. Burkle, Talcott and Bond, Abraham Varick (Ontario Mills) and
Smith, Cole and Company; and the list was still growing.

The business was highly speculative. Grain was purchased during a brief period in the fall. It was milled and
stored through the winter, and delivered by canal to New
York when the market was favorable—if all went well. But
a miller might see his potential profits turn into losses if the
water did not reach his spout, and his stones did not turn.
A sudden fall in the price of flour might be equally disastrous, or a fire, an ever present hazard, might level the
mill in a few hours. On the other hand, the scarcity of flour
after a long winter usually augured high prices, and when

the ice-freed barges, heavily laden with their precious cargoes, reached the market in New York, the miller received handsome returns.

Their control over the "staff of life" was resented by the public, particularly when flour was scarce and expensive, and the warehouses were filled to overflowing. And if the price suddenly fell, and they were caught with their bins full, they received little sympathy. When such a slump occurred in 1838 a local printer gloated, "The flour speculators are in a sorry pickle and we are not sorry. The immense importation of foreign wheat this winter will give the holders of flour a considerable sweat. The article is down to $8 [a barrel] in New York and will probably go lower; the game is up with them for this year."[3]

Edwards' relations with the millers were often turbulent. In the early days they frequently went over his head to deal with Smith. But he learned to handle them, and his employer came to observe a hands-off policy.

Harbor improvements, the Oswego and Welland Canals, the power canals and milling operations combined to expand lake shipping and boat building. "Forwarders" with offices on the docks and connections with Albany and New York, Cleveland and Detroit and Chicago, joined the growing business community, and a fleet of brigs, schooners and sloops, and an occasional steamboat, crowded the harbor. A regular packet service was inaugurated in the 1830's connecting Oswego with Buffalo, Cleveland and Detroit on the western lakes; Lewiston, Toronto, Kingston and Rochester on Lake Ontario; and Ogdensburg on the St. Lawrence River.

Shipyards in the harbor, notably Varick's on the west side, and Andrew Miller's on the east, were turning out vessels at an accelerated rate. In 1833 four schooners came down the ways and two years later an unprecedented fifteen were launched. In 1817 the *Ontario,* the first steamboat to ply Lake Ontario, made its initial appearance in the harbor, and in 1834 the *Oswego,* a four hundred ton steamer, was launched here. In 1836 a registry of seventy-one schooners, one sloop and two steamboats in the Oswego district testified to the vitality of the harbor.

There were also rumors of bigger things to come: a railroad to Utica; a new bank; and most exciting of all, a Niagara ship canal on the American side of the river.

Oswego's situation was not unique in that the entire nation enjoyed a business boom. Jackson had killed the recharter of the Bank of the United States, and state banks had flooded the nation with "wildcat" currency fanning an inflationary spiral. But if Oswego was not unique, it was unusual; only in Cleveland and Buffalo was the boom as spectacular. Land values in Oswego were advertised to the nation in June of 1835, when the village disposed of sixteen lots between West First and Water streets at surprisingly high prices. Four months later state lands on the river and harbor at West First and Schuyler were sold by the Surveyor General. One tract of three acres was struck off for $108,850, and twelve smaller ones for $47,842. Five of the ten purchasers of the latter were "strangers in the village."[4]

The fat was now in the fire. Waterfront property, business lots, residential areas, and even farms lying several miles from the harbor exchanged hands almost as fast as the sales could be recorded. The Oswego Bank and the newly opened Commercial Bank "turned out money in unlimited quantities," accepting the inflated real estate as security.[5]

The climax was reached in the winter and spring of 1836, when price tags on land jumped almost daily. John B. Edwards, seldom extravagant in his estimates, observed in March that property had advanced fully fifty percent and perhaps nearer seventy-five since December.[6]

Something of the spirit of the moment was recorded in correspondence addressed to Joel Turrill, Oswego County's Congressman in Washington, by his business associates. George H. McWhorter, Jacob N. Bonesteel and Ulysses G. White, partners with Turrill in waterfront land on the west side with frontages on Water and West First streets, decided not to sell until they were offered a profit of one hundred percent; White was convinced that it might yield two hundred percent in a short time. He reported the sale of a residential block (where the Oswego hospital now stands) by Bonesteel and Allen for $21,000, and a profit of $5,000 in three weeks.[7] "They sold it to a stranger," he added, "who paid them their profit in cash." Continuing, White noted that Frederick T. Carrington had sold his house to Albany speculators for $15,000, his wharf lot for $20,000, also his two market lots for $11,000. "You say when your Scriba lots will bring $50,000 you think we had better sell. Had we not better sell when we can make a clear profit of $50,000." White also pointed out that the village was thronged with strangers who had come to buy lots, "and thousands and thousands of dollars worth change hands almost daily." He advised Turrill to part with some of his holdings, "only set them high enough. You can judge from the prices here."

Several weeks later another correspondent noted that capital had been invested at the rate of $50,000 per week for the past two months, and real estate was rising "beyond the expectations of the most sanguine, four fold." He reported that "judicious men," estimated Turrill's holdings at $400,000 and he assumed they would reach "half a million at a minimum estimate . . . There are many strangers in the village engaged in buying real estate. The Welland House is remarkably well patronized. The table is full every day."[8]

From Albany an Assemblyman wrote that he "had some disposition to indulge a little in what Governor Marcy calls the 'unregulated spirit of speculation,' and have concluded to turn my attention to Oswego."[9] He asked Turrill to sell him a share of his property sight unseen, "as low as you can afford, taking a fair profit to yourself. [Erastus] Corning of Albany sold his twelfth for an advance of $1700." He noted that he already owned some "wild lands" on the Oswego River, and that if he could obtain Oswego lots he would join others at the next session of the legislature to seek navigational improvements on the river, "which would be of great service to Oswego."

George H. McWhorter, commenting upon Henry Fitzhugh, whose mill had recently burned, observed, "He has sold all of his real estate in Oswego except the business property [dock and warehouse] he occupies, and has made between $40,000. and $50,000 upon it with first rate responsibilities."[10] He estimated that Fitzhugh had cleared a similar sum in his business over the past year, and noted that he had been offered $100,000 for his mill lot and wharves. Finally turning to his own speculations, McWhorter added, "Of the 33 lots [Gerrit] Smith and I bought of Mr. Martin Van Buren [at the western extremity of the village] for $9100 we have sold six for $11,760 and have the rest left, which from the offers must be worth more than the mines of Peru."

McWhorter's eruditon was better than his judgment. The bubble burst, and the pieces were hard to find. An account of the results, written while some of the participants were still alive, provides a terse summary:

"But in the latter part of 1836 the trouble began. Inflation had been carried to its utmost possible extent, and when the reaction set in, the vast volume of the practically irredeemable paper money shriveled up before the hot breath of the panic, involving the whole country in financial disaster which has never since been approached.

The Oswego people could not at first believe that their high hopes were so completely blasted, and for awhile endeavored to breast the tide. But all through 1837 prices continued to sink, and money, of late so plentiful, became scarce beyond conception. Both banks broke, millions of imaginary wealth disappeared. Nearly every business man became bankrupt. The firm of Bronson and Crocker struggled through almost alone. Building ceased, and for years Oswego lay commercially supine under the weight of the terrible 'hard times.' "[11]

Among the numerous bankrupts was Henry Fitzhugh, a few months earlier the envy of his business associates. Gerrit Smith, one of his principal creditors, estimated that he lost $150,000 through Fitzhugh's failure. And for a time even the Peterboro millionaire was pinched. He moved from his mansion house into a small cottage on the lawn, and replaced hired employees in his land office with members of his family. He rode out the storm, however, with the help of extensive credits from John Jacob Astor.[12]

The sudden change in fortunes was brought home to Edwards, who was engaged on an expansion of the Cove Property. He had started the work during the boom, and had found labor scarce. "They got the notion that they will not work but 10 hours of a day and must have $1 for that," he had reported.[13] He raised wages 6¢ a day on condition that the men work "all day." But after the crash, labor was plentiful, and he was so pressed by job seekers that he went beyond his original plans, and put men to work on the roads. "This will enable me to employ some more of the poor men that are begging for work. It is a great charity to employ and pay the poor laborers at this time." He later transferred the workers from the road to the basin, explaining, "One reason why I discontinued this work was that there is no horse feed to be obtained here. None of the mills have done anything this spring [1837] except Mr. Fitzhugh, a little, and his mill stops."

When Smith proposed a wage cut due to the scarcity of money, Edwards dissented, advising that the cost of provisions remained high.[14] But economic necessity ultimately forced his hand.

When the Panic of 1837 came to the nation at large some months later, it was no novelty to Oswegonians.

* * * * *

Insolvencies, unemployment, bank failures, and empty grain bins continued for several years after Oswego's collapse in 1836-37, but recovery was well on its way by 1842, and flush times were back in 1845.

Milling furnishes a graphic illustration of this upsurge. In 1843 the Eagle and Washington mills were built, each with five runs of stone. (A run of stone had a capacity of one hundred barrels of flour a day.) The next year the Empire mill began production. In 1849, a year of unprecedented expansion, no less than six mills took shape on the two canals: The Atlas, Premium, Pearl, Seneca, Lake Ontario and Express, having in all forty-two runs of stone and a capacity of more than 4,000 barrels per day. A year later two more mills, the Crescent and Huron, made their appearance. In a single decade sixteen mills with an aggregate of eighty-three runs of stone and a daily capacity of 7,500 barrels had gone into production. Oswego now ranked with Baltimore, Richmond, Rochester and St. Louis as one of the foremost flouring centers in the nation. The volume of grain required greater lake tonnage and more barges on the canal. It also opened new business blocks and residential areas. Mansions of stone and brick, the homes of the millers and shippers, arose on the two hills beyond the bustling water front.

Meanwhile, harbor facilities kept pace with the milling industry. In 1849 the city built a free bridge across the river at Utica Street, and when the charter of the toll bridge expired in 1856, it was rebuilt as a free bridge also. When the Federal Government failed to deepen the harbor to accommodate larger ships, the city and its citizens combined to do the job. In 1846 Smith again enlarged and deepened the channels and basin of the Cove Property and in 1852-53 in combination with Fitzhugh, D.C. Littlejohn and Edwards constructed a new docking and transfer area north of the Cove. Grampus Bay, as it was called, consisted of six piers extending westward from the shore; a seventh paralleled the stream and shielded the other piers from rough water. Providing more than 3,400 feet of wharf frontage and an extensive storage area, it was well suited for the transfer of lumber, a commodity holding great promise for the future.

A milestone in the history of shipping upon the Great Lakes occurred in November 1841, when the *Vandalia,* the first screw propelled vessel on the lakes, steamed out of Oswego harbor. Its mention recalls John Ericsson, Captain James Van Cleve and Sylvester Doolittle. Ericsson was the Swedish engineer who had demonstrated the feasibility of screw propulsion. He is also remembered as the builder of the famous *Monitor* during the Civil War. Receiving little attention in Europe, he came to New York in 1840, and placed the screw propellor on exhibit. It so happened that Captain Van Cleve, a veteran of twenty-five years' sailing on the lakes, saw the propellor and was excited over its possibilities. Ericsson offered him a half interest in his patent on the Great Lakes, if he would fit out a vessel with the propellor within a year. Van Cleve accepted, and secured the assistance of Sylvester Doolittle, a skilled ship builder, whose boatyard was situated on the west side of the river.

The *Vandalia* was launched in time to fulfill the contract, and made a "shake-down" run to St. Catherines on the Welland Canal. Its cruising speed of six knots was scarcely calculated to drive schooners from the lakes. Nevertheless, it proved the utility of the invention, and side-wheelers, unable to squeeze through the small locks of the Welland Canal, were soon replaced by ships using screw propulsion.

As the trade burgeoned on the lakes, Oswego shippers joined in a movement to ease tariff barriers upon Canadian exchange. The proposal was divisive, arousing the ire of protectionists and latent fears among Canadians that closer ties might result in their absorption by their aggressive neighbor to the south.

But Oswego's merchants were of one mind. As early as 1850 they dispatched a delegation to Washington to lobby for reciprocity and harbor improvements. They obtained neither but continued to agitate. They supported Gerrit Smith for Congress in 1852, ignoring regular party nominees when he endorsed free trade, and he won with assistance from Free-Soilers.

In the House, Smith was unable to participate directly in the drive for a reciprocity treaty, since ratification was a prerogative of the Senate, but he addressed an open letter to Hannibal Hamlin of the Senate, urging its ratification as a step toward the removal of all tariffs. "Free trade in the productions of Nature" he argued, "is an ordination of Nature, which cannot be innocently violated."[15]

Eased by the skillful diplomacy of Lord Elgin the Reciprocity Treaty was signed on June 5, 1854, and went into effect on March 16, 1855. Of greatest interest to local businessmen was Article III which removed tariffs on the natural products of Canada and the United States. The Democratic *Palladium* hailed it as "a glorious consummation for Oswego," and there were few dissents.[16]

The immediate effects of reciprocity were favorable, both exports and imports increasing sharply. However, before two years had elapsed, the Panic of 1857 reversed the trend. It might be noted that Canadian imports into Oswego held up better than exports, and for the first time, the former exceeded the latter in value. The change stemmed from the lumber trade, which became significant during the decade of reciprocity. By 1870 it ranked first in value among imports, and was taking up the slack resulting from the decline of salt and grain.

The year 1848 was a banner one. It marked Oswego's emergence as a city, and witnessed two major developments in its economic growth. One was conspicuous, and attended by the hiss of steam and the belch of smoke; the other went unheralded at the moment, but became the city's largest industry. The first was the Oswego and Syracuse Railroad; the second, Kingsford Starch.

Though the Oswego Canal had served as the main line for Oswego's trade and passengers moving down-state, its mileage represented only a small fraction of the network of highways which supplemented and fed it. Some were turnpikes, offering the user the luxury of a graveled surface in return for the payment of a toll, but most were primitive "dirt" roads maintained by a local path-master. In 1831 Oswego was joined to Utica by a daily stage, which carried mail and hardy souls who insisted on saving time at the expense of comfort. The same year a stage was inaugurated between Oswego and Auburn. Within three years a similar service was introduced between Oswego and Syracuse, Oswego and Watertown, and Oswego and Rochester; another linked Syracuse, Mexico and Pulaski.

Just after 1845 the area participated briefly in the plank road chimera, which seemed to offer a hard-surfaced highway at low costs. One of the first in the nation was built from Syracuse to Central Square; another was constructed between Rome and Oswego; a third connected Oswego and Syracuse; and a fourth led westward from Oswego through Hannibal and Sterling. The Oswego-Hannibal highway until recent years was referred to as the plank road long after the planks had been removed or covered with gravel and concrete.

By 1848 five stage coaches radiated from Oswego on a single morning, furnishing rapid transportation for passengers and goods, and quickening the lives of the villagers and country folk along the way.

But whatever the advantages of the stage, it could scarcely match the appeal of the "iron horse"; and the time was approaching for its consummation. Oswegonians, like their contemporaries across the state, were thrilled by the construction of the state's first railroad between Albany and Schenectady. When the second link of what was to become the New York Central, reached Utica in 1836, Oswego's leaders were prepared to promote a Utica-Oswego route, and thus connect the village with Albany and the Hudson Valley.

They organized the Utica and Oswego Railroad Company the same year, and issued a report extolling its advantages and minimizing the grades and other natural obstacles to be encountered. Gerrit Smith jumped into the promotion with the hope of enhancing the value of his properties on the east side of the river, where he assumed the railroad would reach Lake Ontario. The company had barely initiated a sales campaign, however, when the panic of 1837 closed the books.

Two years later trains were running as far west as Syracuse along the Albany-Buffalo axis, and local promoters set their sights on an Oswego-Syracuse connection. They held a public rally at Market Hall, where Alvin Bronson presented the proposal. Passenger service alone, he argued, would pay interest and dividends, and freight traffic would add a handsome profit. It would be the obvious mail route from Upper Canada to the Atlantic Seaboard. He refused to evaluate several proposed routes for the road, not wishing to discourage support from either side of the river.[17]

But despite Bronson's reputation for integrity and his eloquent presentation, the response was not adequate. Business men were still shaking off the effects of hard times, and the terms of the charter could not be met.

Seven years later Bronson and his associates initiated a second campaign to make the Oswego and Syracuse Railroad a reality. Bronson ranged as far as Albany and Boston, and Gerrit Smith solicited purchases from David S. Jones and William B. Astor in New York, and invested $10,000 himself. When time was about to run out, Jacob Richardson, a local director of the company, made a last-ditch search for funds in New York and returned with the necessary receipts. "Cars should pass between this place and Syracuse before the expiration of 15 months," the *Palladium* boasted. "It can be done and MUST BE!"[18] The forecast was not far from the mark; cars were running twenty months later.

The managers finally selected a route on the west side of Onondaga Lake and the Oswego River as it would obviate crossing the Oswego and Oneida rivers. There was rejoicing on the west side and mourning on the east. Gerrit Smith's enthusiasm collapsed and he considered putting his stock on the block; but an appeal from Bronson stayed his hand. The grading was begun at Syracuse, and the line was soon operating to the railhead, passengers completing the run to Oswego by stage. On Wednesday evening, November 15, 1848 at 5:15 the first train arrived at the Oswego depot at West First and Utica Streets. It was appropriately welcomed by a cheering throng; and for good measure the ringing of bells and the firing of cannon.

It proved to be far more than a successful promotion. Passenger service was brisk from the start, and continued to increase over the next twenty years; freight traffic was more modest at the outset, but multiplied thereafter. In 1854 the line increased its capital stock to reach the wharves to handle grain and coal. By 1862 freight receipts exceeded the income from passengers. Seven years later, recognizing the advantage of a more consolidated system and more direct connections with the coal fields of Pennsylvania, the company agreed to lease the road to the Delaware and Lackawanna Railroad.

Overnight, it seemed, Oswegonians substituted an exhilarating two hour trip to Syracuse for an eight hour or all-night ride on a packet. A businessman might take the cars to Syracuse in the morning and return in the evening with a day's work done; and all along the line a string of "whistle stops" provided rapid transportation into town for countless country dwellers. Life was never the same again.

As mentioned above 1848 was remembered also as the year Kingsford Starch came to Oswego. The founder of what was to become Oswego's largest nineteenth century industry was Thomas Kingsford. Born in Kent, England, in 1799, young Kingsford was apprenticed to a baker in London when seventeen, and worked later in a chemical shop, where he seems to have shown promise as a scientist. But financial reverses followed, and he conducted a school for a few years.

When thirty-two he migrated to the United States and found a position at William Colgate's starch factory in Bergen County, New Jersey. A year later he was able to send for his wife and son.

Colgate manufactured an inferior grade of starch from potatoes. Searching for a higher grade product, Kingsford suggested the use of corn, but he apparently received little encouragement. He began to experiment in his own home.

One Oswego tradition credits his wife with discovering the process in her kitchen. A more likely story is that he attempted to remove starch granules from corn with lye, but failed; he then tried lime water, and failed again. Quite by chance he dumped the one batch into the other, and the starch separated. The formula, whatever its origin, was a close-kept secret.

After producing corn starch on a trial basis, Kingsford decided to manufacture it on his own account. He organized the firm of the T. Kingsford and Son and went into production at Bergen in 1846. The business was immediately successful, and Kingsford decided to start again where conditions were more auspicious for mass production.

He settled upon Oswego. Corn was available in unlimited quantities, and water, and water power, essentials for large scale production, were abundant. With capital furnished in part by investors from Auburn, New York, Kingsford organized a stock company, the Oswego Starch Factory, T. Kingsford and Son, Manufacturers, with a capital of $50,000.

Kingsford built his factory on the west side of the river at Erie Street on the Varick Canal, and in the first year turned out over a million pounds. The initial product was a laundry starch. Several years later he perfected a food product, corn starch, which was soon marketed in Europe as well as America.

In a decade the annual production had increased seven fold, and its initial employment of sixty-five hands had multiplied to seven hundred. Production eventually reached more than twenty million pounds yearly. Kingsford was without a peer.

To process the mountain of corn, twenty-four pairs of burr stones and six pairs of heavy iron rollers were installed. Five miles of shafting were connected by 2,499 gear wheels and 3,000 pulleys; and forty-three miles of steam pipes dried the starch and heated the buildings. Power was supplied by fourteen water turbines and ten steam engines.

Pumps with a capacity of four million gallons a day forced the water and starch solution through ten miles of pipes. These details, supplied by Kingsford publicity, suggest their pride of achievement.

A semi-fluid waste product left in the vats after the extraction of the starch was sold as "starch feed" to farmers, who hauled it away in wooden tank wagons. This putrified gluten could be identified several miles away when the wind was "wrong." It sometimes dripped upon the streets, and citizens complained of its unsavory aroma. Once, when Luther Wright, an officer of the starch company, was asked to intercede to have the nuisance stopped, he is said to have replied, "I do not smell an unpleasant odor, only dividends."

Kingsford and his son Thompson, who worked closely with his father and assumed the headship of the company after the former's death in 1869, did not stop with the manufacture of the snow-white product. They packaged it in boxes manufactured at the plant. They also established the Kingsford Foundry and Machine Works for the repair of machinery. It was expanded to produce stationary, portable and marine engines and boilers; also steam pumps and hoisting machines, car wheels and railroad castings.

The Kingsfords were also store keepers, operating the Kingsford Family Supply Store, a well stocked general merchandise emporium for their employees and the public, but with special emphasis on the former, whom they paid in part in scrip, redeemable at the Family Store. In fact, as the industry grew, they sometimes paid local merchants in the same scrip. Needless to say, the practice was never popular in the community, and despite the recognized quality of the Kingsford merchandise, many a sigh of relief greeted its demise.

In time the Kingsfords became bankers and organizers of the Oswego Water Works. They were also prominent Baptists. Thomas helped to build the Baptist Church on the west side, and purchased pews for it in Germany, carved from hard-wood grown in the Black Forest. They maintained a well trained and equipped fire department, and the huge compound escaped serious fires. They also sponsored the Kingsford Military Band, the finest in the area.

Kingsford identified Oswego as the center of the starch industry. Housewives in Liverpool and Calcutta and hundreds of cities in between asked for "Oswego Corn Starch," and other trade names, including "Silver Gloss," "Pure," and "Laundro." It received medals of excellence at the London Crystal Palace Exhibition of 1851, the Paris Exhibition of 1867 and the nation's Centennial at Philadelphia in 1876. Kingsford packaging had eye-appeal, and its advertising was colorful, replete with recipes and testimonials, and pictures, stories and poems to interest children. *Our Picture Book,* published in 1880 had the features of a comic book. There was also, the *Silver Gloss Waltz.*[19]

The decade of the 1850's was marked by two of Oswego's most destructive fires. At about 2:30 in the morning on July 30, 1850, a fire was observed in a building near the east end of the river bridge. Before it could be extinguished it spread northward, and consumed the Congress and Express mills. Heroic action saved the Fitzhugh Mill next in line. Meanwhile, a shift in the wind drove the fire southward igniting the wooden bridge, one-third of which burned. It continued to the south and consumed the entire block between the river and East First Street. Three schooners were set ablaze, but they were dropped downstream and saved. Empire Company Number Two was caught between two fires flanking Bridge Street, and had to abandon its pumper to the blaze. The local press estimated the loss at $90,000.

On July 5, 1853, fire struck again with even greater fury. The conflagration started in the Fitzhugh Mill and spread to those adjacent to it. All of the mills and elevators on the east side were consumed along with most of the buildings in the Second Ward, the burned over district extending along the river north of Bridge Street to Seneca Street, and east to Fourth Street. Relief committees raised funds and cared for the needy, and the Common Council provided for a fire department.

While the holocaust raged, a young daguerreotypist, George N. Barnard, carried his equipment to the river bank and reproduced the scene. It shows an inferno in the heart of the mill-row, and in the foreground pictures boatmen struggling to push their crafts away from the docks. Barnard later worked for the renowned Matthew Brady, and as official photographer on General Sherman's staff, accompanied the famous march through Georgia, making a pictorial record of the highlights. Just over a century after the fire of 1853 Barnard's daguerreotype was discovered in Rochester. It has been heralded as the oldest surviving American photograph of an action scene.[20]

Both conflagrations, despite their magnitude, left only temporary scars, and while individual losses were high, the city continued to grow at an unprecedented pace. On the first anniversary of the fire of 1853, the *Times* offered the following congratulatory statement:

> One year ago to-day the mills, warehouses and most of the dwellings on the east side of the river in the second ward were burnt . . . The burnt district is rebuilt with stately buildings of increased dimensions and with important improvements. The mills and grain elevators have risen upon the east bank in solid mass, looming high above their predecessors.

The census of 1860 confirmed the recovery and growth, recording 16,815 residents; ten years earlier there had been 12,205.

8

DEMOCRATS AND WHIGS

When Oswego County emerged as a political entity in 1816 the Democratic Republican Party of Jefferson was triumphant, and Federalism was on the wane. Politicians, whatever their views on such national issues as the Second Bank of the United States, the tariff, and the Missouri Compromise, found themselves members of the same party in this "Era of Good Feelings."

Jackson's controversial political career after 1824 tended to divide politicians into two camps: the Democrats, who accepted the General as their leader, and the National Republicans, who cast their lots with John Quincy Adams and Henry Clay. Most of Oswego's leaders became Jacksonians, possibly because of the ascendancy of the party in Albany and Washington by 1828.

But acceptance of the Democratic Party did not preclude a lively competition for local leadership and the spoils of office. Joel Turrill and Rudolph Bunner at the head of one faction and Bronson as a leader of another fought furiously to control party caucuses. Smarting from the barbs of his opponents in a raucous campaign for Congress in 1826 Bunner noted to a friend:

> A specimen of Oswego electioneering talent: I lie, cheat, get drunk, oppress the poor, and can't open my mouth without an oath. [I] break the Sabbath by playing cards after twelve o'clock Saturday night. In fact [Henry] Clay is no gambler. [Erastus] Root [a vitriolic and intemperate New

York politician] very temperate, [George P.] Barker [prominent, but radical New York Democrat] honest, and Tom Paine very religious in comparison with Bunner. What effect all this will have I know not, but fear the result. My friends fight over my dead body like the Greeks.[1]

Despite his misgivings, Bunner won the race.

Democrats basked briefly in the popularity of Old Hickory, but his assault upon the Bank of the United States blew up a political storm. Party leaders had recently secured a charter for the Oswego Bank and had competed to share in its stock; and those remaining empty handed had launched a drive for the Oswego Commercial Bank. They had no heart for an attack on banks, federal or state, the bank veto of Jackson notwithstanding. Bunner, Bronson, and Turrill fell into line as did the *Palladium,* but Henry Fitzhugh, Arvin Rice and others bolted the party.

The parting was painful and before Democrats could lick their wounds they were challenged by another adversary: Antimasonry. Almost overnight this surprising manifestation of political and social ferment swept across New York and beyond. The disappearance at Batavia of William Morgan, after he had threatened to publish the secrets of the lodge, triggered a protest against aristocracy and privilege identified with Masonry. In Oswego there appears to have been no quarrel with Masons until it was fanned by the alleged abduction and murder of Morgan. But the virulence of the "ism" once introduced forced a disbandment of the local chapters of Masonry at Oswego, Pulaski and Mexico. In a short time none remained in the county.

Anti-Masonry's appeal to the "Common Man" is suggested by a letter in the *Free Press* in the closing days of the campaign of 1830. The writer, who identified himself only as "A Granby Farmer," contrasted the "calculating lawyer" (Turrill) with the "honest farmer" (Rice) in the contest for Assemblyman.

I have no objection to an honest, candid, frank and intelligent lawyer to do my business or to represent my interests in the legislature. But I cannot endure your sly, secret, cunning, selfish, calculating lawyer, forever moving about, car-ing for no one but himself, having neither wife nor child; and distrusting everybody, even his nearest friend. Mr. Rice is a farmer, an honest intelligent farmer, having a wife and children and interest in the soil attaching him to the county in which he lives.[2]

The "Granby Farmer" echoed the sentiments of rural people, but the husbandman, so resourceful on the land, was scarcely a match for the lawyer in the more sophisticated atmosphere of the smoke-filled room. In fact Antimasonry's leadership was never commensurate with its potential. National Republicans frequently filled the vacuum in their quest for votes, and astute politicians such as Thurlow Weed used the party to launch careers. Antimasonry was soon sprinkled with erstwhile Masons.

In Oswego Anti-Masons founded the *Free Press* and named Richard Oliphant as its editor. With a penchant for controversy, he filled its columns with attacks upon Masonry and Democrats, goading some of his less articulate opponents into violence. In March 1830 irate Anti-Antimasons returning from a fire wheeled a pumper to the front of the *Free Press* shop, and played the hose upon the windows, breaking them, and deluging the presses. Two frightened journeymen fired pistols, but fortunately did not injure their tormentors. They were arrested, nevertheless, and on the day of the trial the attendance was so large that the hearing was removed from the tiny courtroom to the Welland House. The defense argued that the men had only fired into the air to frighten their annoyers; and that the hosing was an irresponsible act of those entrusted with public property. But the jury found them guilty, and they were fined fifty dollars.[3]

In the election a few weeks later the Democratic nominee for the Assembly, Joel Turrill, won over his Anti-Masonic opponent, Arvin Rice of the Town of Hannibal, by a three to two margin.

The high tide of Anti-Masonry was reached in 1832, when William Wirt, a virtual unknown in Oswego, lost the county to Jackson, the most widely heralded military hero since Washington, by a bare two hundred votes. They did even better in the congressional race, in which Peter Skenandoah Smith, the irrepressible brother of Gerrit Smith, sought to block Turrill's bid for an election.

In the latter's defense it might be noted that he faced opposition from Democrats as well as Anti-Masons. The former had disagreed violently over the patronage of the customs office, and had taken their quarrel to Washington. Turrill, supported by Bunner, A. P. Grant and McWhorter, attempted to remove John Grant as Collector of the Port, and the latter with backing from Henry Fitzhugh, William Dolloway and Daniel Hugunin fought back. The Turrill clique berated the Grant faction for bolting the party's ticket and manipulating the custom house patronage. Grant's partisans retaliated by charging Turrill with a gross violation of his oath as Judge in seeking Grant's dismissal two years earlier. For the moment Anti-Masons were content to permit Democrats to belabor each other, but they found an issue in the last moments of the campaign, a postscript to the "calculating lawyer" theme two years before.

The last issue of the *Free Press* prior to the election contained a letter purportedly written by one Eliphalet Steele to Joel Turrill, accusing him of seducing his daughter. For three years, it alleged, "the beggarly scoundrel" had paid constant address to her under the pretense of marriage.[4] But instead of making her his bride the ravisher had sent her to Albany for the birth of his child. Later, she had returned with the "offspring of her seduction and the image of your congressional candidate." The seducer, it contended, had neither entered his house again nor paid for the care of the mother or child.

Just below this startling accusal was a statement signed by the Anti-Masonic County Committee testifying that Steele was a man of "unimpeachable integrity."

It would be interesting to know how many votes were changed by the sensational charges. Turrill ran more than three hundred votes behind other Democratic nominees and lost the county by about 150 votes, but the deficit was more than offset by his majority in Oneida County.

Anti-Masonry declined rapidly after 1832, most of its adherents being absorbed by the Whig Party. Publisher Oliphant bridged the transition from Anti-Masonry to Whiggery gracefully, and was soon championing the new party in a newspaper appropriately labeled the *Whig*.

The Whigs at the outset appealed to the business community; their advocacy of internal improvements evoking a strong response in Oswego, where harbor appropriations and a Niagara Ship Canal were impatiently awaited. Nevertheless, the county contributed to Van Buren's plurality in 1836, and Democrats seated their nominees, A.P. Grant and Orville Robinson in the House of Representatives and the Assembly, respectively. But "Little Van" was scarcely in the White House when the panic of 1837 swept the nation. By 1838 the Whigs controlled Congress and elected their first Governor, William H. Seward. A year earlier Oswego County elected its initial Whig Assemblyman, the former Anti-Mason, Arvin Rice. But the Whigs were barely established as the opposition party, when an almost extraneous issue played hob with politics as usual.

In 1837 latent unrest in Canada burst into a shortlived revolutionary movement under the leadership of William Lyon Mackenzie. Americans on the border might have been willing to simply offer words of encouragement to the revolutionaries had not the "Caroline Affair" intervened. On December 29, 1837 the *Caroline*, a small American steamship used by insurrectionists to carry supplies across the Niagara River, was seized by Canadian authorities on the American side of the stream, set ablaze and destroyed. This infraction of international law whipped the border into a frenzy. A series of incidents followed, high-lighted by abortive invasions and the burning of a Canadian vessel, the *Sir Robert Peel* in the St. Lawrence River near Clayton. Thousands of residents of the affected area refused to heed Van Buren's call for the observance of neutrality, and affiliated with the "Patriots" and "Hunters" to avenge the insult and abet Canadian freedom, which they hailed as the spirit of 1776.

Since much of the activity was carried on clandestincly, it is difficult to pinpoint it. However, hundreds of Oswego County people joined the various associations of Hunters. A chapter at Oswego had its quarters over a shoe shop. There were cells also in Palermo, Central Square, Constantia, Scriba, Fulton and Richland. Its leaders, meetings and operations appear to have been common knowledge, and what mystery remained served only to glamorize it.

On November 10, 1838, two schooners, the *Charlotte of Oswego* and the *Charlotte of Toronto* sailed from Oswego, presumably for Ogdensburg, preceding by a few hours a regularly scheduled steamer, the *United States,* commanded by James Van Cleve. After entering the St. Lawrence River the Schooners awaited the *United States,* and were taken in tow. When in place on the sides of the steamboat the hatches were opened and scores of armed men appeared. At Morristown the schooners disengaged and turned toward the Canadian shore. The *United States* continued to Ogdensburg, but a few hours later it was seized by the Hunters and used to transport additional volunteers to the Canadian side of the river. In the battle of Windmill Point which followed, the invaders, numbering about three hundred, were soon pressed to the river bank by the larger Canadian force, and in a few hours most of them were prisoners. There were twenty-seven Oswego County men among the captured; and possibly another thirty participated, but escaped.

In Oswego a public meeting petitioned for the release of the prisoners. "We are strongly persuaded that these youths were deluded into the belief that the enterprise was honorable [and] it is impossible that they are not convinced of the grossness of their delusion."[5] But a few nights later another rally dominated by Hunter sentiment repudiated the olive branch.

The temper of the moment is suggested by an incident on New Year's day. Two cannon belonging to the militia,

which had disappeared several months before, were discovered and seized by a small detachment of United Sates
troops. However, when they attempted to remove them, a
mob gathered and enveloped them. McWhorter, who was in
charge of the operation, withdrew to avoid bloodshed;
whereupon the cheering throng fired the cannon in celebra-
tion of the day. The hapless marshal finally escaped from
his dilemma by assigning the guns to the commander of the
local militia. But the strategy backfired when the latter
permitted the cannon to disappear a second time.

Canadian officials were in no mood to release their
prisoners, and instead, brought them to trial. "General"
Neils S. Von Schoultz and his deputy, Dorephus Abbey, an
Oswego printer, were sentenced to death, and others received servitude in Van Dieman's Land. Again passions
were inflamed, but the subsequent freeing of the younger
participants and mitigation of other sentences eventually
helped to ease tensions.

The excitement of the so-called "Patriot War" completely
eclipsed other issues, and both Whigs and Democrats cater-
ed to public opinion, national attitudes notwithstanding.
Obviously, the Democrats had more to lose. They were embarrassed by the conservatism of the Van Buren Administration and in particular by the President's proclamation of
neutrality. The Democrat *Palladium* condoned the Hunters,
and permitted them to print two short-lived newsletters, the
Bulletin and the *Patriot* on its presses.

Turrill tried to explain the need for forbearance in
Albany and Washington. "The feeling is almost universal
among our mechanics, farmers and laborers, a feeling
which rises above party, which grows deeper and stronger
every day, and with the exception of a few old Federalists
all are more or less affected by it."[6]

Senator Silas Wright stopped in Oswego enroute from
Washington to his home in Canton in February to observe
the disaffection. After an interview with Turrill he reported
to Van Buren that any proscription of Patriots or their
sympathizers would be unwise. But he declared that he had

emphasized that federal officers who had participated in the ill-fated Prescott (Windmill Point) incident could not be retained. He admitted that he had been unable to resolve Democratic dissensions.[7]

The protracted border turmoil combined with the panic of 1837 contributed to a Whig ground swell. It was accelerated by the hard cider and log cabin campaign, and Oswego County, like the nation at large, fell into the Whig column in 1840.

A by-product of the Patriot War was the rebuilding of old Fort Ontario; stone replacing the obsolete wooden stockade. Across the lake, meanwhile, British authorities began the construction of a similar defense, Fort Henry at Kingston. Neither was ever required to guard the border, and both became museums in the twentieth century.

Democrats re-won most of the local offices during the early 1840's; Harrison's death and Tyler's alienation of the party, having deflated the Whigs, and momentarily, the county's congressman and state legislators were again Democratic. But fear that the Mexican War might drop thousands of square miles of slave territory into Uncle Sam's lap again shuffled the parties. Oswegonians were accepting the Free-Soil doctrine, whatever their political preferences. Whigs captured the state in 1846, and Oswego sent William Duer, a Whig, to Congress, and elected two Whig assemblymen. They again carried the county in 1847, when Hunkers, allied to the Polk Administration, waged an internecine struggle with Barnburners, committed to the Wilmot Proviso. They repeated in 1848, and also elected James Platt as first Mayor of the newly chartered city of Oswego.

It should be noted, however, that Van Buren's Free Soil appeal in 1848 was greater than Taylor's military aura, the colorless ex-President polling six hundred more votes in the county than "Old Rough and Ready." Lewis Cass, the regular Democratic nominee, was left far in the rear.[8]

Duer soon demonstrated a capacity for leadership. A member of a distinguished New York family, he had a zest for politics, and his trenchant pen and eloquence on the stump added drama to every campaign. He quickly won recognition in Congress.

In the acrimonious debates attending the Mexican War, he condemned President Polk for "unnecessarily and unconstitutionally" precipitating the conflict.[9] He held that Congress had the authority to regulate slavery in the territories, but insisted that he would welcome the war's end without the annexation of Mexican territory. He advocated the admission of California as a free state,and voted against the organization of Utah and New Mexico, objecting to the provision that slavery might be legalized there if accepted by the residents of the territories. However, he did not vote on the two most controversial bills contained in the Compromise of 1850: the Fugitive Slave Act and the abolition of the slave trade in the District of Columbia.[10] The former may have conflicted with his participation in the New York Whig Convention of 1850. But later, as a supporter of President Fillmore, he defended the Compromise, gaining stature in Washington as he lost it at home.

First as Vice President and then as President, Fillmore represented the conservative faction in New York, which was willing to play down free-soilism in order to conciliate southern Whigs and maintain the party nationally. The Weed--Seward faction, meanwhile, accepted the free-soil doctrine, and Seward became one of its leading spokesmen in the Senate. The inevitable showdown between the factions occurred in September of 1850 at the Whig State Convention at Syracuse. Duer came up from Washington as the representative of Fillmore with orders to fight an anticipated Weed endorsement of free-soilism and ward off criticism of the Compromise. At the first show of strength the Fillmore faction elected Francis Granger of Canandaigua as Chairman of the Convention. Later, as Chairman of the Committee on Resolutions, Duer presented a moderate plank on the Utah-New Mexico issue, calling for acceptance of their territorial governments with the confident belief that it would result in the exclusion of slavery there. The tranquillity, which had marked the opening hours, was suddenly broken, when a delegate from Seward's district presented a substitute proposal calling for a prohibition of slavery in the territories and offering commendations to Seward for representing New York so cogently in the Senate. The Fillmore men were at once on their feet, but their protests were overridden by the Weed-Seward majority. The substitute planks were approved by a vote of 70 to 40. At the completion of the roll call, Granger put down his gavel and walked out of the convention, his long silver-gray hair bristling in anger. Behind him marched Duer and the other thirty-nine Fillmore men. Granger's gray-flecked hair provided a spontaneous identification for the faction—the Silver-Grays; Weed-Seward men were labeled Conscience or Free-Soil Whigs. ✓

Duer immediately telegraphed Fillmore: "Affairs at a crisis. Convention split open. Granger and your friends gone to another house." A second delegate wired: "We have nailed the colors to the mast and we'll fight to the last . . . the line is drawn." It was indeed; the New York Whigs were in two irreconcilable camps, and the split would soon spread to the party at large.[11]

Back home Duer was the focal point for attacks upon the Fugitive Slave Act or the "new kidnapping law," as Abolitionists dubbed it. He declined to seek a renomination to Congress, a wise decision, since the Democrats swept the county in November. Duer's services to the Silver-Gray cause, however, did not go unrecognized. In 1851 Fillmore appointed him United States Minister to Chile. Replaced by President Pierce in 1853, he settled in San Francisco, and was elected County Clerk by the People's Party, a Know-Nothing affiliate. But in 1859 he returned to Oswego and to its political wars. In company with other Silver-Gray and Know-Nothing exiles he joined the Constitutional Union Party which supported John Bell of Tennessee for President in 1860.

Oswego Democrats profited from the Whig schism in 1850, but they were equally vulnerable to the sectional tug

The SOUTH VIEW of OSWEGO on LAKE ONTARIO

General Shirley in 1755, strengthend & inlargd this Fort and erected two others, one Westward 170 Square with a Rampart of Earth & Stone, another on the Oppo-site side of the Bason 450 Yards distant from the Old Fort. This which is calld the East Fort, is built of Logs and the Wall is surrounded by a Ditch. The Projec-tion of the Works renders the Channel at the Entr-ance very strait, the Onondaga River very Narrow, and our Vessels are generally warp'd from the Lake into the Bason.

Explanation.
1. The River Onondaga.
2. The Lake Ontario.

Plate I   Oswego on Lake Ontario in 1754
(from William Smith's *History of the Late Province of New York,* New York, 1830)
Fort Oswego, fur traders' cabins and Indian shelters.
The artist exaggerated the elevation on the east bank.

PLAN,

For settling Mexico Harbor, on Lake Ontario, into a village, by the name of VERACRUZ.

This village is situated in the town of Mexico, in the county of Oneida, and state of New York, and borders upon Lake Ontario and Salmon Creek, about 16 miles east from Oswego, 40 miles west from Sacket's Harbor, and but 22 miles from Rotterdam, on the Oneida Lake; at which place large and extensive manufactories of iron, glass, &c. are to be established by incorporated companies. The land on Mexico Harbor has been surveyed and laid out into plats, by streets, from north to south, of 80 feet wide, and from east to west 66 feet, with two public squares, each of four acres of land, named on the map of the village, Washington and Hamilton Squares.

The proprietor gives in trust to three respectable citizens of the county of Oneida, seventy-five acres of land, within one mile of this village, to be appropriated by them solely for the following purposes, to wit:—fifty acres of the same, towards the support of a Clergyman of the first christian congregation who shall build a decent and respectable house of worship in that village; and 25 acres for the support of a Public School; both these tracts of land to remain for ever for these purposes, and for which a deed of trust will be given. The title is indisputable.

This village, from its eligible situation on so extensive a lake, with a good and safe harbor, will command a considerable part of the trade and navigation with the lakes. The timber for ship building is near and convenient, and in quality exceeded by none. It will have also the advantage of two markets in time of peace. The distance to Montreal is nearly of that to Albany, by water—it is also but 65 miles from Utica, and only 34 miles from the Onondaigua salt works; and from its being for the greatest part insulated by a large navigable creek, and fine harbor, and bordering upon Lake Ontario, which here affords at all times an inexhaustible reservoir for the best sort of fish, (of which the salmon fishery is of no small importance) its rapid settlements may be easily conjectured from such numberless advantages; more so, when it will be found that the materials for building are of the best quarry stone, and clay for brick and earthen ware, with excellent timber, which materials almost may be obtained for the labor only. Saw mills are in the vicinity, and excellent mill seats on the rapids of Salmon Creek, (the boundary of the village) on which water works of any extent can be erected. The towns of Scriba, Mexico and Richland, are extensive and populous, and Veracruz is nearly in the centre of those towns. To point out all the advantages in detail, would to many who are unacquainted with the situation, appear to be exaggerated, therefore, suffice it to say, the subscriber now offers to dispose of building lots of divers dimensions, on very liberal and advantageous terms, either to individuals or companies of mechanics or traders, and to societies inclining to settle in this village, for which an indisputable title will be given.

N. B. The terms and conditions may be known, by applying to JOHN W. BLOOMFIELD, Esq. at Rome, or the surveyor of the village, DAVID S. BATES, Esq. at Rotterdam, Oneida Lake. *and David Williams at the Village*

January 4, 1814.   GEO. SCRIBA.

Plate II   Plans for Vera Cruz
Scriba's dream of a metropolis at Mexico Point

Plate III   Carrying the Cable During the War of 1812
Yankee ingenuity delivered the cable from Oswego to
Sackets Harbor

Plate IV   Preparing the Oswego Canal for another season
A view of locks 15 and 14 looking up-stream toward
the high-dam and the Oswego water works.

Plate V   Gerrit Smith
Oswego's oracle, land speculator, builder, philanthropist, abolitionist, prohibitionist and non-denominationalist.

Plate VI   DeWitt Clinton Littlejohn
Oswego's most controversial figure in the 19th century: orator, politician, soldier and railroad builder.

Plate VII   Oswego Harbor in the 1870's
Barges schooners and steamboats, viewed from the
island at Bridge Street

Plate VIII The Canal Basin in the 1870's
From left to right in the background: Gerrit Smith
Library, Church of the Evangelists (Episcopal). Ele-
mentary School, Number 4, Armory of the 48th
Company, New York National Guard.

Plate IX   Loading Railroad Rails for the West in the 1870's
It has often been said that one might walk across the river by stepping from schooner to schooner or packet to packet.

Plate X   Oswego's Grain Elevators in the 1880's
Oswego in transition: slack times for elevators and
colliers as Canadian timber overflows the island.

Plate XI   Toll House on the Plank Road at Brewerton
A section of America's first plank road linking Syracuse with Central Square.

Plate . XII   Dr. Mary Walker
Her proudest moment: Posing for Matthew Brady in
her surgeon's uniform after receiving a Congressional
Medal of Honor from President Johnson.

Plate XIII Dr. Edward Austin Sheldon, Founder of the
Oswego Movement
The vigorous septuagenarian prepares for day's activity

Plate XIV Father Barry; Oswego's Conscience
The Reverend Dean Michael J. Barry, Pastor of St.
Paul's Church, Oswego, 1869-1914.

Plate XV   Fort Ontario (photographed by William H. Leighton)
The third Fort Ontario, constructed between 1839-1866. It was never called upon to defend the Canadian-American border.

Plate XVI Fulton's Flour Milling Center (about 1912)
At First and Oneida Streets, looking north; with The
Oswego Canal in the foreground.

of war. "Hardshells" and Softshells," were soon belaboring one another as vehemently as the rival factions among the Whigs.

Upon the election of Pierce to the Presidency in 1852 the local Democratic factions struggled to seat their favorites in the custom house and post office. Both besieged William Marcy, the newly appointed Secretary of State, who was expected to control the New York patronage; the Oswego letters among the Marcy papers providing a blow by blow account. The Softs pointed to their loyalty in 1848, and to the disloyalty of the Barnburners in deserting Cass for Van Buren. Barnburners, meanwhile, represented their rivals as a small and divisive faction. Pierce apparently attempted to work out a compromise by naming a Soft, Enoch B. Talcott, as Collector, and Samuel R. Beardsley, a Barnburner, as Postmaster. Neither faction was pleased with the outcome.

The confusion was compounded by Nativism, and its political impact as the American or Know-Nothing Party. By the mid-fifties Republicans were recruiting a party from Conscience Whigs, Barnburners, Abolitionists and Know-Nothings. And again, as in the 1820's party labels meant less than personalities on election day.

The decline of Duer's political fortunes was paralleled by the rise of DeWitt C. Littlejohn, the area's most controversial political and financial figure in the nineteenth century, and consecutively, leader of the Whig and Republican parties.

Littlejohn came to Oswego from Albany in 1839 at the age of twenty-one to work as a clerk in the office of Henry Fitzhugh. The business association proved beneficial to both. Littlejohn was an indefatigable worker at whatever he turned his hand. As partners in the Old Oswego Line they developed extensive forwarding operations. They also expanded Fitzhugh's milling business, and purchased an interest in Smith's Grampus Bay property. Littlejohn married Alida Tabbs, a niece and ward of the Fitzhughs.

Both Fitzhugh and Littlejohn mixed business with politics. The former was mayor, assemblyman and state canal commissioner. The latter first served as a trustee of the village and later as its last president, while still in his twenties. He was twice mayor of the city. In 1851 he received a temporary setback when the defection of the Silver-Grays defeated his bid for mayor, but he was elected to the Assembly in 1852 despite the county's preference for Pierce and Seymour in the national and state elections.

In the Assembly he displayed talents of high order. He was earnest and forthright, yet courteous and affable. Tall, dark and slender, graceful in his movements, possessing a voice which was deep and resonant, he had few peers as an orator or debater. When emphasizing a point, he would thrust his right arm forward and point his index finger directly at his hearers. It became the most familiar mannerism in his oratorical bag of tricks.

In Oswego, a notice that he was to speak was the guarantee of a large house, and in Albany it often filled the gallery of the assembly chamber. It should be remembered in passing that this was an era when oratory was held in high esteem, and a speaker worth his salt was expected to hold the attention of his audience for two or more hours. This, Littlejohn did almost daily during the closing days of a campaign. From the platform he radiated a magnetism which might have made him a national figure, had not business frequently relegated politics to a secondary position.

At Albany he attracted the attention of Thurlow Weed, the Whig "Dictator," who made him one of his trusted lieutenants.

During his first years in the legislature Littlejohn's primary interest was an enlargement of the Oswego Canal to match one already provided for the Erie. He found that his best chance for success was not by obstructing appropriations for the Erie, but through supporting them on a *quid pro quo* arrangement with legislators from districts along the Erie. By such bargaining he secured appropriations for his local project, and saw it completed simultaneously with the Erie in 1855.

During his third term he emerged as a state leader. With Weed's backing he was elected Speaker, an office which soon seemed to belong to him. The climax of the session was the balloting for United Sates Senator. Seward, the incumbent, had the support of the majority party, and his election would have been a formality, had not an undetermined number of Whigs been tinged with Know-Nothingism. As Governor more than a decade before he had shown a willingness to use state funds to support Catholic schools, and thus, with nativism rampant, he was extremely vulnerable. For a time Know-Nothings and Democrats combined to prevent an election, and as the contest intensified, all other business ceased. "When at last DeWitt C. Littlejohn, vacating the Speaker's Chair, took the floor for the distinguished New Yorker, the excitement reached its climax. The Speaker's bold and fearless defense met a storm of personal denunciation that broke from the ranks of the Know-Nothings; but his speech minimized their opposition and inspired Seward's forces to work out a magnificent victory."[12]

Littlejohn's assault upon Know-Nothingism was circulated widely. Excerpts appeared in newspapers and were incorporated into resolutions at Whig rallies. It is doubtful whether so partisan a discourse changed many minds; but Seward's election followed, and jubilant Whigs celebrated with fireworks and bonfires.

Back home, Democrats and Know-Nothings raised a storm of protest over Littlejohn's behavior, and he responded in a dramatic appearance before an over-flow audience of friends and foes at Doolittle Hall. "Hundreds who went there to mock and denounce went away to cheer and vote for D. C. Littlejohn," boasted the partisan *Times*.[13]

Littlejohn accompanied the Weed-Seward faction into the newly organized Republican Party, and was caught up in the Presidential campaign of 1856. He pleaded business pressures in declining Weed's invitation to tour Central New York for Fremont, the Republican Presidential nominee, but accepted a nomination to the Assembly, running against the Democratic incumbent and Speaker of the previous session, Orville Robinson.

The campaign of 1856 was filled with imponderables. The Republican Party tried to attract Free-Soilers and Know-Nothings, and capitalize upon Fremont's reputation as the "Pathfinder of the West." Democrats insisted that "Bleeding Kansas" was largely a fabrication of the Republican press, and that free-soilism obstructed the organization of the West, which would reject slavery if left to its own choosing. Perhaps the most uncertain factor was the strength of Know-Nothingism.

On election eve Republicans staged a giant rally, where Seward and Littlejohn exhorted from the same platform. The strategy paid off. Fremont carried the county, as did John A. King, the Republican nominee for Governor. Littlejohn won his race for the Assembly, though his margin in the district was a thousand votes less than Fremont's. Yet his majority of 750 reversed one of 1500 given to his opponent the year before. Elated by his victory, he observed to Weed, that fearing the loss of the district, "Our friends put me in nomination against Speaker Robinson to beat him. *He was beaten,* and I am to pass another winter in Albany. Of course it is natural that I should desire to hold the same position as when last in the Assembly. Am I not warranted in asking, and shall I not have your influence?"[14]

He received Weed's backing, and despite allegations that Oswego did not merit the office for three consecutive terms, he was elected on the first ballot. Nevertheless, the session could scarcely have been a rewarding one. Pressing financial problems, stemming from the panic of 1857 awaited him at home, and politics had to go into a temporary eclipse.

In a letter to Seward, of particular interest because it

contains a self-evaluation of his personality and service, Littlejohn elaborated upon his plight.

> The commercial storm of last autumn found my affairs so extended (imprudently so), that nothing could ease me from shipwreck. From being worth $150,000 as I believed myself to be in the fall of 1856, I am now utterly ruined, so far as property is concerned. My property has nearly all, and all will be, turned over to my creditors. I have the battle of my business life to commence again, and at the best [there] are great disadvantages. My history is that of many thousands of our most liberal and most enterprising men; those who by their energy are always foremost in developing the wealth and resources of our country, often times at great hazards.
>
> Nothing is to be gained by restraining the energies of this class of men either to the country or their creditors. There seems to be no relief except in a general commercial bankrupt act, one that should be permanent and lasting.
>
> I need and must have its benefits, for I chafe at the thought of even one year of inactivity. Can you give me any assurance that such a measure will pass this session?[15]

It might be noted that no general bankruptcy act was forthcoming for another decade, and Littlejohn was forced to struggle along without its benefits.

His monetary distress finally put him in prison for a few hours;"an oppressive creditor" having obtained a judgment against him and his partners, Fitzhugh and Andrew Miller, in a propellor case. Families and friends hurried to the little county jail at Pulaski to offer aid and comfort; among them Mrs. Gerrit Smith and Mrs. James G. Birney, sisters of Fitzhugh. The defendants were released after several days, but Littlejohn's creditors continued to plague him for many months.

The election of 1856 was a turning point in Oswego County politics in that it revealed that the rural areas had been weaned from the traditional preference for the Democratic Party to a loyalty to Republicanism. The Republican ascendancy would continue for a century and beyond. On the other hand, the city of Oswego, with its Irish vote attached to the Democratic Party, frequently cast majorities for Democrats. In the spring of 1857, for example, the city elected a Democrat, Lucius B. Crocker, as Mayor, and in the fall it went Democratic again, threatening Littlejohn's bid for a reelection. He won, however, when Republicans piled up majorities in the rural sections of the district. He repeated in 1859, and gained his third and fourth election as Speaker.

During the 1859-60 session he cooperated with the Weed machine to grind out a series of bills for the chartering of street railways in New York City. When Governor Morgan vetoed them the Republican-controlled legislature repassed them by decisive majorities, and they became laws. Morgan objected to the lack of regulations to safeguard the public, and charged that the state was giving away privileges worth many thousands of dollars. During the contest there were allegations of high pressure lobbying and corruption in the legislature, and of payments totaling $25,000 to $500,000 for services rendered. Greeley's *Tribune* led the assault on the Weed juggernaut.

Following Lincoln's nomination for the Presidency in 1860 the Greeley and Weed factions fought bitterly to control the expected patronage in the state, and in the midst of the campaign Greeley returned to the railway controversy. He charged Littlejohn with responsibility for the "give away bills," and declared that he was corrupt and unfit to be reelected.

It is difficult to evaluate Greeley's motives in choosing the last weeks of the campaign to rend the party. Acknowledging his sincerity in combating corruption, a recent biographer concludes that his immediate purpose was to replace Seward in the United States Senate when his term expired that winter. "His attacks upon such Seward stalwarts as Littlejohn . . . fitted altogether too well with his ambition to be merely coincidental."[16]

Coming at a time when he was actively campaigning for Lincoln as well as his own re-election, Littlejohn found Greeley's allegations extremely embarrassing, but he hesitated to challenge his formidable critic lest he involve

Weed, and jeopardize the Republican campaign. In a "burn this letter" appeal to Weed he asked for his counsel. "Shall I prosecute Mr. Greeley for libel? I am told he has expressed a wish that I should do so, that he might place you on the stand as a witness. Suppose he does? Between us nothing has occurred that could injure either of us.

"Shall I write out my reasons in full for the support of the railroad bills or shall the subject drop until after elections?"[17]

After consulting also with Seward and Governor Morgan Littlejohn withheld legal action, and for the moment, simply addressed a denial to Greeley, who published it, but then renewed his charges.

Despite the internecine quarrel the Republicans carried the county and state, and Littlejohn was returned to Albany. But the intra-party strife was not relaxed. In fact Lincoln's procrastination in naming his Cabinet intensified it.

Strategists for the rival factions arrived early in Albany determined to control the choice of the Speaker and the election of a Senator. Littlejohn as usual received the backing of the Weed faction, while the Greeley forces agreed upon Lucius Robinson of Chemung County, a future Governor of the state. The caucus was heated. On the first ballot Robinson led by four votes but lacked the majority required for election. On the fifth Littlejohn edged ahead, whereupon the Greeley men dropped Robinson and threw their strength to a third candidate who had received a token vote. But the move failed. Littlejohn gained several votes to win by a bare majority. His election in the Republican-controlled Assembly was a formality. It was his fifth term as Speaker, a record to that time.

A Greeley man lamented that rural members had been convinced that "Thurlow [Weed] is the person that will deal out the soup for New York, and every person who is expecting to share in the good things of Lincoln's administration from the Empire State, must apply through him and at his favor. Upon this point alone, was Mr. Littlejohn nominated and Mr. Robinson defeated."[18]

Littlejohn repaid his debt to Weed a few weeks later when the legislature prepared to name a successor to Seward, who had been appointed Secretary of State.

The harassed "Dictator" was fighting for his political life, and never waged a harder battle. He backed William M. Evarts in the caucus, and the Anti-Weed coalition countered with Greeley. A few, committed to neither, voted for Ira Harris. For eight ballots Greeley gained slowly, and it appeared that another would give him the victory. Henry B. Stanton, the distinguished journalist, in his *Random Recollections* preserved a bit of the drama which followed:

> Pale as ashes, Weed sat smoking a cigar within ear shot of the bustle in the crowded assemblyroom where the caucus sat. Littlejohn stalked over the heads of the spectators and reported to Weed. Unmindful of the fact that he had a cigar in his mouth, Weed lighted another and put it in, then rose in great excitement and said to Littlejohn, "Tell the Evarts men to go right over to Harris; to Harris; to Harris!" The order was given in the caucus. They wheeled into line like Napoleon's Old Guard, and Harris was nominated.[19]

Again Littlejohn had demonstrated his worth as a lieutenant. As a reward for his labors Lincoln offered him an appointment as Consul to Liverpool, reported to be the most lucrative foreign post in the diplomatic service. He considered it, but finally declined; there was too much to be done at home.

When the first shots were fired at Fort Sumter, Littlejohn secured the adoption of resolutions in the Assembly pledging the power of the state to support Lincoln in the defense of the nation. He then hastened to Washington to deliver them in person. He boarded the same train which carried the Sixth Massachusetts Regiment, and at Baltimore witnessed its assault by a mob. Continuing his journey he carried the news of the rioting to Secretary Seward. With Washington virtually defenseless he enlisted in Casius M. Clay's improvised military company, and helped to guard the public buildings until troops arrived.

Back in Oswego a few weeks later, he prepared to settle the score with his tormentor. When Greeley again refused to retract, he initiated a libel suit for $25,000. Gerrit Smith urged him not to be vindictive, and reminded him of Greeley's poor health; but he would not be dissuaded.

The case was tried in Pulaski in September. The village had never hosted such an array of notables or legal talent; and it took on a festive air. Crowds gathered at the street corners awaiting the latest reports as they filtered from the well-packed little court room. Greeley offered no proof of Littlejohn's corruption, and insisted that he had only repeated current reports about improper influences in the legislature. But he used the opportunity to indict the Weed machine for corruption, and identified Littlejohn as a pliant tool. He reminded the jury that the Speaker had a responsibility to avoid suspicion. Yet he had left the Speaker's Chair to argue for the passage of the bills.

His clever counter-offensive tended to place the Weed faction, and Littlejohn in particular, on trial, and though the case ended in a hung jury, it was in reality a victory for Greeley. He gave the trial conspicuous coverage in the *Tribune*, and hailed the outcome as a vindication of the freedom of the press.

Littlejohn's feelings require no comment. He declined to seek a re-election to the Assembly, and busied himself in the recruitment of soldiers.

Politics in the area was eclipsed momentarily by the emergency. But it revived and remained very much alive through the war.

9

RELIGION IN THE VALLEY

The traditional picture of Americans trekking westward, clearing land and building homes; and after pausing only to take a second breath, erecting schoolhouses and white-spired churches is an oversimplification. Land and homes were necessities, whereas schools and churches were often luxuries, which a frontier community could not afford. The absence of clergy, lack of money, and remoteness from the older communities had to be overcome. And thus, while many Oswego pioneers were God-fearing people, they were physically unable for a time to duplicate the churches or meeting houses which they had left behind.

Years later Edwin W. Clarke of Oswego recalled that he had attended religious meetings but once during 1808: a Baptist service conducted by Elder Jeffers, a lay minister, on a weekday afternoon. However, others of his family had walked through the woods to meetings at the home of Theophilus Baldwin on the lake shore. Eleven years later Clarke reported only occasional Methodist meetings and a single Presbyterian sermon during a period of several months. Churches did not come to the frontier automatically; they arrived piecemeal and required labor and sacrifice.

Notable in the process were the contributions of the missionaries or itinerant clergy. Poorly paid, lodging wherever warm hearted people took them in, traversing primitive trails at the risk of life and limb, these dedicated enthusiasts made their unappointed rounds—baptising, burying, preaching or counseling according to the need. One such missionary was John Taylor, a Presbyterian, who visited Sandy Creek in 1802. "Preached to about 40 people September 2nd," he recorded. "The most I can say is that they behaved with tolerable decency. Three or four left the house sermon time. Gave one Bible and a half a dozen Catechisms to such persons as I thought would receive them. The people are in general nothing—Arians or fatalists, or Methodists and Baptists, who are the worst of all."[1] Taylor's animadversion toward the latter was not atypical of the older sects toward the upstart Methodists and Baptists.

A second bearer of the gospel was Chandley Lambert, a Methodist circuit rider, who was in Oswego County before 1812. Identified by his followers as "Father" Lambert, he is said to have preached with equal fervor against the Devil, Congregationalists, Baptists, and especially, Universalists, and to have been an inflexible man, and a good disciplinarian, "a fine example of the pioneer preacher."[2]

Another Methodist, Jonathan Heustis rode into Mexico unannounced, with a Bible and hymn books in his saddle bags. The "tall, solemn and neatly dressed and equipped" cleric, though probably not sartorially correct at the moment, wandered into a Presbyterian meeting, sat through it, and inquired for Methodists. He was directed to Mrs. Leonard Ames, who hastily spread the news of his arrival, and Heustis preached the first Methodist sermon delivered in the town in the Ames' cabin. He remained for some time, and helped to organize a Methodist congregation. Mrs. Ames converted a sheepfold into a meeting room, "and the first class for the central portion of Oswego County was soon organized, and found a safe and pleasant fold in the sheep-pen, which, like the log house to which it was attached, was always kept as neat as a band box."[3]

Still another circuit rider, the Reverend Tuller, preached in Fulton as early as 1809. He also covered Mexico, Sandy Creek, Sackets Harbor and Oswego on his rounds.

In 1817 Mrs. Catherine Hawley, who has been called the

"Mother of Methodism in Oswego," learned that three itinerant preachers were holding "revival" meetings at a camp
five miles southeast of the village. With Mary Cooley (a
Presbyterian) she walked to the meeting and begged the
clergymen to come and preach "in benighted Oswego,
where there was neither Church nor minister." Enoch
Barnes responded, organized a class, and helped bring the
First Methodist Church into being (The First Presbyterian
Church had been founded in 1816).[4]

Alvin Bronson, a Presbyterian, recalling the early days
after the passage of a half-century, had some good words
for itinerant Barnes and others, who had ministered in
the Fulton area.

> [Their] field of labor was Oswego Falls, and a more
> barren and forbidding field could not be found. The boat-
> men and fishermen were as a class inebriates or hard
> drinkers.
> These worthy men with starving stipends, the labor of
> galley slaves, and the devotion of martyrs, made converts
> among the humble, the degraded and the vicious; and for
> many years past, no part of our country, has stood better in
> its moral and social position, or in its industry, thrift and
> prosperity . . . And I may be allowed to say without offense,
> that this worthy class of preachers [has] improved and
> elevated themselves with their disciples and proselytes. The
> Methodist clergymen of our day is a better educated preach-
> er than his predecessor, and equally zealous and effect-
> ive.[5]

In one instance emigrants organized prior to departing
from New England, and brought a clergyman with them. In
1810 nine Congregationalists in Pawlett, Vermont, framed
a preliminary association and engaged Oliver Leavitt as
their pastor before departing for Pulaski. Leavitt remained
at Pulaski for eight years, and in his spare time preached at
New Haven, Fulton, Mexico, Central Square and Sandy
Creek. In 1819 he moved to Volney to become pastor of the
Congregational Church.[6]

In other cases preachers or lay preachers settled in the
infant communities, and were instrumental in founding
congregations. Joshua Johnson was a pioneer in Redfield,

and founded a Congregational Society there in 1802, the first in Oswego County. Five years later Elder Gamaliel Barnes, who had built the first log house and barn in the Town of Parish, organized the Baptist Church of Mexico. This congregation erected the first church building in the county at Colosse in 1823. With the interior substantially altered in 1873, this fine old building served as a sanctuary until the 1960's.

In the inevitable competition for adherents among early sects the Congregationalists had an initial advantage in that it was the traditional church of many of the pioneers. However, its decentralization and the virtual independence of each congregation left it without an effective means of propagation in regions removed from New England. The Presbyterians helped to fill this void. They had the hierarchy to initiate missions and support missionaries in the West; furthermore their Calvinistic doctrines were congenial to Congregational tastes. The Plan of Union of 1801 coordinated the missionary work of the two denominations, and it was not unusual for a congregation to switch its affiliation from one to the other.

Both Congregationalists and Presbyterians were handicapped, however, in competition with Baptists and Methodists by their insistence that clergy be college-trained and ordained, only after a lengthy preparation. Baptist lay preachers worked at trades during the week and preached on Sundays, while Methodist clergy, also licensed with the bare rudiments of a formal education, ministered to many congregations. Both operated on slender budgets.

The Presbyterians seem to have organized initially in Mexico as a Congregational Society in 1811. They engaged the Rev. Oliver Leavitt of Pulaski for a series of sermons, and appealed to George Scriba for his "aid in procuring a piece of land for the support of the Preached Gospel in said Society." Scriba shrewdly offered them fifty acres "on condition that each Member of the Society shall work or cause to be worked three days labor on the public highway between Rotterdam and the 23rd Town [Parish] in one month from date." The Congregation accepted, performed the work on the road, and obtained the "Glebe Lot."[7] After several years the Society obtained a minister, David R. Dixon, a Yale graduate. In 1818 the church reorganized to become Presbyterian.

Meanwhile in 1816 Dixon joined John Davenport, pastor of societies at Baldwinsville and Lysander, to organize a Presbyterian congregation at Oswego. There were seventeen charter members: two men and fifteen women. The society built its first edifice near the center of West Park in 1825. The small Georgian structure with its graceful bell-tower offered a favorable contrast to the nondescript buildings of the village. In rough weather a light was hung in the steeple, and it is said that it guided many a navigator to port. Its bell was the only one in the community, and it was rung at stated intervals to indicate the time of day. It was also a fire signal and the beacon of special events.

In 1841, the meeting house burned to the ground; only the bell escaping injury. They rebuilt at West Fourth and Bridge streets rather than in the park; opposition having arisen in the village to its use for churches. The new building, completed in 1844, was a spacious stone structure with massive columns and an imposing tower. It stands, sans-cupola after more than a century. James Abell became the first settled pastor in 1825; and six years later Robert W. Condit was installed. He remained for forty years, to become one of the community's outstanding leaders.

In 1872 the founders of Grace Presbyterian Church separated from "Old First" and erected a gothic edifice at West Fifth and Oneida streets, where the pews were not to be rented or sold. "Anyone can have all the room he wishes by asking for it; and that, regardless of whether he pays much or little, or anything towards the support of the church."[8]

During the 1820's the Methodists (First Methodists) and Episcopalians (Christ Church) organized congregations at

Oswego, and by 1832 had constructed churches in West Park. In 1848 the Methodist Society was divided, and the East Methodist (Trinity) was founded. A year later the little Methodist Church in the park burned, and the First Methodist erected a church at West Fourth and Oneida Streets. An African Methodist church was formed in 1847, and for a time, listed as many as thirty-seven members.

Episcopalians susbequently erected a new edifice at West Fifth and Cayuga streets. It was an imposing structure of gothic design with green sandstone facing. Meanwhile, the Episcopal Church of the Evangelists was organized in 1850 by east-siders, who erected a substantial stone house of worship at East Second and Oneida streets.

The Baptists who were the first to found a society on the east side erected a church at the southeastern corner of East Park in 1831.

A Congregational society was founded at Oswego Falls in 1818. It later became the Presbyterian Church and Society of Fulton and Granby, and built its first church at the corner of Oneida and Second streets in Fulton. Episcopalians (Zion Church) in Fulton organized in 1835.

In Hannibal Presbyterians and Baptists were in the vanguard, and in New Haven Congregationalists and Methodists furnished the initial leadership. In Scriba, the presence of Asahel Bush, a pioneer preacher who came from the East on an ox-sled, gave the Baptists an early start. In Schroepel Methodists and Baptists organized at Gilbert's Mills, and Congregationalists and Methodists were first on the scene at Phoenix. In Sandy Creek Methodists, Congregationalists and Baptists had erected churches by mid-century.

By contrast Episcopalians, aided by a gift of land from Frederick W. Scriba, son of George Scriba, were the first to erect a church at Rotterdam (Constantia). George Scriba, his brother-in-law, Burnet Dundas, George Scriba, Jr., and Frederick W. Scriba were members of the vestry. At Bernhard's Bay, nearby, a small society of Friends organized in 1846.

That early generations of Oswegonians took their religions seriously needs little documentation. Hell was a reality awaiting the sinner, and the hand of God was seen in the daily events. Death was an all-too-frequent reminder of the omnipotence of the Creator. Intolerance, and a denominational approach to heaven were not uncommon. At times congregations refused to share their meeting houses with others, and hecklers were prone to interrupt the earnest and occasionally boisterous sermons of the circuit rider. A few Presbyterians in Mexico went so far as to board up their pews rather than permit Methodists to occupy them on alternate Sundays.

But there was at least an occasional spirit of tolerance. Surely, Nancy (wife of Deodatus) Clarke exemplified it in an exchange of views with her uncle in Vermont. Writing after a hard day's work, with a swarm of moths fluttering around the candle, this frail forty-six year old mother of ten observed:

> I am no foe of Episcopalianism: The thirty-nine articles contain my creed. I do not think religion consists in *modes* and *forms,* but in genuine affections of the heart. The heart is not affected by the position of the body, yet I think a kneeling posture when addressing our Lord is altogether proper, and so is standing while singing his praise. I say it is not Episcopalianism that I dislike, but a corruption of its pure and genuine doctrines. Many of my favorite authors are of that denomination, Wilberforce, Scott, Buchanan and Horne, with a host of others. So honor the Christian name, and manifest to the world that their minds have been enlightened and their hearts renewed by the Holy Spirit. I think I love Christians in whatever denomination I find them, for the difference in real Christians lies wholly in nonessentials. The party spirit which rages in some of all denominations, is so far from belonging to Christianity, that it is the very spirit of the adversary.[9]

Church raisings, of course, were highlights in the life of the times. One such raising, carried through without the stimulation of the jug, is remembered as an exception to the rule. Even so, it was accomplished only by knocking the bottle of a would-be-user to the ground. When Prattville (east of Mexico) Congregationalists affixed the steeple to their church, a workman, scanning the horizon, observed the shining waters of Lake Ontario several miles away. His shout attracted others to the ridge pole. One, who was possibly a bit more jubilant than the others, hurled a whiskey bottle from his lofty perch. Years later it was recalled that the neck of the bottle had buried itself several inches in the ground—evidence of the height of the steeple and the exuberance of the thrower.

The pioneer churches assumed a responsibility for the conduct of the flock. Delinquencies and back-slidings, drunkenness, intemperance and folly, parental failures to prevent children from attending public dances, profane language, theft, and communing with Presbyterians were among the charges aired before the Baptist Board at Colosse; and Elder Barnes was rebuked for not attending services. But he refused to accept the jurisdiction of the Board, and was later reinstated to preach for two dollars per week.

Mexican Presbyterians also disciplined their members. Charges were preferred against one woman for "treating her husband with habitual disrespect, and not obeying her husband in the Lord," and a male parishioner confessed to the sins of falsehood, slander and Sabbath breaking. A third member was excommunicated for neglecting his covenant obligations and being disrespectful to the pastor; a fourth was taken before the Session for intemperance, neglecting his family, and absence from public worship. A member who built a dam in the village, and allegedly flooded his neighbor's land, was tried by the Church Board and disciplined. Thus church authority embraced the gamut of social relations.

The work of the clergy was supplemented in the early years by the activities of the American Tract Society, which distributed thousands of religious tracts in the region. Edwin W. Clarke for a time was an agent of the society, and traveled extensively in New York and New England.

Clarke also assisted in fostering the Sunday School

system. His secretarial report for the Oswego County Sunday School Teacher's Association in 1831 indicated that dozens of Sunday Schools had been established in the district school houses; there were twenty-six in the Town of Volney, thirteen each in Scriba, Granby and Hannibal, and eight in New Haven.[10] Later the various denominations took the movement under their own care.

With the coming of the canals and railroads, Roman Catholic Irish and French Canadians arrived in the valley; and by 1840 they constituted a sizeable minority in Oswego and Fulton.

As early as 1830 a handful of Catholics in Oswego, finding that they could finance the traveling expenses of a Priest, invited Father O'Donahoe of Auburn to visit them. He accepted, and for a time conducted services every three months in a private home on the west side. Several years later they purchased a lot from Gerrit Smith on East Fifth Street and erected St. Paul's, the first Roman Catholic Church in the county. They enlarged it in 1844 and a decade later added a brick schoolhouse.

In 1869, Dean Barry, a man with remarkable leadership qualities, was appointed pastor. Under his direction a handsome stone edifice was constructed, much of the labor being contributed by the men of the parish. He subsequently added a recreation hall and installed a fine organ. He attracted organists from Europe, and the quality of the church's music was known far and wide. He was a bitter foe of vice, intemperance and the desecration of the Sabbath, and waged a forty-five year battle against them. His vigor in civic as well as spiritual affairs remains unforgotten a half-century after his death.

An incident, which occurred late in his life, will illustrate the awesome majesty of his presence upon teenagers of his parish. A large number of young people had been attending dances in a grove on Mitchell Street, and it was reported that several saloons in the neighborhood were doing an unusual turn-over. Father Auger of the St. Louis Church went to the grove and appealed to the adolescents to leave the festivities and return to their homes. It had little effect. The next night the stately form of Father Barry appeared suddenly in the midst of the liveliest music, his long white hair flowing over his shoulders from the brim of his tall silk hat. There was a wild rush to get away, and in a twinkling of an eye he stood alone in the grove.[11]

The local press in its report of the affair used the apt heading: "The Dance Was Ended;" and so it was.

Meanwhile in 1848, St. Mary's Roman Catholic Church was founded by Father F.E. Foltier at the request of French Canadians in the Oswego vicinity. They constructed a frame edifice the following year at the corner of West Sixth and Cayuga streets. In March 1859 tragedy struck suddenly, when the floor sank under the weight of an overflowing audience attending a mission of the Order of Redemptorists. The fall was gradual, and apparently no one was seriously injured; but in the ensuing rush toward the doors a panic developed. Before clergy and police could restore order four were killed and many others injured.

For a time the French shared the church with Irish, German and English parishioners, but finding themselves outnumbered, they sought a church of their own. In 1870 they organized the St. Louis French Catholic Church, moved to the east side to be near the French quarter, and erected a building in the Roman basilica style.

By 1860 the German element was numerous enough to seek a National Church. With the assistance of Father Joseph Wissel, the first German Priest to labor among his countrymen in Oswego, and the St. Boniface Society, St. Peter's German Roman Catholic Church was formed. They erected a sanctuary at East Seventh and Albany streets in 1862.

The English and Irish influx was reflected in a third parish in the southwestern part of the city, and the erection of the Church of St. John the Evangelist in 1871.

In forty years Roman Catholicism had attained a majority status in Oswego.

Meanwhile in Fulton the Church of the Immaculate Conception had its inception in services initiated there by Father Kelly of Oswego in 1850. A magnificent brick and stone edifice replaced an older structure in 1895.

A little French island in a sea of Protestantism was the setting for a Roman Catholic Church at French Street in the southern corner of the Town of Mexico. A small colony of French emigrants had settled here between 1820 and 1840. There were both Catholics and Protestants in the community, though the former predominated. Just after 1840 the Catholics erected St. Ann's Church, a small frame building with a tall, graceful steeple. For a time it enrolled more than a hundred families, but with the decline of the rural population and the withdrawal of Mexico Village communicants to St. Mary's early in the twentieth century, the little church was closed. Only the cemetery with its French inscriptions remains. A similar tiny French Catholic Church was organized at Little France in Hastings.

The rise of the Seventh-Day Adventists is closely linked with the Oswego area. Small groups were attracted to the preachings of William Miller, who forecast the second coming of Christ in 1843, and at least several of these bodies gathered in the open air to await the momentous event. Crestfallen at its failure, Miller's followers accepted a second date only to be disappointed again. The initial movement subsided, but several Adventist congregations, including the Seventh-Day Adventists endured.

A little congregation occupied the basement of Gerrit Smith's tabernacle property on West Second Street in 1844. "The Millerites are much pleased at yours and Mrs. Smith's proposition to charge them no rent until the first of April," Edwards reassured his employer.[12] They seem to have moved elsewhere before 1848. By that time, however, a number of Adventists were living in the Roosevelt Cemetery section of Schroeppel and neighboring Volney.

In August of 1848 one of the first conferences of the church was held in David Arnold's barn near Mount

Pleasant. About thirty-five delegates discussed their Biblical interpretations and then celebrated the Lord's Supper, the first recorded in Seventh-Day Adventist history. The conference was largely responsible for the stabilization of Adventist doctrine.

Adherents were soon added to the growing movement in West Monroe, New Haven, Scriba, Mexico, Richland and Oswego; and at the latter James White, one of the founders, published a series of tracts, and initiated *The Present Truth*, one of the official publications of the denomination. Conferences were held in Oswego in 1849, 1851, 1854, and 1855, where plans for a more formal organization were formulated. In 1858 the congregation at Roosevelt was given permission to build a sanctuary. It was dedicated the next year, and still stands today as the oldest church building still in use.

At meetings at Roosevelt in 1862 and 1863 the denomination's noncombatant military position was defined. Adventists were not permitted to bear arms, but might serve in the medical corps.

Churches were eventually established in more than a dozen communities in the county; most of them in the rural areas.[13]

Universalists were organized in several communities by 1850. They were particularly active in Mexico, Fulton and Oswego, but eventually lost momentum, and their buildings were taken over by other denominations.

For a time at mid-century Spiritualism attracted adherents. Because many people gave lip service to it without actually affiliating with an organized group, its acceptance is difficult to measure. But the sensation created by the Fox Sisters at Hydesville and Rochester stimulated the movement across the state, and Oswegonians were soon turning out to view demonstrations.

One in a district schoolhouse at Prattville was said by a witness to have been "beautifully perfect and absolutely demonstrative. A perfect cluster of spirit hands were re-

peatedly exhibited in a clear, bright light and long continued, and most harmonious music on five different instru-
ments were played at the same time by the spirits, while the
mediums were perfectly tied."[14] The promoters of the
meeting were later fined for unlawfully entering the building and trampling the grass.

A few weeks later they were convicted at Phoenix for
failing to secure a license and committed to the Oswego jail.
However, no unpleasant repercussions followed a seance
conducted at the home of Orville Robinson in Oswego. In
fact a local paper hailed it as the greatest manifestation
since the Rochester rappings.

Spiritualists were numerous enough in 1861 to sponsor a
boat excursion to the Bay of Quinte, where Oswego Spiritualists met with their brethren in Canada. The experiment
was so successful that they took a similar jaunt the following year to Pultneyville and Charlotte, and mingled with
Rochester adherents of the cult. Enroute the travelers were
entertained by a brass band; there was also dancing and
singing as well as speech making.

Spiritualism receded thereafter, although as late as 1900
the Reverend Susannah Harris held a seance in the parlor of
Dr. Mary Walker for the edification of neighbors along the
Bunker Hill Road.

For many years Gerrit Smith attempted to foster non-
sectarianism in Oswego. Convinced that denominationalism
was an evil, he resolved to assist in founding a church based
on Christian union, "simple and liberal, yet scriptural in its
principles, without any denominational name or distinction,
to be called, 'The Church of Oswego worshipping on
Second Street.' " It would have "the whole Bible, and
nothing but the Bible for its Creed."[15]

He purchased a building formerly used by a disbanded
Congregational society on West Second Street (the Tabernacle), installed Samuel Mills as pastor, and guaranteed to
make up any deficiencies in his salary for two years, and if
the experiment failed to pay him an additional one hundred

dollars to move his family to another community. With an attendance which fluctuated from seven to twenty Mills was soon discouraged. Smith urged him to persevere, however, even though he received but a half dozen members. Mills waged the battle for nondenominationalism for six months, then gave up the struggle.

Several years later Smith withdrew from the Presbyterian Church and organized a nonsectarian church in Peterboro, but it failed after a short trial. Smith's missionary zeal soon had Edwards wavering between Methodism, his denomination for twenty years, and nondenominationalism. He declared his objections to the divisions within the family of God, but acknowledged his attachment to many of the Methodists.[16] Edwards balked, however, at Smith's acceptance of Saturday as the proper Sabbath day. In 1850 Smith sponsored an anti-sectarian convention in Oswego. After some difficulty in finding a meeting place, Edwards obtained the Second Presbyterian Church.

Lewis Kellogg, pastor of the Second Presbyterian Church, undertook the defense of denominationalism at the convention and from his own pulpit, and affronted the non-denominationalists by refusing to permit them to preach a rebuttal in his church. Kellogg's arguments do not appear to have stimulated his parishioners, for the society disbanded a few months later. His flock formed a nucleus for the founding of the Congregational Church at East Fourth and Oneida streets in 1857.

By 1850 Smith stopped giving money for church buildings, and his views became more and more unorthodox. But he made little headway in Oswego despite a quarter-century of activity. In his last years, possibly wearied by controversy, he attended Methodist services.

Shortly after he had determined to reject solicitations from churches Smith offered $25,000 to Oswego for a public library, specifying only that it be built on the east side and that its privileges be conferred upon all persons without regard for race or color. His generous gift, with an additional $5,000 for books was accepted, and the institution continues to be one of the region's cultural centers after more than a century.

Perhaps the most colorful figure in the history of religion in Oswego was Ned Lee. Born in 1846 of Scotch-Irish parents in the "Flats," a sailor's hang-out at the lower end of West Seneca Street (where Lee once observed that no officer of the law or respectable person of another ward dared to tread at night), and left an orphan at six, he sailed the lakes when he was not in the toils of the law. During the Civil War he was freed from jail on the condition that he enlist in the service. He did a two-year term in the navy and later joined the army. He was captured in the Battle of the Wilderness, and was a prisoner of war for almost a year. Later, he went west, and spent time in prisons in Milwaukee and Detroit.

To a woman who presented him with a bouquet of flowers while he was incarcerated in Syracuse, he attributed "the great change" which came to his life. He was converted to Christianity, and became an evangelist, a crusader for temperance, and a social worker. He labored at a mission in Albany, and then toured the towns of up state New York from Syracuse to Buffalo preaching temperance. In between times he returned to Oswego, where he operated The Peoples' Mission and conducted services at the county and city jails. During hard times after 1873 he added a soup kitchen to his establishment. He left Oswego in 1887 to work for the New York City missions in the Bowery, ·but he returned two years later. He subsequently added the superintendency of the Society for the Prevention of Cruelty to Children, and the Society for the Prevention of Cruelty to Animals to his multifarious responsibilities.

Elder residents still recall his athletic figure, colorful and dynamic delivery, volatile temperament, resonant voice and love of children as well as the down-trodden. His book, *Prison Camp and Pulpit, the Life of a City Missionary in the Slums, Talks and Tramps Here and There*, still affords interesting reading.

The late Dr. Lida S. Penfield summarized his life in these felicitous words:

> A veteran of three great struggles, the rebellion against law and order of his ill-disciplined, tempestuous youth, the Civil War, and the crusade to bring men to the good life, he proved himself the good sailor who pulled for shore and reached the fair haven where he would be the brave soldier who held the fort for his captain.[17]

The colorful evangelist died in Davenport, Iowa, in 1927.

10

THE ANTI-SLAVERY CRUSADE

The tradition of the anti-slavery movement and the Underground Railroad in the Oswego Valley has lingered into the twentieth century. Five generations of children have listened wide-eyed to the tales of tunnels reaching to the harbor from the cellars of the station-keepers. The stories have lost little in the telling but if the tunnels are imaginary, the stations are real, and their operators deserving of their immortality.

That Oswego should have participated in abolitionism is not surprising. New Englanders and their descendants were receptive to its appeal. Canadian captains and crews, embarking almost daily during the navigation season for Canadian ports, were more than willing to whisk fugitives across the lake to freedom. Finally, Gerrit Smith, one of the national leaders of the anti-slavery crusade, centered his operations here.

The region's first convert to abolitionism cannot be determined, but it may have been "Quaker" Alfred Wells of Colosse or James Caleb Jackson of Mexico. The two participated in a series of debates on the merits of abolitionism in the district schools prior to 1835. The latter, a farm boy in his early twenties with a flare for oratory, participated in the inception of the New York Anti-Slavery Society at the home of Gerrit Smith in 1835. With financial help from Smith he left his farm to preach abolitionism, and was employed by the Massachusetts Anti-Slavery Society as an agent and spokesman. His rustic appearance in sophisticated New England elicited the sobriquet, "Farm Boy Speaker." He later accepted political abolitionism, and parted company with the Garrisonians who spurned this expedient. Returning to Central New York he edited the *Madison County Abolitionist,* a Liberal Party organ, and lectured at anti-slavery rallies.

During an illness he experimented with the dietary reform of Sylvester Graham and the Priessnitz water cure at Cuba, New York, and after his recovery studied medicine and set up his own water cure at Sanatoria on Skaneateles Lake. Later at Dansville he manufactured one of the first health cereal foods, "Granula," and a cereal beverage, "Soma." Competitors enlarged upon the idea at Battle Creek, Michigan, and changed breakfast habits of millions of Americans. Jackson's ventures in dietary reform removed him from the anti-slavery movement, but meanwhile, others carried on.

Gerrit Smith's conversion was a boon to the movement in both the Madison and Oswego areas, and his impressionable agent at the latter, John B. Edwards, was soon a recruit also. There were, in addition, the Clarke brothers, Edwin and Sidney in Oswego, Hiram and Andrus Gilbert at Gilbertsville, and Asa Wing in Mexico. Wing was a younger contemporary of Jackson, who also had the gift of oratory, and lectured before anti-slavery audiences in New York and New England. Unfortunately, his promising career was cut short by consumption, and he succumbed at the age of thirty-eight.

An obituary in the local press attested to the quality of his contribution:

> The first time we saw him was ten years ago. We heard of him before, that he was a young man of great heart, abilities and eloquence; but then we saw and heard him holding thousands of men and women by the force of his logic in the great grove of Syracuse, pressing the claims of the noble Birney against Van Buren and Clay, breasting the storm of 1844 pregnant with Texas annexation and continental despotism. From that time he was a public man and identified

with the first class of anti-slavery orators in the State, including Gerrit Smith and J. C. Jackson, certainly inferior to
none in innocence, purity, benevolence and all that is lovely
in human character.[1]

A year after his death abolitionists gathered at Mexico to
dedicate a monument in his honor. The principal eulogy
was reserved for Frederick Douglass, the outstanding Negro
lecturer and publicist. "He poured out his life for the perish-
ing slave," he declared, "pleading for him with an eloquence and earnestness which could have scarcely been
more direct, pathetic, and touching, had his own wife and
children been on the auction block . . . He dared to be called
an abolitionist when mob violence howled from one end of
the state to the other."[2]

The first reference to a local anti-slavery association
appeared in the press in 1835 just prior to the founding of
the New York Anti-Slavery Society. "A few abolitionists
among us," it lamented, "have resolved upon calling a
meeting in this county—not that the meeting will tend to
promote their principles or add converts to their cause, but
that it is calculated to stir up a spirit in this community
which will not be quieted until much ill feeling is en-
gendered among our citizens . . . Verily, these men are as-
suming a dreadful responsibility, and we hope every citizen
who has one spark of humanity or would save this union
from dissolution, will pause and reflect before he gives his
aid in the work of destruction . . . We hope [the meeting]
will be avoided by every citizen who wishes the peace of the
community.[3]

Most readers accepted the paper's advice and simply
turned their backs upon the rally, but a hard corps was
organized, which continued to agitate year after year
despite public apathy. Other local cells were established in
Pulaski, Mexico and Fulton, but membership was always
limited to a small, hard-bitten band of enthusiasts; it did not
appeal to the casual or the lukewarm.

Taking their cue from Smith, who saw potential in
political action by some three hundred local anti-slavery

societies in the state, Oswego abolitionists turned to politics. In 1839 at a convention in the Presbyterian Church of New Haven they agreed to use every constitutional means to remove the abominable system of human bondage. To give substance to this principle, they resolved to support no candidate for office, who had not given evidence of his regard for freedom by accepting membership in an anti-slavery society.

They addressed queries to the nominees for the Assembly to ascertain whether they would support a trial by jury for fugitive slaves: and where replies were unsatisfactory or not forthcoming, they made nominations of their own. On election day they polled 240 votes in the county. Thus they were in the vanguard of the Liberty Party movement in the state and nation, and the first in the former to run independent candidates.

The following year Oswego abolitionists participated in the nation-wide campaign of the Liberty Party in support of James G Birney for President, and Gerrit Smith for Governor. Though admittedly a lost cause, New York abolitionists waged an aggressive campaign. Of the six thousand votes polled across the nation for Birney, New York contributed 2,700 and Oswego County, 166. Volney abolitionists made the best showing, casting thirty-eight votes. Scriba, including Oswego east of the river, polled eighteen, Oswego Village, ten. It was hardly a significant achievement, but they were not easily discouraged; and far from despairing, turned their sights on 1844.

The nomination that year of James K. Polk, a Tennessee planter, by the Democrats, and Henry Clay, a Kentucky slaveholder, by Whigs, was grist for the anti-slavery mill. Edwards distributed hundreds of pamphlets throughout Oswego County and parts of Jefferson as well. They held rallies in Oswego, where Gerrit Smith was the chief attraction, and at Fulton, where Wing's oratory thrilled his listeners.[4] Results were gratifying; the Liberty vote for Birney and for James Brown for Congress exceeding eight hundred. Volney again led the way, followed by Richland

and Mexico. Whigs were "exceedingly angry" at the abolitionists, Edwards noted, their vote having defeated the
Whigs and handed the county to the Democrats.[5]

Anti-slavery forces continued to agitate through 1845
and 1846. During the latter they found a new issue in the
Constitution of 1846, which denied the ballot to Negroes
who could not meet property qualifications. Overlooking
democratic features in the new document, they blasted the
franchise clause and carried their battle to polls. They lost
again.

But repeated failures did not alter the pattern of political
anti-slavery. In 1849 Frederick Douglass lectured in Oswego; and a short time later, S.R. Ward, a fugitive from
slavery, addressed the annual abolitionist county convention at Fulton, and found lodging in the home of John B.
Edwards.

Oswego momentarily became the focal point of anti-
slavery in the nation, when local abolitionists played host to
the Liberty Party's annual convention in 1850. Delegates
from points as distant as Michigan and Massachusetts
meeting in Market Hall heard addresses by Dr. James
Caleb Jackson, S.R.Ward and Gerrit Smith. The recent
passage of the Compromise of 1850, including the controversial Fugitive Slave Law, gave immediacy to the
deliberations.

Having found their most explosive issue in the Fugitive
Slave Law, abolitionists pursued it relentlessly. They thrilled to observe thousands of Whigs and Democrats, who had
heretofore remained cool to anti-slavery, denounce the law
and agitate for its repeal. "Anti-Slavery is working glori-
ously in this place now," Edwards observed to Smith.[6]

But the opposition to the Fugitive Slave Law did not win
converts to the Liberty Party. Instead, it helped to lay the
foundation for the Republican Party, and the Liberty vote
dwindled to insignificance.

Yet they persevered. In 1857 national leaders of the Gar-
risonian faction including Susan B. Anthony and Frederick

Douglass participated in a county anti-slavery convention in Oswego.

As 1860 approached abolitionists were reluctant to trust the issue to the Republican Party. Writing to Smith, Edwards noted that "Republicans have the impudence to ask me if I will not go for Lincoln. I tell them I should look beautiful voting for a President, who would be for sending a Marshal after me for helping the fugitive slaves to Canada."[7] But he could not overlook the trend. Republicanism was swallowing abolitionism. In the ensuing election only sixteen abolitionist votes were cast in the county; eight of them in Granby. Abolitionism had failed; yet their goal through the instrumentality of the Emancipation Proclamation was less than three years away.

The beginnings of the Underground Railroad in the Oswego area are cloaked in secrecy and folklore, but it seems to have begun in the 1830's, shortly after its main lines had been coordinated in Ohio and Pennsylvania. It was stimulated by a New York statute in 1840, which provided a jury trial for fugitives, and its pace was again quickened by the Fugitive Slave Law of 1850.

While there may not have been a typical case, Gerrit Smith established a well-worn branch with his home serving as a station. Fugitives were relayed from Peterboro to Canastota on the Erie Canal and forwarded to Oswego. When the canal was too conspicuous the slower overland route was substituted. Arriving at Oswego they were housed with one of the small coterie of abolitionists while their passage to Canada was arranged.

The first reference to the underground in the Edwards-Smith correspondence appears in 1845, when on July 17 Edwards noted that "nine poor fugitives from slavery's prison left this port last evening for Canada. They were, I am told, in much fear that pursuers were after them."

Two years later Edwards reported a second case in greater detail. "On Saturday last, that slavery maimed and branded man and Brother, Robert Thompson, called on me with his subscription book and letters. By considerable effort I raised in this place $31.25 for him, and this morning put him on the steamboat for Lewiston." He reminded Smith that the fugitive's family would soon arrive at Oswego and that he had agreed to provide a house for them.[8]

Edwards' next reference occurred a short time after the passage of the Fugitive Slave Law. "Fugitive slaves," he noted, "have become almost contented to remain in this place, and [Benjamin] Hockley will probably remain." But four months later Hockley departed for Canada, "afraid of the fugitive law." He hoped to return to Oswego in the spring, Edwards added, and wished to retain the house and lot which Smith had provided for him.[9]

In April, 1852, Edwards reported that the "fugitive Dorsey came to me today with your letter. I have put him aboard a vessel bound for Canada and gave him $1.00. He appears more intelligent than a slave-holding family by the name of Dorsey with whom I was acquainted in Lyons when I was a boy."[10]

The next year Edwards observed that he had not seen a fugitive whom Smith had forwarded, but that another had arrived, and he had taken him to Hamilton Littlefield for housing. Two years later he reported that he had placed ten runaways, five women and five children, aboard a steamboat for Canada. Then in April, 1860, he advised Smith that the "smart colored man, Henry, arrived here last evening. I will see to getting him underway for Canada."[11] And finally, several weeks after Lincoln's inauguration, he noted that "the young colored man that was at your house last week arrived at my house last evening. I shall keep him a few days to recuperate a little from the effects of his hard travel."[12]

Edwards made no further references to the underground; it might be equally interesting to know what remained unwritten.

A second source of information on the Underground Railroad is a reminiscence written in 1931 by John J.

Clarke, son of Sidney Clarke.[13] Too young to have been an eye-witness, he based his account upon conversations with his mother more than a half century before. Details, therefore, may be questioned; but there is no doubt that the Clarkes were participants. Sidney Clarke lived on the family farm just east of Oswego, and his brother Edwin, in the city; both were ardent abolitionists.

Clarke wrote that the fugitives usually arrived at his Uncle Edwin's house, and were then delivered to the farm. He identified Syracuse, Auburn, Sterling and Mexico as relay stations. At the farm they were hidden in or about the barn until their transportation on the lake was arranged. Ship captains were usually cooperative, and carried the refugees for as little as one dollar each. The fugitives were ordinarily delivered after dark; they usually walked from the farm to the docks, following Sidney at a safe distance. If speed or security were required they were loaded into a wagon and covered. Their best known "guest" was the famous "Jerry" of the "Jerry Rescue" at Syracuse.[14] They lodged him for four days, then shuttled him to Canada.

Clarke also reported that the farm was searched on several occasions, but no hideaways were discovered. Once a timely warning from Edwin permitted them to remove runaways to the woods at the rear of the barn. His father had estimated the number of fugitives hidden on the farm at more than eighty; but his mother's recollection enlarged the figure to 125.

A third source, a study made in 1907, indicates the pivotal role of Hamilton Littlefield, who maintained a hideaway for fugitives in his cellar, and delivered them to Canada on his lumber ships.[15]

There is also the story of the child in the home of Judge Orville Harmon, who unsuspectingly opened a closet door to see two eyes gleam from the murky interior; and her father's reproach that she never speak again of the incident. The house and closet are still identified.

Tunnels are also said to connect the Edwards, Littlefield

and Clarke homes with the harbor. The veracity of the Edwards tradition would seem to be impugned by the fact that he occupied this house after the Civil War. Yet the story lingers.

For good measure, there are additional tunnels associated with the homes of Civil War heroes, though none was identified with anti-slavery prior to the war.

In the village of Mexico Elizabeth Simpson uncovered more than a dozen reputed underground stations. The headquarters was the store and house of Starr Clark, which were connected by a passage between cellars.

The Underground Railroad remains one of the traditions of Gilbertsville. A grandson of Andrus Gilbert recalls a story told by his father more than fifty years ago.

> Mrs. Griffith [who lived a short distance from the Gilberts] came to my grandmother after church one Sunday asking her help with a colored girl, whom she was hiding in her house. The girl was depressed because she had become separated from her family, who had escaped with her. She feared that all of the others were lost. Grandmother suggested that she bring the girl to her house to visit with a girl whom she was secreting. Mrs. Griffith agreed; and when the two girls met, they rushed into each other's arms. They were sisters![16]

An attic room in the Griffith house, where fugitives were said to have been hidden, adds authenticity to the tale.

Most of the churches in the Oswego area remained aloof from the abolitionist controversy during the first twenty years. A notable exception, however, was the Second Presbyterian in Oswego, where the Pastor, Charles Jones, advocated abolitionism from his pulpit. His position divided the congregation and impaired the society's income. "It is pretty close times with him in getting support," Edwards commented. "The proslavery part of his church are much dissatisfied with him on account of his faithfulness in showing the people their sins." Five months later Jones was dismissed for "doing his duty too well for wicked Oswego."[17] The decision was subsequently reversed by his supporters, but the church languished.

The Fugitive Slave Act ended the apathy of the churches. "We had a sound, whole-hearted, political anti-slavery sermon preached by our local preacher [H.Colborn at the Trinity Methodist Church]," Edwards exulted.[18] West Methodists called a special protest meeting, where they condemned the law as opposed to "the mandates of Heaven and subversive of the most sacred rights of man."[19] Baptists and Presbyterians in Oswego registered similar protests. Trinity Methodists also took up an offering to aid those charged with complicity in the "Jerry Rescue."

But the issue remained divisive. When Mason Gallagher of the Church of the Evangelists (Episcopal) delivered a series of anti-slavery sermons, he found that the majority supported him, but he "unfavorably affected some dozen families." He weighed the financial losses which might result should the disaffected withdraw to the west side (Christ Church), but decided to continue with the sermons. "I have given offense to all the so-called Conservatives in town," he reported, "but I believe there is virtue enough in this place to sustain the untrammeled and fearless preaching of the gospel. I shall persevere with the help of God." One of Gallagher's backers was the ubiquitous Gerrit Smith, who answered the rector's appeal with a "generous response."[20]

The controversy became involved in politics, when the Fremont Club sponsored a service in the First Methodist Church. Democrats charged that the rally was out of place in a church sanctuary, and scored the participation of a Fremont Glee Club. But an overflow crowd turned out, and the Republican press responded enthusiastically, "Right eloquently did the preacher explode the atheistical doctrine that religion had nothing to do with politics by examples from the Prophets . . . Thank God we have one free pulpit in Oswego."[21]

But even as late as 1861 just before Lincoln's inaugural, Anthony Schuyler from the pulpit of Christ Church declared that slavery was "no heinous sin," and that the Almighty had never denounced it. He called upon his congre-

gation to observe forbearance and peace.[22] The resulting
furor was cut off only by the call to arms.

Surprisingly, the opprobrium attached to abolitionism
endured beyond the war years. In 1866 Edwards, as a
candidate for Alderman in the Fourth Ward of Oswego,
was the subject of the following editorial in the Democratic *Palladium*.

> The Republican candidate for Alderman of the Fourth
> Ward is an out and out Abolitionist, and has been for the
> last thirty years, and he says openly that he is in favor of
> Negro equality; of allowing the Negro to vote; of the Whites
> amalgamating with the Blacks; that the Negroes north and
> south are a better class of citizens than the foreigners. He
> says that there are Negroes of his acquaintance 'whose
> hands he is unworthy to kiss.' He says the only reason that
> he employs foreigners at all is, that there are not Negroes
> enough seeking employment in the city. He is in favor of
> foreigners remaining here twenty-one years before they are
> allowed to vote.
>
> Electors of the Fourth Ward, do not vote for such a
> fanatic. His election would be a public calamity. Vote for
> Alanson S. Page, a good Union Andy Johnson Democrat,
> and elect him by a rousing majority, and thereby say to the
> wire-pullers that if they force such names as Mr. Edwards'
> before the people they must take the consequences[23]

Despite this undisguised appeal to prejudice Edwards
won the election.

11

OSWEGO IN THE CIVIL WAR

While it is commonplace to refer to the Civil War as an "Irrepressible Conflict," its inevitability escaped Oswegonians right up to the firing on Fort Sumter. It was not that they did not see the war clouds. They followed the press releases detailing the violence in "Bleeding Kansas" and at Harper's Ferry, witnessed the election of President Lincoln by a sectional, party amidst threats of secession, and saw the slave states of the Deep South rend the fabric of the Union, and organize the Confederate States of America. Yet a fratricidal war seemed unbelievable, and the public awaited a last-ditch accommodation.

The first cannon ball to hurtle across the leaden skies at Charleston ended this dream-world; and its psychological effect can hardly be overemphasized. War was a reality; the rebellion must be crushed, and the Union preserved.

Undoubtedly the vitriolic editor of the *Oswego Times* expressed the climate of opinion in his first editorial after the bombardment of Fort Sumter.

> Grim visaged war is upon us. Our dispatches today disclose the fact that the rebel authorities have assumed the responsibility of opening a causeless, senseless warfare upon the government of the United States. The days of bullying are passed. The slave holders who for the past ten years have kept this otherwise peaceful country in a constant uproar, have at last proceeded to the dire extremity of war. The die is cast. Let party differences be thrown to the winds. Perish dissension when our country is in peril! All to-

gether let us stand ready to accept the consequences and do
our duty like men in whose minds yet lingers the recollection of Bunker Hill, Yorktown and Saratoga. To arms![1]

When President Lincoln called for 75,000 troops, Oswego County's response was almost spontaneous. The uncertainty had ended, and Republicans and Democrats, and
city and country folk closed ranks to join in the preparations for armed conflict. War meetings were called in every
town in the county, and local units were soon competing to
be included in the initial regiment.

The enthusiasm of the moment, however, should not be
confused with preparedness. Excepting the 17,000 residents
of the city of Oswego, 3,000 in Fulton, and about 1,000
each in Pulaski, Mexico and Phoenix in 1860, the population of the county totaling more than 70,000 was rural. The
Oswego Canal and the Oswego and Syracuse Railroad and
a few miles of the Rome and Watertown Railroad on the
eastern fringe of the county were assets, but the left most
of the area dependent upon the horse and wagon for transportation and communication.

Isolation was tempered by the local press: Pulaski,
Mexico and Fulton had weeklies, and the Oswego dailies
issued weekly editions which circulated in the county; but
recruitment would require strenuous and protracted campaigns to tear the farmer from the plough, and equally
concerted drives would be needed to provide for dependents
and to supply the servicemen with a variety of necessities
not available through the commissary.

Oswego's local militia, the Forty-Eighth Company of the
Old Oswego Guards, eased the problem of recruitment at
the outset. Volunteers from its personnel quickly formed
nuclei for several companies, and during the course of the
war the company supplied more than forty commissioned
officers, six of them from two families: the Raulstons of
Southwest Oswego and the Olivers of the city supplying
three each. Oswego also had Fort Ontario, which was used
as a recruiting center for a number of companies prior to
their departure for regimental headquarters in Elmira, Albany or New York.

A single line from the report of a rally suggests the initial martial spirit. It had been scheduled to meet in the West Baptist Church, but the crowd could not be contained, and it adjourned to Doolittle Hall. Here "for three hours the fires of patriotism glowed brighter and brighter as each [clergyman] took a turn at the bellows."[2]

The county's quota of ten companies (the Twenty-Fourth New York Infantry) was filled in a few weeks, leaving several units without billets. It rendezvoused at Elmira, and proceeded to Washington; and though not called upon to do battle at Bull Run, it crossed the Potomac to intercept the Confederates should they follow up their victory by a march upon the Capital.

Being the first regiment to enter the conflict, it received more than its share of attention during its two year enlistment. Letters from camp circulated from hand to hand, and proud parents passed them along to the local press; and while it remained in the periphery of Washington, a stream of visitors added their impressions.

The Twenty-Fourth saw little action until the second battle of Bull Run. But in this debacle their battalion was enveloped by a superior force, and crushed by a galling cross fire. Survivors endured a forced march across the Potomac only to find themselves in the "bloody corn field" at Antietam a few weeks later. "I never knew the horrors of war until now," Adjutant Robert Oliver advised his young wife. "It is past description."[3] After further action at Fredericksburg and Chancellorsville the much reduced regiment returned home to a hero's welcome and its final muster a full month before the battle of Gettysburg.

Meanwhile the route at First Bull Run had precipitated Lincoln's call for 500,000 troops, and Oswego County organized a second regiment. The initial enthusiasm was cooling, and the Eighty-First Infantry had to be consolidated with companies from Oneida County to bring it up to strength. The Eighty-First faced its baptism of fire on the Peninsula in General McClellan's abortive campaign against Richmond in the spring of 1862. They marked time on the Carolina and Virginia front until Grant's push against Lee in the spring of 1864, when they endured the carnage at the Wilderness, Cold Harbor and Petersburg. In the last hours of the war these veterans had the satisfaction of being the first infantry to march into the fallen Confederate Capital, where amidst the fires which engulfed the city they released Union soldiers from Libby Prison. When they returned to Oswego they brought back the prison's key as a trophy.

After McClellan's failure Lincoln ordered the recruitment of 300,000 more. War-weariness was setting in by this time, and bounties and the threat of conscription were required to supplement the roll of the drum and the waving of Old Glory. But the county's war committee led by the persuasive D.C. Littlejohn not only recruited the 110th Infantry, but organized the 147th, as well. Littlejohn added the prestige of his own enlistment as Colonel of the 110th and State Senator Andrew Warner of Pulaski did as much for the 147th. "Under the spell of the fiery eloquence of Littlejohn," a local historian recorded, "the farmer left his field, the artisan his bench; all pursuits gave way to the extreme necessity of the hour, and the men hastened to enroll their names under the sacred banner of their country."[4]

The personnel, of course, included all ethnic groups, but Irish and Germans were especially active in the recruitment of the 147th. The "Irish ladies of the Third Ward" presented a colorful silk banner to Captain Patrick Regan of Company I, a company which was Irish from "A" to "Y". And not to be outdone, the "German ladies of the city" fashioned a banner for Company G, an outfit with a pronounced Germanic flavor, and tendered it to Captain Delos Gary. Scarcely an able-bodied man, it was noted, remained in the German Lutheran Church; and its pastor, Jacob Post, enrolled the following year as Chaplain of the 184th Regiment.

The 110th was assigned to the Army of the Gulf, and shipped to New Orleans, where more of the troops succumbed to disease than bullets. They saw limited action on an expedition into the bayou country, and several companies participated in the siege of Port Hudson. They spent their last year at Fort Jefferson, a remote Florida Key, policing a prison camp. Sun, sand and water have become Florida's principal assets, but they spelled only boredom for the men of the 110th, and probably no other local regiment hailed the coming of peace with as much fervor.

The 147th Regiment, as long as the veterans survived, was identified with Gettysburg, and though it served until the war's close, everything after July 1, 1863, was in the nature of an anticlimax. The regiment, a unit of General Reynolds' First Corps, marched from the village of Gettysburg on the morning of the first day of the battle to delay the Army of Northern Virginia until the Union army arrived. They clashed in the open fields just west of the Seminary buildings and held their ground, standing for a time almost alone against the Confederate frontal attack. When they at last retreated, they left sixty per cent of their personnel on the battlefield, either dead or wounded.

The huzzas for Gettysburg and Vicksburg had scarcely ceased to reverberate, when the county was forced to face up to the conscription law. Between July 13-16 New York was paralyzed by mob violence, and it was feared that the draft would touch off bloody reprisals up-state. The Democratic *Palladium* reported that Republican leaders were carrying weapons, and that they justified their behavior on the "higher law" principle. It speculated whether they would wear them to Church on Sunday. The *Times* accepted the statement at face value, pointing to the Pilgrims who held a Bible in one hand and a musket in the other. However, it belittled the likelihood of violence.[5]

In Fulton the *Patriot* noted that there were mutterings of a draft riot, and that "well known citizens" would be held responsible. The village trustees immediately called upon the editor to divulge the sources of his information, but he refused, and demanded that the officials respect the freedom of the press.[6]

Seeking to allay misgivings the *Times* listed the pecuniary advantages which would accrue to those possessing
the "lucky numbers," emphasizing that federal, state and
county bounties in addition to a private's pay would net
almost two dollars per day through the first year. Soldier-
ing, it insisted, would be the best business in the future.[7]

The implementation of the draft was staged on August 4
in Oswego in front of the Provost Marshal's office on West
First street. The area was jammed with potential draftees,
their families, and others more detached, but equally curious. The atmosphere was tense, and a sense of foreboding
hovered over the officials. When all was in readiness, the
Marshal, flanked by just thirty-seven members of the Invalid Corps, veterans whose disabilities had washed them
out of the regular service, signaled that the drum be spun. A
local man, known to have been sightless since youth, after
being blindfolded, according to law, withdrew the first
name.

It was that of an ex-soldier, who had already lost a leg on
the battlefield. Why his name was among the thousands in
the drum has not been explained, but that he should be
drafted seemed so ridiculous that the crowd laughed; then
applauded his name. The tension was broken, and a more
relaxed audience listened to the two thousand additional
names as they were announced.

That evening the conscripts held a "regular jollification."
After a round of speeches the marchers were supplied with
Roman candles for a prodigious display of fireworks. The
fun continued until a late hour, when "all retired in good
humor," and the fateful day was behind them.[8]

At Phoenix, also, draftees celebrated their new status.
Equipped with old guns, some from garrets where they had
lain since the War of 1812, and led by the local band, they
staged a torch-light parade to the amusement of the citizenry.

The publication of the lists at once precipitated reports of
draft dodgers "skedaddling" to Canada, and of "sharks"

who victimized drafted men seeking deferment. The *Times* noted that the draft had activated "several half-starved lawyers, who don't often get any business. [They] have been taking advantage of the anxiety of drafted men to become exempt, to charge the most exorbitant rates for their services in making out the necessary papers, charging $50 for a service ordinarily costing 50¢." Seeking to curb this evil, the Enrolling Board issued a statement advising draftees that anyone charging more than fifty cents "was seeking to impose upon and defraud you."[9]

Despite the draft's unpopularity, it proved to be more of a gadfly to encourage enlistments than a means of raising troops directly. Of the several thousand names in the drum only about 150 were called upon to serve; and of these, eighty-eight were paid substitutes. The effects of conscription are suggested by its second application the following year. Preferring to avoid it, the towns intensified their recruitment and raised their bounties; and most of them thereby obtained their quotas prior to the deadline.

Of course, bounties reaching as high as one thousand dollars, at a time when ordinary labor commanded but one dollar per day, were temptations to the unscrupulous, and "bounty jumping" was soon a much used expression. It might be noted, however, that it was never as serious as desertion. The yearning for loved ones at home after a long winter in camp when the farms were turning green was apt to be overpowering.

Later in the war, with Grant's casualties exceeding those at Gettysburg and Chancellorsville, Oswego County was asked for another regiment, the 184th Infantry. Boys in their teens, scarcely fifteen at the beginning of the conflict, made this regiment possible, for there were few others left to serve. Six of the companies were assigned to camp detail behind the lines near Petersburg, but companies A, B, D and F were diverted to the Shenandoah Valley to intercept "Old" Jubal Early's surprise offensive. They had their finest moments here with General Sheridan, joining the colorful leader at the end of his famous ride at Cedar Creek.

Thirty-four years later Hiram Dutcher recalled:

> We had retreated about six miles and the thousands of
> men were scattered in all directions, when suddenly there
> was a shout that Sheridan was coming. I was in the field
> about a quarter of a mile from the turnpike. As Sheridan
> saw the group of stragglers he turned his horse from the
> road, jumped a low-rail fence and came up to where we
> were standing. He rode a black horse with a white hind
> foot. I was tying a handkerchief around the fingers of a
> Pennsylvania soldier when Sheridan came along. He heard
> one of the boys call me 'Dutch,' and called out, 'Come
> along Dutch, help me rally these men, and we'll be sleep-
> ing on our old camp-ground tonight.' He was good as his
> word. At eleven o'clock that night we had regained our
> position.[10]

Perhaps the tales and poems of Sheridan and his black
charger, Rienzi, had over-jogged Dutcher's memory. But if
he exaggerated the details, he might be forgiven; for the
men of the 184th thrilled at the mention of Sheridan or
Rienzi as long as they lived.

Meanwhile, smaller detachments, including the First
Artillery, Battery G, and the Twenty-First Independent Battery, and also companies of the Twelfth and Twenty-Fourth
Cavalry had been recruited locally. The First Artillery
spent four years in Virginia with the Army of the Potomac,
while the Twenty-First Independent Battery accompanied
the Army of the Gulf to Louisiana. The Twelfth Cavalry
joined the army of occupation on the North Carolina Coast.
For a time they were so remote from combat that officers
invited their wives to join them. But an unexpected Confederate counterattack, spearheaded by the ram, *Alber-
marle,* at Plymouth, left a sizeable number of the regiment prisoners of war; the wives escaping on the last boat
to Roanoke Island. The prisoners were sent to a living hell
at Andersonville Prison; few surviving.

The Twenty-Fourth Cavalry, with its leadership supplied
in part by veterans of the Twenty-fourth Infantry, fought as
infantry on Grant's drive against Richmond. But they were
eventually mounted, and in the final moments harassed the
retreating Confederates until they halted at Appomattox.

For people of the Oswego area, responsibility for the soldier went beyond recruitment and bounties. Since the government provided no special allotments for dependents, and a private's pay was inadequate to care for them, voluntary contributions were solicited. Two weeks after Lincoln's first call for troops the Pulaski *Democrat* reported about fifty enlistments and a sum of $1,100 for the families.[11] In Oswego the Common Council supplemented private donations, voting sums of $5,000 on at least three occasions, and between September 1862 and May 1863 Oswego distributed $4,429 to 130 families.

Women in the villages organized Soldiers' Aid societies to coordinate their services. The Oswego society held a festival in July of 1862, which yielded eighteen large boxes of dry goods, clothing, bedding and books. The following spring they forwarded boxes of clothing, dried fruits, wine and jellies to the wounded of the Twenty-Fourth Regiment. They made similar gifts to the sick of the Eighty-First Regiment, including a sum of money for lumber and sash for a camp hospital at Yorktown, Virginia, where the regiment was in winter quarters. They offered special thanks to the "little children of the primary school on the east side, and to their teacher, Miss Davis . . . most hearty thanks for the beautiful quilt . . . made by those children in their leisure hours at school."[12]

In response to a request from the 110th Regiment for havelocks, the Oswego Ladies' Society, headed by Mrs. John E. Lyon, purchased 272 of them and 500 straw hats to help protect the soldiers from the Louisiana sun.[13] The Mexico chapter of this organization, through its Secretary, Luther H. Conklin, responded to a similar request from the Twenty-Fourth Regiment. They also dispatched prodigious quantities of foods and materials for the sick and wounded to the Sanitary Commission; one shipment including 341 pounds of dried fruit and liberal quantities of shirts, socks, drawers, handkerchiefs, lint and old linen.[14]

Oswego also supported a local chapter of the Christian Commission, which distributed religious tracts and fresh fruits to the sick and wounded. Still another agency with at least one local chapter, was the Freedmen's Relief Association of Mexico. Organized in 1863, it contributed generously to the care of the Negro in occupied areas of the South.

In any appraisal of woman's work in the war, special mention should be given to Elmina Spencer, forty-three year old Oswego housewife and school teacher, who joined her husband when he enlisted in the 147th Regiment in September of 1862. She accompanied the regiment to Washington, and made herself useful in improvised kitchens and tent hospitals. She was a stone's throw from the battle front at Gettysburg, helping to ease pain and anguish.

Later, she set up headquarters at Belle Plain to aid the wounded streaming in from the Wilderness; and when General Grant's base was moved to City Point, she went there also.

She was appointed to the New York Agency for the Relief of the Sick and Disabled Soldiers by Governor Seymour, and entrusted with the distribution of provisions, foods, clothing and medical supplies. In this capacity she visited the various Oswego regiments and often served as an intermediary between the soldiers and their families. At City Point she was struck by flying debris, when an ammunition ship exploded, and was partially paralyzed for a time. She refused to retire, however, and was still serving selflessly at the war's close.[15]

The intensity of the struggle made dissent an extremely difficult problem. It was accepted in theory, but the line between criticism and obstructionism was difficult to define. The term "Copperhead" was used loosely, and was applied to almost any type of nonconformity. One prominent citizen with enough money to indulge a whim, used the following expedient to embarrass alleged Copperheads among the members of the Presbyterian Church. He secretly arranged to have the choir sing the "Battle Cry of Freedom" at a Thanksgiving service without previous announcement, upon the assumption that the Copperheads would not participate, and be made conspicuous by their silence. He paid the members of the choir a liberal sum to gain their cooperation, and obtained the consent of a deacon, who showed his mettle by replying, "Sing it if it drives every Copperhead from the shed." At the appointed time "the song was sung with soul-stirring energy with the full power of the organ as accompaniment."

> The Union forever,
> Hurrah! Boys, Hurrah!
> Down with the traitor,
>   up with the stars,
> While we rally 'round the flag boys,
>   rally once again,
> Shouting the battle-cry of freedom. . . .

"The singing of that patriotic song on this occasion set all minds at rest, who before may have had doubts as to how [this church] stood affected on the great question of the hour." [16]

The Oswego newspapers with almost daily telegraphic reports from the battle fronts featured the military action from beginning to end. The *Times* published an "extra" to report the assassination of Lincoln:

PRESIDENT LINCOLN ASSASSINATED
HE WAS SHOT WHILE IN THE THEATRE LAST
NIGHT
SECRETARY SEWARD STABBED AND EXPECTED
TO DIE
MR. SEWARD'S SON ALSO STABBED
HIS RECOVERY CONSIDERED DOUBTFUL
ARREST OF THE ASSASSINS[17]

Later in the afternoon the regular edition of the paper appeared with its columns shaded. Seven columns, a rather remarkable achievement in news gathering, detailed the assassination and the events which followed.

At noon the City Hall bell tolled a solemn dirge. Flags on public buildings, homes, and ships in the harbor, were displayed at half-staff. A special prayer service was announced for the next afternoon at Doolittle Hall.

The Oswego area reflected the panic and frustrations following John Wilkes Booth's escape. On April 27 the *Mexico Independent* reported that a very suspicious appearing man had passed through Colosse on the previous Sunday; that he seemed to be in an unusual hurry, and told an improbable story. Some people believed that he was Booth or one of his men making his way to Canada. The paper doubted this, declaring that there were reports every day of Booth's arrest.[18]

A final glance at local opinion as Vice President Johnson assumed the presidential responsibilities for reconstruction is of interest. Writing to Gerrit Smith, John B. Edwards observed that in numerous discussions with his townsmen, it was generally agreed that the leaders among the traitors should be dealt with severely.

Some people, he noted, believed that God had removed the "Great and Good Lincoln" because he would have been too indulgent to traitors, and that Johnson, with a touch of Andrew Jackson's spirit, would act more vigorously.

Smith disagreed, declaring that a truly religious attitude was one of mercy, and that vengeance was the result of spurious religion. The North, he insisted, was but a little less guilty than the South in causing war. In defense of his position he forwarded copies of a recent speech titled, "No Treason in the Civil War," to the local papers.

"Our wicked *Palladium* condemns your position of mercy to all Rebels," Edwards replied a few days later. "Yes, your late writings are very unpopular, excepting the Copperheads; but you are used to unpopularity."[19]

A few months later Edwards reported to Smith that he hesitated to publish the most recent of Smith's addresses, since people felt that he had already published too many.[20]

The detached Gerrit Smith might propose tolerance to the vanquished, and go so far as to offer to pay Jefferson Davis' bond to release him from prison, but the rank and file in Oswego would have their pound of flesh. Four terrible years of sacrifice could not be forgotten overnight.

12

REPUBLICANS AND DEMOCRATS

As has been noted the loose coalition identified as the Republican Party by 1856 had scarcely entered the political arena before it was beset by schisms. The Weed-Seward–Littlejohn faction in Oswego, supported by the business community, was dominant at the outset of Lincoln's Administration, but there were not enough loaves and fishes to satisfy the hopefuls; furthermore, there were others desirous of leadership. Greeley's attacks on Littlejohn found a sympathetic audience among those who would soon be known as radicals, and the distribution of spoils in the customs office, post office and along the line of the canal made more enemies than friends. Littlejohn also alienated the only Republican daily paper in the county, the *Oswego Times,* which heretofore had been his consistent supporter. He had subsidized it to ease its financial problems, but he had no office for the editor.

The growth of radical Republicanism can be followed in the editorials of Ira Brown in the *Times*. In September 1861 he hailed Fremont's proclamation calling for the confiscation of Rebel property, including slaves, in Missouri, and condemned Lincoln's repudiation of Fremont. He was wary of a Union ticket, insisting that there was "no better Union Party than the Republican." But he accepted Richard K. Sanford, a Fulton Union nominee, for the State Senate and Littlejohn as the Union choice for the Assembly. Both were Republicans. Littlejohn declined the nomination, leaving

178   OSWEGO: FROM BUCKSKIN TO BUSTLES

Republicans and Democrats unable to agree upon a substitute. Both subsequently made their own nominations, and the voters were treated to three choices: Republican, Democratic and Union.

After the election the *Times* insisted that Republicans had been duped into supporting Union nominees, and announced that they were taking leave of the humbug, and "the miserable business of buying loyalty."[1] Democrats, also fed up with the Union experiment, showed no regrets over its early demise. The unlikely honeymoon was over.

The *Times* joined the radical chorus against General McClellan, and advocated that the war aims be broadened to encompass the confiscation of southern property, the freeing of the slaves, and the use of Negro troops. It found the Lincoln Administration remiss on each point.

It accepted Littlejohn's nomination for Congress in 1862 despite "certain differences," which had arisen between them during the past year. Later, it charged him with duplicity, alleging that he had manipulated the nomination after he had promised to serve out a three-year enlistment as Colonel of the 110th Infantry. But for the moment it insisted that the nomination was feasible since he would not assume his duties in Congress for thirteen months, and by that time the rebellion would be crushed. Then, just before the election, with the explanation that Democrats were saying that Littlejohn had made private pledges that he would adopt a conservative course in Congress, the *Times* published an open letter addressed to him at Camp Patterson in Baltimore, asking for his position on the various radical-conservative issues; with an added word of advice, that they expected his endorsement of the radical position in each case.[2]

Littlejohn wired back, "Your letter received. I am a Union Republican, in favor of the President's [Emancipation] Proclamation, opposed to any compromise with Rebels except upon unconditional submission to the United States Government."[3] His terse reply sidestepped the more controversial issues, but his interrogators could scarcely repudiate it. The *Times* expressed satisfaction, and affirmed that he stood with Wadsworth (the Republican nominee for Governor) and the President.

Meanwhile Democratic fortunes had deteriorated following the call to arms. Without patronage, charged with responsibility for the war and identified with Copperheadism they were in a sorry plight. Their position was further weakened by the suspension of the *Palladium*, their only daily paper in the county. High costs, loss of government printing and a paucity of advertisers contributed to its failure. But the prolongation of the war and dissatisfaction with its administration, as well as the radical-conservative split among Republicans, contributed to the party's revival. The *Palladium* resumed publication long enough to cover the last weeks of the campaign of 1862. It did not prevent the city and county from going Republican, but Democrats celebrated Seymour's victory for Governor.

In March, 1862, the Democrats won the mayoralty election in Oswego, the much named Lathrop Augustus George Bradley Grant replacing Daniel G. Fort. But that fall Republicans piled up a substantial majority for Littlejohn and carried the two assembly districts in the county. One bit of Democratic strategy misfired when their hastily nominated candidate for the Assembly, Captain John D. O'Brian, who had lost a leg at Antietam, went down to defeat.

The *Times* continued to press for radical objectives in the months which followed. In April 1863 it forecast the military occupation of the conquered South and the punishment of traitors.[4] It was critical of Halleck's handling of the army and condemned Lincoln's mitigation of the sentence of Clement L. Vallandigham, the notorious "Peace Democrat" after his arbitrary arrest by General Burnside and his trial by military court. It also castigated the President for removing General Hunter after he had stretched his military authority to declare slaves freed in occupied South Carolina.

The newspaper's inevitable showdown with Littlejohn
occurred in November of 1863, when the latter attempted
to expel the management by foreclosure. The newspaper
was offered for sale, and Littlejohn imported Thaddeus S.
Brigham, a printer from Mohawk, to take it over. But at the
last moment James N. Brown, who had published the paper
for six years, fought to retain it. He had Brigham forcibly
removed from the plant, barred the doors, and went to
press, delivering that afternoon's edition from a partially
lowered back window. Brigham managed to slip warrants for
the arrest of the publisher and the vituperative editor
through the same aperture, but his strategy failed when the
former raised sufficient funds from his radical friends to
pay off the debt. Littlejohn was beaten.

The *Times* now poured out an almost unceasing stream
of abuse upon its former benefactor. It represented his
action as an attempt to "squelch" the paper because it was
"too independent," and called his pressure "malignant and
unrelenting."

It hammered away at his alleged duplicity in leaving the
army and abandoning his soldiers, and reminded the families that the men had left the community under the
command of one, "who by artful persuasion and plausible
rhetoric succeeded at the time in deceiving a confiding
public by his loudly spoken and oft repeated professions of
patriotism . . . Fathers consented, Mothers believed, wives
entrusted." But instead, "you ingloriously resigned and
came home . . . Cooling zephyrs of Lake Ontario are far
more healthful than the hot and death-dealing blasts wafted
over the Gulf of Mexico, [and the] invalid as he lays
burning with fever in the hospitals of New Orleans thinks of
the pledges which were made to him."[5]

During Littlejohn's long absence from congress between
December 1863 to May 1864 the *Times* pilloried him for
feigning illness and for accepting pay without serving. It
called upon him to resign so that the district might be represented. Later, when it was reported that he was seeking a

renomination, it called upon the public to reject this bid to gratify his "inordinate ambitions, lusts and hates."[6]

Having failed to silence the *Times* Littlejohn assisted Brigham in founding the *Daily Commercial Advertiser,* and the two Republican papers went after each other with hammer and tongs. The *Palladium* now revived to enjoy and exploit the intra-party hassle.

In the fall of 1864, Littlejohn received a signal honor when he was elected Chairman of the State Gubernatorial Convention at Syracuse, where Ruben Fenton was nominated for Governor. But the Radicals defeated his bid for a renomination for the House of Representatives, a blow to his pride and to the prospects for a Niagara Ship Canal which he had sponsored. The *Palladium,* from its detached position could chortle:

> A certain ex-editor [Ira D. Brown] slept soundly last night after routing his arch enemy 'horse, foot, and dragoons' [in the nominating convention] . . . The outrage suffered by fond fathers and doting mothers, betrayed and deceived by solemn protestations of the Colonel-Congressman, had been avenged . . . the debt of the *Times* coterie had been paid.[7]

Littlejohn saw no humor in the paper's banter. Veterans seldom invited him to deliver his "matchless" oratory at their encampments, and their vote was always elusive on election day.

In the Presidential campaign of 1864 the Democrats attempted to capitalize on the popularity of General McClellan with the soldiers and the lack of enthusiasm for Lincoln's renomination. A local Democratic spokesman declared that one candidate was "a clown, mountebank, and obscure jester and reckless tyrant; the other a soldier, statesman, patriot and Christian gentleman."[8] Apparently his hearers had no difficulty in deciphering which was Lincoln and which was McClellan. But the latter's glamour was somewhat tarnished by election time, and Governor Seymour was charged with obstructing the war effort and responsibility for the New York draft riots the previous year. On election day Oswego's majorities for McClellan and Seymour were more than balanced by the heavy Republican vote in the county. In fact the latter provided Lincoln with 2,500 of his 7,000 majority in the State. Thus the war ended with Republicanism triumphant.

The hegemony of radical Republicanism after the war was virtually unchallenged for a time, though Oswego's concern for its huge investment in the Midland Railroad enabled Littlejohn to return to the Assembly in 1868 and 1869. But his candidacy exposed him to the heated blasts of his political enemies. In 1867 he had apparently decided to wash his hands of politics, and had moved to Buffalo; but he was back in Oswego in less than two years. He was now taunted as the "Buffalo Candidate," with the inference that his loyalty belonged to the region's traditional rival.

In 1872 the Liberal Republican movement challenged thousands of Americans who were shocked by the scandals and ineptness of the Grant Administration and were prepared to call off military reconstruction in the South. Liberal Republicans in Oswego began to organize Anti-Grant clubs in February, and a month later their defection permitted the election of a Democratic mayor. But the nomination of the eccentric Horace Greeley for president brought the movement to a halt. And as soon as it was apparent that Grant could not be stopped, most Republicans hastily returned to the fold.

But not Littlejohn. Seeking a vehicle to humble the radicals, and never one to do things by halves, he jumped into Liberal Republicanism with both feet despite warnings from his friends. So it was, that on July 18, 1872, Oswegonians viewed a spectacle which bordered on the incredible: Liberal Republicans and Democrats in a joint rally at Doolittle Hall, with Littlejohn the featured attraction!

To an audience which overflowed into the street, Littlejohn reviewed his life story. "Some of my old political friends call me a traitor to my party, but I call it patriotism when men shake off the shackles of a corrupt party organization."[9]

After a lengthy denunciation of the Grant Administration, he turned to the Liberal Republican and Democratic nominee, the man he had sued eleven years before for libel. "I support Greeley because he is kind-hearted; of generous impulses, has a massive intellect; but above all, because I know him to be honest."

Littlejohn appears to have assumed that the Republican Party was breaking up as the Whigs had done in the 1850's, and that a coalition of Liberal Republicans and Democrats was the party of the future; and his misgivings, if he had them, were lost in a torrent of oratory delivered from platforms across the length and breadth of the county.

He still had another surprise for the bewildered community. In October the district convention of the Liberal Republicans and Democrats placed his name in nomination for the Assembly to oppose the Republican incumbent, Daniel Fort, whom he had endorsed and escorted about the county just twelve months before. During the two weeks between his nomination and election day, Littlejohn's past was torn to shreds by his long-time political associates, while Democrats, his equally long-time opponents, came to his rescue.

Republicans brought Conkling, "the Magnificant," now New York's most powerful politician to Oswego to enlist his oratory in behalf of Grant and in condemnation of Littlejohn. It seems only to have spurred the latter. "Mr. Littlejohn," the partisan *Palladium* reported, "swayed the multitude, whose tumultous cheering was like the voice of the tempest. His noble bearing, his tremendous energy, his honest unswerving purpose, challenges the admiration even of his enemies."[10]

Later, the *Palladium* recalled that Grant and Greeley had been almost forgotten during the contest for the Assembly, "while the swarthy Midlander with his 'finger of fate' loftily shaking, his voice of wondrous resonance and magnetism, from many a crowd-crushed platform called forth the clamor of approbation. That was a great fight."[11]

After the closing of the polls on election day, crowds remained, awaiting the count. And as it became clear that Littlejohn was carrying the city, his partisans went wild with joy. But "then a 'solitary horseman' from the town of Hannibal arrived on the train with his disgusting 300 odd majority for Fort."[12] Littlejohn's majority in the city was more than offset by Fort's plurality in Hannibal, and the latter carried the district by 129 votes.

If there was no turning back, neither was there the stagnation of inactivity. The opposition press was soon referring to Littlejohn as the leader of the Liberal Republican-Democratic coalition in the county, J. B. Edwards phrased Littlejohn's new position more picturesquely, when he wrote that he had wedded himself to the "whiskey loving and negro hating party."[13]

Two years later he was chosen as a delegate to the Democratic Gubernatorial Convention at Syracuse, and was welcomed with open arms. Responding with an address, delivered with his usual flourish, he promised 30,000 votes from the Liberal Republicans. And after Samuel J. Tilden had been nominated for Governor, he mounted the platform a second time to place the name of William Dorsheimer in nomination for Lieutenant Governor. The convention accepted his candidate unanimously, and he returned to Oswego flushed with success.

His Republican opponents were awaiting him. In a satirical editorial entitled "Adieu Mr. Littlejohn," the *Times* gave him its dismissal from the Republican Party:

> Now that [he] has buried himself to his old political friends let us remember him kindly . . . He has been a stout and efficient advocate of good, sound Republican principles . . . From every school house platform in Oswego County, Mr. Littlejohn's 'clarion voice' has rung out in vehement denunciation of the Democratic Party, Democratic principles and Democratic leaders . . . And what must be his sensations today as he takes his seat in the very sanhedrin of Democracy in Syracuse?[14]

The campaign was spirited with the issue Littlejohn, even though he was running for no office. Democrats carried

Oswego, and helped sweep Tilden into the Governor's chair. Littlejohn was again in evidence the following year at the Democratic State Convention, where he nominated John Bigelow for Secretary of State, and defended his eligibility as a Liberal Republican. Bigelow was nominated and subsequently elected to the office.

Meanwhile, up-state Democratic leaders quarreled with Governor Tilden over his investigations of the Canal Ring, which they seemed to resent as much as the Republicans. They were dissatisfied also with his handling of the patronage, and as the campaign of 1876 approached, they organized to oppose his bid for the Presidential nomination. Littlejohn joined the stop-Tilden movement, and as a delegate to the Nominating Convention at St. Louis, joined with a few of his up-state partisans to defy the unit rule. When the maneuver failed, "The Midlander . . . put on his stovepipe and left the hall."[15]

Back on his home soil he completed the walk-out he had initiated at St. Louis. He denounced the nomination of Tilden, and offered his support to Hayes. He had thus gone the full circle.

Hayes's election was Littlejohn's opportunity to restore his leadership in the Republican camp after four years' service with the enemy. He conferred with the President and his advisers in Washington, and when Oswego's appointments were announced, Littlejohn men were found in the key offices. News spread like "wildfire" that the Conkling Ring in Oswego had been overthrown, and as the *Palladium* observed, it was "wonderful to contemplate the change of Republican sentiment toward Mr. Littlejohn since his visit to Washington. He is now discovered to be a man of remarkable ability and high influence in the councils of the administration."[16]

His return to Republicanism coincided with an internecine struggle between the Stalwart and Half-Breed factions. The former were identified with Grant and Conkling, and the latter, with the fortunes of James G. Blaine, and for the moment with the Administration of President Hayes.

The latter's appointments had hurt the Stalwarts, but with Conkling at the height of his power, they could afford to await the next election.

In the Republican convention of 1880 Conkling and other state bosses boomed Grant for a third term but in the end were forced to accept James A. Garfield, the choice of the Blaine faction. Stalwarts were permitted to name a henchman of Conkling, Chester A. Arthur, for Vice President. Garfield was duly elected, and proceeded to appoint Half-Breeds to the key posts, despite Conkling's bitter opposition. When the latter failed to block their ratifications in the Senate, he resigned, and took his colleague, Thomas Platt, with him. New York Republicans were thus given a choice of backing Conkling in his impetuous and unprecedented action by re-electing him and Platt to the Senate or supporting Garfield. The issue served to propel Littlejohn back into the political arena.

Half-Breeds in Oswego drew up resolutions supporting Garfield's appointments, condemning the resignations of the Senators, and urging the Legislature to reject their re-election. Littlejohn endorsed the resolutions, and urged that Conkling and Platt be returned to private life. He was thus critical of the state's most powerful Republican politicians, and was courting oblivion.[17]

Subsequently, the Half-Breeds had the satisfaction of seeing Conkling and Platt defeated in their bids for re-election. But in Washington, the assassination of Garfield placed Arthur in the Presidency. Stalwarts were soon replacing Half-Breeds in the offices.

In 1882 the Half-Breeds backed Littlejohn for the Assembly, with the hope that his prestige and relative inactivity for several years might win sufficient Stalwart support to put him over. Stalwart leaders, as expected, sought to block the move, contending that Littlejohn would not get fifty votes in the towns which had bonded themselves for the Midland Railroad.[18]

Once again, Republicans fought each other more furiously than they battled Democrats. The *Palladium* saw the opposition to Littlejohn stemming from the leaders, who knew they could not run him.[19]

Littlejohn gained the nomination and was soon back in harness. But the old Midlander had chosen the wrong year for his "comeback." Buffalo's reform mayor, Grover Cleveland, swept the state as the Democratic candidate for Governor, and carried the city of Oswego by just over four hundred votes, and the county by a few less. Though he ran ahead of his party, Littlejohn lost the city by ten votes and the district by 187 to the incumbent, William A. Poucher. Democrats were in command in Washington and Albany for the first time in thirty years.

A year later with factional lines unchanged, Littlejohn again was the least controversial of the candidates, and received the nomination. During the campaign he called for the removal of tolls from the Welland Canal and the revival of Oswego's trade. He recalled the battle for the enlargement of the Oswego Canal in 1853. It was won; and Oswego handled one-third of the western trade. "When the Vanderbilts and Goulds shall have killed your canals, it will be a fearful day for this country until the people shall rise against monopolies. It is in the interest of the people to keep the waterways open." (This from a railroad builder!)

Admitting that he had made enemies in the past, he called upon them, as he did his friends, to consider his practical experience. "Do with Littlejohn," he said, "as you hire a man to do your work, and if you believe that I can be made useful, and can add to the value of the town, though you hate Littlejohn, vote for him (applause)."[20] "It was plain," a sympathetic hearer recorded, "that he had lost none of his old-time earnestness."[21] On election day he triumphed over his Democratic opponent, J. A. Baker of Volney, by nine votes.

His election almost automatically made him a candidate for Speaker, and his friends rallied to his banner. Even his old Nemesis, the *Oswego Times,* recommended him without reservations:

Tall, erect and thoroughly self-possessed, he carries the weight of his 65 years as if it were unfelt and unthought of. His voice has in it a tone of command, and yet a winning sound. There is courtesy and even courtliness in his manner. He has magnetism, grace and dignity. He is every inch a speaker.[22]

His entry into the canvass created a three-way contest, which included also Titus Sheard of Little Falls, and young Theodore Roosevelt. Sheard was the favorite, but in the opinion of the *New York Tribune* Littlejohn's friends "fairly broke the backbone of Mr. Sheard's strength." Its tabulation of Republican sentiment indicated about twenty votes each for Littlejohn and Roosevelt, and thirteen for Sheard, with seventeen scattered.[23] Incidentally, Roosevelt was flattered by the *Tribune's* forecast, and solicited votes, though he believed that Littlejohn and Sheard would join forces if he showed strength.[24] Conflicting rumors of shifts and deals continued to the opening of the legislature. In the end Littlejohn withdrew rather than carry the issue into the caucus; and Sheard was the winner.

The following year Littlejohn was ready to undertake the rigors of another campaign. But he appears to have made no attempt to line up support, and was passed over for a younger man.

✳ ✳ ✳ ✳ ✳

As noted, Cleveland's popularity as a reformer made possible a Democratic revival in 1882. His majority in Oswego County was the first for a Democratic nominee since the rise of Republicanism. But it was not sustained. With Cleveland in the White House and David B. Hill succeeding him as Governor, Cleveland and Hill men split into warring factions, and frequently nominated rival slates of candidates. Republicans lost little time in restoring their traditional majorities. Only the city of Oswego remained pivotal; and even here the second generation Irish were shifting to the Republican party. Democrats had little more than their tradition to sustain them. But for those who could wait, better times were coming in the twentieth century.

13

FROM MAIN STREAM TO TRIBUTARY

In retrospect the Civil War was a turning point in the history of the Oswego River and harbor. The change was not so much the conflict itself, but the technological revolution which it accelerated. Inventions, mass production, the nationalization of industry and railroad trunk lines served to feed the metropolitan centers and starve the satellites. The trend was not immediately apparent in Oswego. In fact, it enjoyed the post-war boom, and milling and forwarding prospered for a time. But the population of the region remained stationary, and it began to decline in the rural sections. Western competition made much of the soil sub-marginal, and hundreds of farmers turned from diversified farming to dairying.

Beginning with the depression year of 1873 commercial decline set in. Perhaps the most succinct picture of this deterioration is offered by the tonnage handled at the port of Oswego. In 1870 it was just over 100,000 tons; at the turn of the century it had shrunk to 30,000. The recession was sharp between 1873 and 1875; more gradual between 1876 and 1890, but again severe during the 1890's. Rotting wharves and empty mills were mute evidence of evil times.

Oswego's commercial decline is easier to demonstrate than explain. But several causes are now apparent. Numerous improvements were made upon Canadian waterways, which facilitated the flow of goods from Lake Ontario to the Atlantic Ocean by way of the St.Lawrence River and Montreal. But the Welland Canal was not enlarged for a half-century, and by the post-war era only the smaller vessels could pass through it; and in time, even these ships had less incentive to use it. In 1871 New York began to reduce the tolls on the state canals. Lower per mile rates tended to off-set advantages stemming from Oswego's shorter route. In 1875 they were further reduced, and in 1883 all charges were removed. Oswego was now at a distinct disadvantage in its competition with Buffalo and the Erie Canal. In 1870 the Oswego Canal carried 900,000 tons of freight; in 1900 it totaled just over 30,000.

Railroads also cut into Oswego's water traffic. Trunk lines carried more of the western trade, and while the area was crisscrossed by a variety of lines which served the harbor, the water front was not revitalized; its decline was only prolonged.

Policies of the Federal Government added to Oswego's woes. Despite the construction of a new breakwall along the west side of the harbor in 1883, western storms played havoc with the docks, and ingress and egress remained hazardous in gusty weather. A breakwall on the east side initiated in 1882 proved so inadequate that it was later removed. On November 15, 1893 the *Flora Emma* crashed against the rocks east of the channel. A year later the *Baltic* went down on the same rocks; and within twenty-fours the *D.G. Fort* suffered a similar fate. And more damaging than inadequate breakwalls was the government's decision not to construct a Niagara Ship Canal, a project close to the heart of Oswego for many years.

After the passage of a century it is difficult to appreciate the hopes which Oswegons attached to a Niagara canal. Proposals for such a waterway were voiced prior to the construction of the Erie and Oswego canals, and though the Canadian-built Welland Canal subsequently linked Lake Erie with Lake Ontario the glitter of an "all American Canal" on the American side of the falls remained untarnished.

Five years after the opening of the Welland, Congress-man, Joel Turrill advised President Van Buren that an American canal would make Oswego a city at once; but an Oswego delegation received a cool reception in Washing-ton. In the 1850's the inadequacy of the Welland gave immediacy to the project, but it was not until the Civil War that it made real headway.

Then, overnight, the Mississippi River outlet was closed, and thousands of tons of western grain were diverted east-ward by water and rail, overloading facilities and intensify-ing the need for additional routes.

The Oswego Board of Trade sent lobbyists to New England and the West to agitate for the canal, and resolu-tions in its support began to appear in the press. The New York Legislature recommended it to Congress and to Presi-dent Lincoln, and in June of 1862 a host of Oswego leaders participated in a national canal convention at Chicago.

In the first session of the Thirty-Eighth Congress Little-john prepared to champion a canal bill, but Congress had scarcely convened when illness forced him to withdraw. A year later, however, he headed the drive for congressional approval, and delivered the principal address in its support. He pictured a ten-fold expansion in grain production during the next quarter-century and an ever growing need for additional transportation facilities. He also stressed the canal's utility should war with Canada close the Welland Canal to American shipping. In an eloquent peroration he foresaw the eventual supremacy of New York over London as the financial capital of the world—a supremacy made possible by the network of canals and railroads in the United States. At the close of his spirited justification, the bill passed the House by a vote of 95-51. It was perhaps Littlejohn's finest hour, and he hastened to the telegraph office to wire the result to his eager fellow-townsmen. It was another story in the Senate, however. Lacking the support of New York's members, it went down to defeat.

Unsuccessful in Washington, Littlejohn's backers hastily

elected him to the Assembly to salvage the canal as a state project. He won the support of the lower house but was unable to avoid crippling amendments in the Senate. Nevertheless, grateful citizens gave him a hero's welcome upon his return from Albany, and presented him with a magnificent 18-piece silver service.

Finding the law useless, Littlejohn was willing to try again in Congress, but he was unable to overcome the opposition of the radical Republican faction to his nomination. And thus the canal was lost.

Interest revived in the 1880's, but an enlargement of the Welland eased the pressure. In the twentieth century the St. Lawrence Seaway provided fringe benefits anticipated from the century-old project, but a canal along the south bank of the Niagara River under the shadow of the stars and stripes remained unfulfilled.

Prevailing high tariffs were also destructive to Oswego in the post-war era. During the war the threat of Anglo-American hostilities following the *Trent* affair, rumors of invasion along the Canadian frontier, and the popularity of the Southern cause in Canada cast a shadow over the Reciprocal Trade Treaty of 1854. Furthermore tariff concessions had been unpopular among manufacturers, who alleged that Canada received greater benefits than the United States.

Congressmen from the Great Lakes area, however, rallied to the defense of reciprocity in Congress, and in the debate in the House of Representatives in May, 1864, Littlejohn made one of the most telling addresses against its abrogation. He emphasized the utility of Canadian-American commerce, and warned that its curtailment would impose a strain on other transportation facilities already overtaxed by the war. Why destroy a profitable trade across the lakes, he asked, and inflict pecuniary distress upon the entire northern frontier. Friends of reciprocity ultimately saved it from destruction, and Littlejohn dashed off a hurried note to Gerrit Smith with the glad tidings. "I am so

elated that I can not refrain from writing again to say that
after a sharp contest we defeated the resolution of Elijah
Ward by a majority of eight . . . The matter is disposed of
for the present."[1]

But the next year the raid on St. Albans, Vermont, may
have tipped the balance. The House "in a moment of frenzy
and passion," Littlejohn advised Smith, "passed a resolution
to rescind the Reciprocity Treaty for which you labored so
hard and so successfully. So intense was the feeling against
the Canadians on account of their participation in the raids
upon our frontier, that it would have been folly to have
attempted to stem the current."[2]

The resolution for abrogation passed the Senate by a
decisive majority, and thus reciprocity ended. Oswego was
the loser.

Tonnage and customs receipts reveal the degree of
Oswego's commercial decline, but an analysis of the com-
modities and changing times is required to give it meaning.
As some businesses faltered others moved ahead, at least for
a time.

One of the earliest casualties was salt. Western sources
gradually eliminated markets for Salina salt, and lower
tolls on the Erie Canal attracted much of what remained to
the main line. Oswego's share of the trade fell off slowly
between 1860 and 1868, and then dropped sharply between
1869 and 1873, when it virtually ceased.

The grain trade also deserted Oswego. In 1870 more than
thirteen million bushels were transferred to the mills and
canal barges; in 1900 less than a half-million bushels were
brought to the harbor. In the former year about eight percent of the western Canadian and American grain trade
passed through Oswego, measuring about one-half of the
volume handled at Buffalo. But with the rise of Minneapolis
and other milling centers in the Middle West, the traffic
slowed down, and railroads absorbed much of that which
remained.

Milling at Oswego declined proportionately. At its height

in the 1860's twenty mills had turned more than one hundred runs of stone. But after 1870 facilities outstripped demand. The downward trend was slow but steady until 1885; then it plunged to insignificance.

A notable exception among the grains was Canadian barley. This trade became active after the Civil War, and expanded until 1883, when Oswego was the largest Canadian barley market in the United States. The barley attracted malsters, and by the 1880's malting houses dotted the water front. In 1890 more than three million bushels entered Oswego harbor—about one-third of the total imported into the United States. The prevailing tariff of ten cents a bushel did not appear to discourage imports.

But the trade was altered drastically, when the Republican Congress in 1890 adopted the McKinley Tariff. An Oswego delegation descended upon Washington during the debate on the bill, and came back with the impression that the increase on barley would be limited to fifty percent. But instead, it was hiked to thirty cents, or an advance of two hundred percent. The Republican *Oswego Times* called the rate prohibitory, and observed that barley "is nearly the only remaining source of profit to the elevators, and there are a large number of malting establishments here which depend exclusively upon Canada for their supply of barley . . . In addition to the elevators and malt houses, the handling and boating of the barley gives employment to a large number of men. It can scarcely be expected that the people of this city whose interests are thus endangered will quietly submit with no further effort to protect themselves."[3]

It hastily added that it supported "judicious protection," a cardinal principle of the Republican Party, but insisted that a rate of ten or fifteen cents would serve the purpose. It also called attention to the tariff's threat to the coal trade. Coal was exchanged for barley, it noted, and if the latter were curtailed, it would pile up at the docks without ships to carry it to Canada.[4]

When the tariff became a reality in October the *Times*

could not condone the duty on barley, but sought solace in
the over-all benefits of protection; and to bring its value
home to its readers cited local manufactures which were
dependent upon it for survival: starch, wood and iron products and knit goods. It also quoted Thompson Kingsford
and other local oracles upon the virtues of protection, and
reiterated the charge that the Democratic Party was the
party of free trade as championed by such "notables" as
John C. Calhoun and Jefferson Davis. "Tariff reform [re-
vision downward]," it concluded, "means a loss of $80 on
every horse the farmer raises to sell, and $70 on every ox or
cow."[5]

The *Palladium* showed no such ambivalence, and condemned the tariff from the first rumor from the Ways and
Means Committee to the day of its consummation.

October 4, 1890, was an exciting day at the harbor—not
altogether unlike a twenty-four hour reprieve from the gas
chamber. A *Times* reporter picked up much of the drama of
that Saturday, and what spilled over to the Sunday which
followed.

> If the appearance of Oswego harbor today was its general
> appearance, Oswego would be a lively port. Old timers who
> stood on the bridge looked at it with delighted eyes and said
> it looked like the good old times, when the harbor was
> crowded with shipping, and vessels had to drop down below
> the island before making a turn. All day Saturday white
> sails gleamed on the distant horizon and the smoke of com-
> ing vessels could be seen. The Canadians had evidently
> picked up everything on the north shore which would hold
> grain and hurried it across, and a delighted look swept a-
> cross the countenance of every skipper as his vessel came
> between the piers. Every captain as he came in had his
> papers ready and made a wild rush for the custom house,
> and was only happy when his entry had been regularly
> made.

The entire staff of the customs house had a strenuous day,
and Collector Lyman, the former adjutant of the heroic one
hundred forty-seventh regiment at Gettysburg, gave the
importers an extra day of grace since it fell on Sunday. The
last vessel arrived at eight o'clock that evening; it was the

thirty-eighth in the thirty-six hour period. Over a half-million bushels of barley had been unloaded; and duties totaling $55,641.40 collected. The *Times* noted that the same entries the following day would have cost $166,-942.20. It forecast additional arrivals, but "not at the rate heretofore carried." It was the understatement of the year![6]

In November Oswego gave a five-three majority to the Democratic nominee for Congress, but the Republican incumbent, Sereno E. Payne of Auburn, carried the county in a tight squeeze.

The malting industry, as anticipated, languished. A subcommittee of the United States Senate Committee on Finance, which held hearings in Oswego in the fall of 1891 received a poignant presentation of the woes inflicted by the tariff:

> A.H. Failing: Spurred on by favorable duties in the tariff bill of 1883 malsters had come to Oswego and had erected substantial malt properties with an annual capacity of 1,500,000 bushels. "Now elevator-men would almost give away their elevators to anyone who would take them."
>
> Oren F. Gaylord: Just 15,000 bushels of Canadian barley had arrived during the year, compared with more than a million the year before.
>
> A.H. Failing: Three of the larger mills were worthless, leaving from five to six hundred workers seeking employment elsewhere.
>
> Dudley Irwin: One elevator had already been abandoned to the city for taxes.
>
> J.B. McMurrich: Investments in ships, elevators and canal barges had been lost. Coal might be exported at a profit if the old barley fleet were available to transport it.

Manufacturers such as Thompson Kingsford dissented from the shippers and malsters. The corn-starch industry, he insisted, could operate only if protected from New Brunswick potato starch.[7]

In 1894 the Oswego Board of Trade and local newspapers urged a lower duty on barley in the Wilson Tariff bill. "The existing state of our idle malt houses speaks as emphatically as anything I can possibly say on the subject," was Theodore Irwin, Jr.'s response to a reporter.[8] But the bill did not bring relief.

The malt houses were abandoned one by one. The last empty hulk with "FRANCIS PEROT'S SONS" still visible under the eaves was razed in 1961 after the refusal of a policeman to stand duty under its crumbling walls had raised a momentary tempest.

The row of empty mills and elevators which had lined the lower east side river front for so many years came down in a spectacular blaze on May 20, 1892. There were whispers of "arson" and "insurance."

For a quarter-century the lumber trade sustained the activity of the port. It was first freighted to Oswego from the adjacent lake shore, but local sources were dwarfed by Canadian timber from the forests of Ontario. It reached its zenith in 1873 when almost 300,000,000 board-feet were imported; four-fifths of it incomparable white pine. In fact, for several decades the port was one of the largest pine markets in the world.

Simeon Bates seems to have been the first importer, and in partnership with Peckham H. Smith and John K. Post, handled up to eighty million feet yearly. Kingsford Starch was also a major buyer, the Standard Oil Company purchased millions of board-feet for its box shook factory, and the Diamond Match Company milled hundreds of cargoes into boxes and matches.

The greatest importer, was the E.W. Rathbun Company. Owners of thousands of acres along Ontario's shores, it sawed the logs at Canadian mills and transported the timber in its own twin steamers, the *Resolute* and the *Reliable,* with the regularity of clockwork between the Bay of Quinte and Oswego. Their extensive docks on the west side of the lower harbor and on several islands near-by were piled high with the fresh-sawed pine.

Most of the timber was transferred by canal to markets in the eastern states, but the stout planking in the older houses of Oswego attests to the abundance and the quality of the product.

A local historian some twenty years ago recalled that the

waste lands along the western margin of the city, where it is said James Fenimore Cooper gathered cranberries to garnish his game, became the depository for tens of hundreds of tons of shavings and sawdust. Night skies were lighted by the flames rising from it, and the district was known until recently as the "Shavings."

The lumber trade receded during the panic of 1873, rebounded in the 1880's and then edged downward. Like the barley trade it was hurried into its grave by the McKinley tariff. When the Wilson Tariff of 1894 again removed the duty its corpse could not be revived.

The depth to which the trade had fallen is suggested in what may have been John B. Edwards' last letter to the heirs of Gerrit Smith, written in 1891, when he was eighty-nine. He noted that he was seeking a lower assessment upon the Grampus Bay Property, which was listed at "a plump one and one-half times its value . . . I talked a little about the present and prospective worthlessness of the property, and the expenses of keeping up 1700 feet of pier."[9]

Edwards did not live to see the "Great Wharves" disintegrate to mounds of stone and rubble frequented only by a few fishermen when the perch or pike were running. But his spirits would have been lifted could he have returned a half-century later to see its restoration by the Oswego Port Authority after the St. Lawrence Seaway had opened the port to the Atlantic Ocean.

One commodity, which reversed the trend in the late nineteenth century and continued to grow into the twentieth, was coal. Limited quantites of anthracite from Pennsylvania were brought to Oswego by canal as early as the 1840's. It found markets in Upper Canada and helped to fill the holds of the grain fleet. Rail facilities stepped up the operation, and by 1870 more than 50,000 tons were handled annually. In 1876 the Oswego and Syracuse Railroad, which had become a unit in the Delaware and Lackawanna system, tunneled to the river, where it constructed a trestle. But finding the site unsuited for larger vessels, it extended its tracks to the lake front, and built a trestle into deep water. The New York, Ontario and Western Railroad, successor to the New York Oswego and Midland, constructed a trestle along the north shore of the Cove Property; and the Delaware and Hudson Company erected a third trestle parallel to it. By 1900 the export coal trade totaled more than four hundred thousand tons. It continued to grow until 1913, when it reached seven hundred thousand tons. It then declined, and where there had once been three trestles, there remained but one.

14

THE MIDLAND AND A RASH
OF LESSER RAILROADS

Sensitive to the potentialities of rail transportation Oswego's leaders contracted "railroad fever" more frequently and with higher temperatures than most of their contemporaries in this fabulous age. The Oswego and Syracuse line had only whetted appetites for more.

The region's second railroad stemmed from promotions in Rome and Watertown to join the North Country with the Mohawk Valley, and after several false starts the Rome and Watertown moved across the eastern towns of the county in 1851, creating the villages of Richland Station and Lacona.

The panic of 1857 discouraged railroad schemes for several years, but in 1862, in the midst of the Civil War, Oswego's promoters undertook the Rome and Oswego Railroad, designed to link Oswego with the Rome, Watertown and Ogdensburgh Railroad in the Town of Richland. It was one of the least pretentious of the promotions: twenty-seven miles at an estimated cost of $500,000.

The company called attention to the potential market in the eastern towns of the county. "Ten men from Pulaski visit Watertown and Rome where one visits Oswego", it noted, "and this is because they are more accessible. The completion of the road would instantly reverse the tide."[1] It also argued that it would increase manufacturing and utilize the "noble harbor and immense waterpower."

Stock sales justified construction immediately after Appomattox. The track was laid from Richland Station to Pulaski, and thence to Mexico and New Haven, with the labor force of French-Canadians and Irish working from the eastern end of the line. A reporter who visited the mess hall was impressed by the appetite of the gang: steaks and mutton chops, with bread, boiled potatoes and raw onions. "The quantities of these articles which were mowed away were sufficient to explain to all the grumbling stockholders where their money goes."[2] Except for the accidental death of a worker, incurred when a train of cars plunged into a herd of cattle, and the "runaway" of a string of cars when a coupling failed, the work proceeded on schedule.[3]

The first run from Oswego to Richland Station on January 4, 1866, was a banner day for the villages along the line. A profusion of omnibuses rolled into the village of Mexico early that morning; each seemingly overflowing with curious occupants. The report of the event in the local paper indicated that they were not disappointed:

> A little before 8 o'clock the shrill whistle of the western train was heard, re-echoing over hill and plain as the cars came thundering in at the depot. The advent of the first regular messenger of civilization into this hitherto, unblest region, caused quite an excitement; and when it is remembered that this people have traveled in stage coaches over horrible roads for the last forty years, it will be admitted there was occasion for rejoicing at the first train of cars.[4]

Few in the crowd moved from the station after the train departed for Pulaski, preferring to await the arrival of the initial westbound cars three hours later.

The excitement at Mexico was echoed along the length of the road. In the words of a reporter:

> All along the route at the different depots and many of the cross-roads crowds were assembled and welcomed the train with all sorts of manifestations of joy. At New Haven an aged veteran palsied with the breath of death, was drawn down to the track, where he sat, shielded from the rough winds by an umbrella held over him. He desired before he died to see a locomotive draw a load of passengers over the soil of his native town, and his friends gratified his dying

wish. We are told that as the night train was passing Sand Hill, a stranger who had never seen a railroad, unexpectedly chanced to see the fiery, snorting, screaming locomotive as it went pulsating by, and actually fainted. On being restored and asked what ailed him, he stated that he never saw anything of the kind before, and his first thought was that the monstrous Slave Power had some how got loose, and was coming North on a raid.

We learn that an excursion train will run over the road at half-fare, some time this month.

The Stage Coaches have been hauled off, and the mails will be carried in buggies till spring, or until the Railroad makes a contract with the department.[5]

Within a few weeks the local press noted that flour, grain and feed were flowing along the railroad between Oswego and Jefferson and Oneida counties. And during the first year more than thirteen thousand passenger tickets were purchased at the Mexico depot, and almost six thousand tons of freight were handled there. Four passenger trains were running daily each direction between Oswego and Richland Station.[6]

While the Rome and Oswego was under construction four additional railroad ventures were launched: The New York and Oswego Midland, The Ontario Lake Shore, The Syracuse Northern, and The Syracuse, Phoenix and Oswego.

The promotion of the Niagara Ship Canal inevitably raised the question of a railroad from Oswego to tidewater to complete the lake to sea outlet. The Oswego and Syracuse Railroad already connected with the New York Central system at Syracuse, but Oswegonians looked upon the latter with the same misgivings which they had always viewed the Erie Canal. It was a Buffalo route. A direct line with its western terminal at Oswego was far more attractive.

But a feasible alternative route to tidewater posed a knotty problem. The New York Central was entrenched in the Mohawk Valley; and south of it, the Catskill Plateau barred the way. One possibility remained, a route west and south of the Catskills. There were formidable grades; and rugged spurs of the Catskills blocked an easy approach to the Hudson River. The route, no matter where it might ultimately be located, would cross a thinly populated region scarcely touched by industrialization. Finally, the cost would be high, and, with so many railroad schemes hatching, much of the capital would have to be raised along the line.

Oswego was looking for a Moses, and found one in DeWitt C. Littlejohn.

Having lost his bid for a ship canal in Congress, he turned to the railroad, trusting that the two projects might yet be coordinated. If he had doubts, he kept them carefully guarded, and entered upon the promotion with all of his indefatigable energy. And having taken the plunge, he pursued it relentlessly. He was soon identified as the "Midlander," an association which clung to him as long as he lived.

The paperwork on the railroad was launched at Delhi in Delaware County on October 4, 1865, and a more formal organization was consummated at the St. Nicholas Hotel in New York on the following December 13. Littlejohn reported the articles of association at the latter and was elected to the original board of directors. The promoters set the capital at $10,000,000, drew up the necessary articles of incorporation, and petitioned the legislature to permit towns and municipalities to aid financially.

They opened their books for subscriptions, seeking to raise one thousand dollars per mile, with ten percent payments as required under the laws of incorporation. Littlejohn, stock in hand, toured the Oswego area speaking at rallies and interviewing prospective clients. He obtained the initial sum in less than a month. His services were so outstanding that when the company was formally incorporated on January 10, 1866, he was elected President.

Shortly thereafter the legislature complied with the company's petition with "An Act to facilitate the construction of the New York and Oswego Midland Railroad, and to authorize towns to subscribe to the capital stock thereof." It permitted the borrowing of sums up to thirty percent of the assessed valuation of real and personal property in towns, and fifteen percent of the assessed valuation of any city, at interest not to exceed seven percent, and for terms not exceeding thirty years, provided it met the approval of a majority of the tax payers owning more than one-half of the taxable property, excepting that in Oswego two-thirds of the voters participating should signify their consent.

The act offered an additional favor to the road, in that it waived all property taxes "until a single track is completed or for a period not exceeding ten years."[7] A year later the Midland secured additional help from the state. Bonds sold by the municipalities to purchase stock were exempted from taxation, and for the first time savings banks were permitted to invest in these bonds. Finally, the issuance of such bonds by municipal officials, once it had been authorized by the voters, was made mandatory. The previous measure had left it optional.[8]

That the municipalities were not unreceptive to the blandishments of the promoters is borne out by the results. Collectively, they purchased ninety-seven percent of the stock of the company, and bonded themselves for $5,704,707.

In the sales campaign which followed Littlejohn offered his hearers an opportunity to live on the mainline of America. He pointed to the expansion of the western grain trade. The Great Lakes were already whitened with the sails of some two thousand vessels, and since water was the cheapest mode of transportation, these ships would inevitably seek Oswego, the nearest point to the seaboard. Should the Niagara Ship Canal be delayed, Canada could be expected to enlarge the Welland Canal. In either case Oswego would capture much of Buffalo's trade, and the latter's preeminence, based only upon an obstruction (Niagara Falls) in the Niagara River, would cease. Oswego's prosperity, in turn, would be Midland's prosperity.

Benefits from the railroad, he argued, would not be confined to the lake-sea traffic. Local service would expand to swell the volume. Farm and dairy products were abundant along the line; and lime, plaster and salt would provide cargoes in the Syracuse-Oneida sector. Branches were contemplated, which would reach the lumber of the Catskills and coal fields of Pennsylvania. With all of these advantages, the system should never pay less than ten percent.

With its stock widely disseminated along the right-of way the Midland would be a people's road.

Despite these honeyed words, it was soon evident that communities would not bond themselves unless they were on the line; and even with this assurance they sometimes showed resistance, if they were already served by a road, or had prospects of obtaining one.

Hence the managers were tempted to delay the determination of the route, and to offer it to the highest bidders. Syracuse, for example, situated on one of the more feasible of the proposed survey lines, but athwart the New York Central, refused to purchase stock. A route further east was thereupon given priority, and Syracuse's fate was broadcast as a warning to communities which hesitated to bond themselves. And once a tentative route had been selected, the company would hint at a reappraisal if bonding lagged. On the other hand, if the situation required, the promoters might offer special inducements: the promise of a car repair shop was dangled before Middletown and Oswego to gain cooperation; others were won over with prospects of becoming terminals for branches. And so it went.

Once the Midland had succumbed to the temptation to alter the line in search of bonds, its efficiency could only be a secondary consideration. Its critics were soon referring to it as "Mr. Littlejohn's Roundabout," and in other terms equally unflattering.

Gerrit Smith's reaction is of interest in this respect. With an investment of a million dollars in Oswego, he was vitally concerned with its railroads, particulary on the east harbor, which thus far had no connections to the south. During the early stages of the promotion he supported it, and subscribed to $20,000 of stock. When the decision was made to by-pass Syracuse, and follow a line on the north side of Oneida Lake, however, he became a formidable opponent. Midland spokesmen attributed his about-face to the decision to take the road through Stockbridge in Madison County rather than Peterboro.

Smith broadcast his criticisms in open letters which he circulated across the state. One of his early productions addressed to Littlejohn underlined the importance of a direct route from Oswego to New York. "Will your company build this road," he asked. "I fear it will not. It will perhaps build a road. But I fear it will not build *this* road." Pressure to accommodate intermediate localities, he insisted, would prevent it. The required road would have to be direct, with easy grades and fifty miles shorter than the Utica, Albany, New York route. Capital would be forthcoming from private investors, he maintained, if the road were direct. "You told me the other day, that I must increase my subscription to twenty-five thousand dollars," he continued. "I did not demur. I believe all Oswego will testify, that I have evinced a submissive spirit under the numerous and sometimes heavy demands she has made upon me." He conceded rich benefits if the line were direct, "but if your road shall zig-zag here and there, to please an individual, or to accommodate a town or a county, then your road may, indeed, be still worth much to people who live along it, but the stock in it will be worthless."[9]

As the details of the line took shape, Smith became more hostile. After property holders had sanctioned the bonding of Oswego, but prior to its implementation, he made a formal offer of a gift of $20,000, the sum he invested in the Midland, to the City, "if the Common Council and the City can, by fair means prevent the construction of the contemplated Midland Railroad on the route now designated, and the issuing of the $600,000 City bonds."[10] The City Fathers ignored the communication.

Later in an open letter to Alvin Bronson, Smith insisted that through a "penny-wise and pound-foolish" course they had thrown away the benefits of a shortest route, a policy which promoters in Boston, Philadelphia and Norfolk would not have permitted.

"Alas, that our old and esteemed friend Littlejohn, usually so large, as well as clear-sighted, should now be expatiating before audiences kindled by his magnetic eloquence upon the immense advantage of turning aside the Midland Road some ten miles in order to reach a lot of cordwood, a few saw mills, tanneries and glass factories [on the north shore of Oneida Lake]! Who would have expected to find *him* amongst the little men that 'hold at the spigot whilst it runs at the bung.' "[11]

Smith's efforts to scuttle the railroad can be followed in Edwards' correspondence. The latter reported that Oswego people were "infatuated" with the line north of Oneida Lake, believing that it would open trade with this area and unite the county. He could get no critical comment from the newspapers, since Delos DeWolf, a Midland promoter, controlled the Democratic *Palladium,* and Littlejohn, the Republican *Times.* "The strength of this place now consists in the millers and produce dealers," he advised. "They are unanimous for anything in the form of a railroad; whether it goes crooked or straight they seem to have no care; and this winter the same price is charged carrying flour from Oswego [to New York] that is charged from Buffalo, that is, $1 per barrel. This is a circumstance for making the people furious for Midland."[12]

Smith carried his battle to Albany, where he obtained a hearing before the Assembly committee considering municipal bonding. But he could find no one from Oswego to corroborate his criticisms.

The decision to by-pass Syracuse was a boon to Littlejohn's sales campaign in Oswego County, where the route would cross three additional townships along the north shore of Oneida Lake.

One of his earliest successes was the City of Oswego. After a spirited promotion in the local press he obtained the

unanimous approval of the Common Council for a referendum upon the issuance of $600,000 in bonds for the pur-
chase of stock. The ensuing referendum was an emphatic
endorsement of the railroad; 1,477 voting for it, and but
twenty-six in opposition.[13] He was equally successful in
West Monroe, where $40,000 in bonds was voted. During
the following year Volney with $300,000, Hastings with
$80,000, Constantia with $87,000 and Scriba with $20,000
fell into line; and he was now freed to roam beyond the
confines of the county.

Fortunately, several descriptions of his methods have
survived. In Skaneateles, where a branch line was under
consideration, an observer declared that "his flowery speech
bewildered the audience in such a manner that they were
ready to bond immediately. The manager, anticipating this
result, had previously prepared to receive signatures to the
petitions." A newspaper reporter covering the same meeting
noted Littlejohn's persuasive arguments: It would bring
Skaneateles seventy miles closer to New York, cheapen the
price of coal two dollars per ton, reduce freights, and cut
passenger fares to New York. It would attract manufactories and make the village the center of a thriving
economy. Finally, taxes on the railroad would provide a
sinking fund to pay off the $250,000 in bonds which would
be required.

When the meeting adjourned, "A raid was made on the
Secretary's Office, E. Bean, Esq., to sign the bonding act.
Names were obtained, we might say voluntarily, of individuals that were opposed to bonding up to the time of the
meeting. The effect was electrical. About all of our business
firms and men have already signed the enabling act, so that
it may be safe to announce that, so far as Skaneateles is
concerned, the road will be built."[14]

Littlejohn was particularly effective when teamed with
State Senator Henry R. Low, a Director, from Monticello.
They toured the route and addressed dozens of meetings,
and also joined forces in the legislature. Low introduced the
bill in the Senate which permitted municipalities to bond

themselves, and Littlejohn facilitated its passage in the Assembly. In the ensuing session Low introduced the bill to exempt municipal bonds from taxation. With other legislators from districts adjacent to the road, they presented a host of petitions requesting such tax relief. Littlejohn, meanwhile, reported the bill from the Committee on Railroads, and guided it to a successful conclusion.[15]

Three years later, Littlejohn resumed the drive to secure state aid for the Midland. In association with promoters of other lines he helped to obtain the passage of an appropriation bill totaling $5,500,000 to be paid to the Midland and other specified companies. The measure was greased by an unusually large number of petitions in its behalf: six Senators and twenty-five Assemblymen presenting one or more such entreaties. In the end it was vetoed by Governor Hoffman, and lost. Again, a year later, Littlejohn and his associates tried to exact a subsidy from the state to "aid and expedite the construction of unfinished railroads in the State which are intended to connect the chain of western and northern lakes and rivers with tidewater, or to develop the resources of unimproved portions of the State." The bill was broad enough to draw support from most sections of the state, and the Midland's portion of one million dollars was the guarantee of its popularity along the road. The bill passed both houses by substantial majorities, but was killed by the executive axe.[16]

By the spring of 1868 stock sales permitted construction. Beginning at Oswego, it skirted the north shore of Oneida Lake and crossed the New York Central Railroad at Oneida. Continuing southward, it reached successively Norwich, Sidney, Hancock and Middletown. Here a connection with the New Jersey Central at Unionville, designed to give the Midland access to Jersey City, was begun. There were also branch lines linking Ellenville, Delhi, New Berlin, Rome and Utica to the main line; an Auburn and Buffalo branch was completed only as far as Scipio Center in Cayuga County. The branches were added at enormous cost, pushing the total sum far beyond original estimates.

From a forecast of $8,000,000, expenditures by 1873, when trains first ran along the entire main line, soared to $26,000,000.

Earth was moved on June 25, 1868. Sixteen months later, on November 1, 1869, the track was in place between Oswego and Norwich. The last spike between these two points was driven at Seneca Hill, just south of Oswego, amidst the roar of one hundred guns discharged by a local battery. Early the next morning, "three visitors" the *Oswego,* the *Orange* and the *Fulton,* decked in bunting, puffed into Oswego. Hundreds turned out to enjoy the festivities. Noting the locomotives and the rising terminal and shops, the local press hailed them as "monuments of the enterprise, industry and influence which has given us the Midland."[17]

Progress was won more slowly, however, from this point, and at a higher cost. The line reached Sidney during the summer of 1870, but another full year was required to tunnel through Shawangunk Mountain.

Meanwhile, Littlejohn had accepted ever increasing responsibilities in the building of the Midland. To his promotional and legislative activities of the early years were added countless duties attending construction, which kept him moving along the line with frequent junkets to New York and Albany. He negotiated with delegations seeking branch lines and entered into arrangements to reach the coal mines of northeastern Pennsylvania. He also supervised the purchase of rails and rolling stock, including substantial quantities of Belgian and Welsh iron and steel. He prepared numerous press releases and drafted detailed reports for the stockholders. The confidence of the directors in his mangement is reflected in his reelection to the Presidency year after year with no more than token opposition.

No definite compensation for his services seems to have been fixed for a number of years, a motion to determine a salary, having been postponed by the directors in 1867. A rumor in 1869 places the figure at $10,000 per annum.

Finally, in January 1873, seven years after he had assumed the Presidency, the directors, with Littlejohn abstaining, resolved "that the salary of our President, Hon. D.C. Littlejohn, be twelve thousand and five hundred dollars for the first two years from his election January 10th, 1866, and twenty-five thousand dollars per annum for the subsequent five years. Unanimously adopted."[18]

Whether any of this $15,000 award had already been drawn as salary, whether it was a last-minute attempt to line his pockets from the depleted treasury, or whether the money was available and paid to Littlejohn remains a moot point. An expert on early New York railroads assumed that it was another instance of "shameless profiteering" by the promoters.[19] But Littlejohn seems to have ended his connection with the Midland with his personal finances as precarious as they had been at the start.

While the Midland inched its way southward, its promoters seem to have left no stone unturned to expedite it. At the eleventh hour in 1869, Littlejohn was boomed for the legislature, and the incumbent, Benjamin Doolittle, asked to withdraw, despite the fact that he was a Republican and hitherto a supporter of Littlejohn. The latter, it was argued, was required to safeguard the railroad and the City's $600,000 investment. Doolittle refused; and the issue was taken to the district convention, where a battle-royal developed. The result was the splitting of the party, and separate nominations.

The ensuing election was one of the most bitterly contested of Oswego's many political battles. Democrats sat back, offering no candidate of their own, to enjoy the spectacle of Republicans vilifying Republicans. Few of Littlejohn's many political and business activities escaped the critical scrutiny of his opponents. He was said to have been nominated by a "bloated aristocracy," "a money ring," "a silk stocking gentry, which sat upon satin sofas, in rooms carpeted with velvet."[20]

His opponents belittled the alleged "crisis" facing Oswego, insisting that it was manufactured each of the many times Littlejohn aspired to office. They accused him of having too many irons in the fire and of mixing politics and business. They predicted that both the railroad and the party would suffer. "Should DeWitt C. Littlejohn be elected to the legislature at the cost of the disruption of the Republican Party in this district," they argued, "his weakness in the Assembly will be measured by his infamy."[21]

Littlejohn's adherents were not without weapons. Two releases circulated a few days before the election could not have been better timed; and they may have been decisive. First, the Midland shops were to be located in Oswego and would employ about three hundred men; second, service would begin immediately, as far as Norwich.

Littlejohn won decisively, carrying all of the wards in the city. Again he had demonstrated his amazing capacity as a vote getter. It should be noted, however, that his displacement of the incumbent Assemblyman hardened the organized opposition within the party; it would not be forgotten.

With the Democrats victorious across the state and in control of the legislature, Littlejohn's stature in the latter was circumscribed. Nevertheless, he was frequently mentioned for governor, and might have made a strong bid for the nomination if Conkling and Fenton had not been wary of his independence.

Littlejohn returned to the legislature in the fall of 1870, but did not accept a third nomination in 1871. The legislative work was done, and he preferred to give his undivided attention to the railroad.

In the summer of 1873, as the Midland approached completion, it ran out of funds. And with the panic closing in its management was forced to yield control of the line to a syndicate with $4,000,000 to invest in its securities. Littlejohn stepped down as President, but remained a director, in charge of a western extension of the line from Cortland to Buffalo. Two months later the main line was completed with appropriate fanfare near West Field Flats in Delaware County. E. P. Wheeler of Middletown, who had turned the first spade of earth, drove the final spike. The western section of the last rail bore the inscription "D. C. Littlejohn," the eastern section, "George Opdyke," for his successor. There were cheers from fifteen hundred throats, the shrieks of four locomotives, and the roar of howitzers. Littlejohn was toasted for "indefatigable services." But the former President was not present to acknowledge the tribute. He had forwarded his regrets, with an explanation that his work on the Buffalo connection prevented his attendance. It would be safe to assume that he would not have missed the celebration if it could have been held a few months earlier.[22]

The rolling stock had scarcely begun to move when it halted. On "Black Friday," September 19, the stock market broke, initiating the panic of 1873. On the same day the syndicate managing the Midland threw in the sponge, and the road passed into the hands of a receiver.

Littlejohn thus ended his career as the Midlander, though he was never permitted to forget it, since Oswegonians continued to identify the Midland with its builder. Property owners,who had earlier petitioned the railroad to run its tracks on streets adjacent to their homes and businesses, expecting that it would augment real estate values, saw only its disadvantages. They accused the company of neglecting its responsibilities for maintaining streets and crossings, and sought compensation for alleged injuries. Most irate were residents of East Schuyler Street, where the tracks ran to the harbor.

In November 1873, with wages in arrears, a crowd of women and children, families of employees it was reported, with winter on the way and fuel bins empty, raided the company's stock pile of ties and lumber. Neither explanations nor threats from the officials turned them back, and the enraged women continued to haul the wood away until the pile was gone.[23] Workmen were soon threatening to stop the trains until their wages were paid.

Though the town and city investments in the company were wiped out, the need for taxes to meet payments on the bonds, of course, continued. In fact, this onerous duty extended long beyond the life-span of its principal builder. The last Oswego bond was not paid until 1918 at which time the $600,000 indebtedness had cost the city $1,204,-500 in interest. There had been no dividends. Such were the fortunes or misfortunes of the Midland. Scarcely noted was the fact that the line was in operation, and that it offered employment to several hundred local people.

Next to the Midland, the Ontario Lake Shore was the area's most ambitious railway scheme. With lines already linking Oswego to the south and east, the projectors envisioned a road along the Lake Ontario shore to Rochester and Lewiston, with connections to Detroit and Chicago; and in more optimistic moments they looked eastward to the Mohawk Valley and the Hudson River. From the outset it was primarily an Oswego promotion.

Ignoring competition from the New York Central—but ten to thirty miles farther south along the entire route—the sponsors forecast plump dividends and an unparalleled performance: "And what a line we shall have," one release boasted, "seventy-three out of our seventy-six miles west of the Genesee River, as straight as the proverbial ruler-edge; and a maximum gradient of but twenty-six feet to the mile! What opportunities for fast and efficient operation!"[24]

Again, one of the leaders was Gerrit Smith, who as early as 1864, while providing sustenance for the Rome and Oswego line, advised Edwards that he would invest $50,000, and as much as $75,000, if the line were extended westward to the Niagara River. Edwards urged caution, since railroads had already proved costly for him.[25] But Smith became its largest stockholder and its first President.

Preliminary meetings were held as early as June of 1864, but a formal organization was not effected until March 17, 1868. Subscriptions were solicited in the spring of that year, and Oswegonians barnstormed the proposed route with newly printed stock in hand. The names of the subscribers, neatly listed in an old ledger, total just over five hundred, and represent 1,395—$100 shares.[26] Most buyers took a single share on which they made payments of ten dollars each. Almost half of the shares were purchased in the Oswego area, and Smith's 226 shares represented almost one-sixth of the entire stock. Niagara County, at the far end of the line, subscribed the second largest sum, followed by Wayne. Already served by the New York Central the populous Rochester area turned a cold shoulder to the project. Only forty-one shares were purchased in Monroe County, most of them in Webster. Rochester's rebuff was not forgotten; the city was by-passed.

Failing to sell sufficient stock the company turned to Albany for help. A compliant legislature agreed that the towns along the route might bond themselves up to twenty percent of their assessed valuation.

Resulting stock sales to the municipalities dwarfed the sum raised by individual subscription, and eventually yielded close to two million dollars. Even so, a special dispensation had to be sought from the state to permit piecemeal construction, *i.e.*, whenever twenty thousand dollars per mile for twenty-five consecutive miles had been subscribed, and ten percent paid in.[27] The persuasive D. C. Littlejohn, who had been elected to the Assembly to aid and protect the Midland, graciously steered the bill through the legislature.

In the spring of 1871 the Lake Shore appointed Isaac S. Doane as Chief Engineer, and began construction. By July fifty-five miles were being graded. A year later the track was in place from Oswego to Hannibal, and director and guests celebrated the achievement with the residents of Hannibal. They repeated the formula in October at Sterling, where a junction was made with the Southern Central, a railroad connecting Fair Haven Bay with Auburn.[28] In January the road reached Sodus.

By the following spring, however, the company had exhausted its funds, and construction stopped on the east bank of the Genesee River at Charlotte. There was no bridge to carry it to the other side.

Finding no alternative, the company agreed to transfer control to the Rome, Watertown and Ogdensburgh Railroad, with the stipulation that they bridge the Genesee and complete the line to Lewiston. The agreement provided no compensation for the stockholders, but bondholders were to receive eighty-three cents on the dollar.[29]

The mountainous debt at seven percent interest hung like a pall over Oswego, Oswego Town, Hannibal, and points west.

The work, however, was resumed, and in June, 1876, the trains were running. Oswegonians might leave the local depot at 6.20 A.M., and see Niagara Falls by early afternoon. The Lake Shore or Western Division of the Rome, Watertown and Ogdensburgh became a fruit, produce and dairy line, and, coordinated with the Midland, a passenger and immigrant line to Chicago. But no cities mushroomed along its route, and it earned few dividends.

During the promotion of the Ontario Lake Shore road Oswego's civic leaders were hosts for the area's most advertised railroad meeting, the Trans-Continental Railroad Convention, designed to foster nothing less than a trans-continental railroad. Impetus came from John A. Poor, a railroad magnate of Portland, Maine. Oswegonians eagerly seconded his proposal, and staged the spectacle in a manner worthy of its name. They extended invitations to hundreds of municipalities from the maritime provinces of Canada to the Pacific Ocean; 125 newspapers; more than one hundred railroad executives; 127 members of Congress from eleven states; the governors of eighteen states; and hundreds of business executives.

The official call signed by Mayor Alonson S. Page, Robert R. Sage, President of the Oswego Board of Trade, and Gerrit Smith, for the moment President of the Lake Ontario Shore Railroad, pointed out that a trans-continental railroad across the broadest part of the continent would become the quickest and least expensive transit between the commercial centers of Europe and Asia, and emphasized that it was more feasible than heretofore due to the completion of the Union Pacific Railroad. It proposed a line due westward from Portland, Maine, to the head of Lake Champlain, thence to the "basin" of the Great Lakes at Oswego, and along the south shore of Lake Ontario and across the Niagara and St. Clair rivers to Chicago. From the latter it would connect with the Union Pacific to San Francisco, and in the future with Puget Sound, by way of the Northern Pacific Railroad. Its consummation, it proclaimed, would reduce the passage from England to Hong Kong from forty-two to thirty-three days, an advantage which even the completion of the Suez Canal could not erase.

Notices of the Convention, scheduled to convene on October 6, 1869, were carried in newspapers from Maine to Chicago, and, while only a fraction of those invited made an appearance, the meeting focused the attention of the business world upon Oswego. Dealing only in generalities, the convention was marked by enthusiasm and harmony. Lake Shore promoters were elated to see their embryo viewed as an integral part of this magnificent trunk line.

But, despite the fanfare and good intentions, the road did not materialize, and the main lines went elsewhere.

While railroad magnates from far and near dreamed of a trans-continental road, residents of the towns in the eastern part of Oswego County were working on a line which would follow the old salt road—a trail blazed by pioneers who had used it to transport salt from Salina as far as Watertown in exchange for country produce. The Oswego Canal, the port at Sackets Harbor, the Rome and Watertown, and the Rome and Oswego railroads had facilitated transportation at various points, but a railroad along this line was calculated to do a great deal more. Much of the initiative was furnished by Syracuse, but local people joined the project enthusiastically. Residents of Brewerton, Central Square, Hunt's Corners, Union Square (Maple View) and Pulaski turned out to listen and approve. Dissent came from the villagers of Mexico, who assumed correctly that they would find themselves several miles from the tracks, though its exact location, as usual, was withheld as long as possible. Some Pulaski citizens were also alarmed lest the right-of-way should run through the center of the village to the ruination of the Academy, the churches and the business block, but these protests were scarcely heard amidst the tumult.

Sponsors of this road also used the newly discovered magic of selling stocks to the towns, and a vigorous sales campaign left Sandy Creek bonded for $80,000, Richland for $60,000, Parish for $35,000, and Hastings for $25,000. The latter would undoubtedly have done better had the Midland not loaded it with $80,000 of its stock. The City of Syracuse added $500,000 in stock and the Town of Salina in Onondaga County the sum of $120,000.[30]

The contract for ties was given to Captain R.W. Slayton of Parish, who delivered them while the sleighs were running in the winter of 1870. Construction began in the spring, and, with easy grades and but two sizeable streams to span (the Oneida and Salmon rivers), the first trains ran on November 9, 1871. After leaving Syracuse the line crossed the Oneida River at Brewerton, and, proceeding through Central Square and the eastern fringe of Mexico and Richland, crossed the Rome and Oswego Railroad at Pulaski and merged with the Rome, Watertown and Ogdensburgh at Lacona in Sandy Creek. Four years after its completion it was sold on foreclosure to the Rome, Watertown and Ogdensburgh, and shortly thereafter, the northern end of the line between Pulaski and Lacona was disbanded, and a junction made with the Rome, Watertown and Ogdensburgh at Pulaski. The road drew the eastern towns of Oswego County into the Syracuse orbit, a situation later reinforced by the highway network. Along with other properties of the Rome, Watertown, and Ogdensburgh. it was leased to the New York Central Railroad in 1891 and incorporated into the system in 1898.

During the building of the Syracuse Northern residents of Schroeppel and Volney in Oswego County and Clay in Onondaga projected the Syracuse, Phoenix and Oswego Railroad, a spur from the Syracuse Northern to Phoenix and Fulton, and thence to Oswego on the tracks of the Midland.

The scheme was heartily endorsed by the Midland, which envisioned it as a connection with Syracuse. Littlejohn joined the promotion, and in addresses at Liverpool and Phoenix predicted a bright future for it as an outlet for Liverpool's salt and iron, and Phoenix's flour and wood products. He indicated that the Midland would be interested in leasing the right-of-way, and thereby enable the company to pay its interest and relieve the residents of a share of their taxation.

Stock sales were limited, the public having recently subscribed more than $25,000 toward the Baldwinsville, Phoenix and Mexico Railroad, which had failed without laying any track. Again, the principal purchasers were the towns: Schroeppel, $50,000, and the village of Phoenix, $20,000. The work was scarcely underway when it halted, a victim of the panic of 1873. It languished for a decade, but was revitalized by the Rome, Watertown and Ogdensburgh as a branch of the Syracuse Northern, and trains ran for the first time on September 7, 1885. When completed, it branched from the Syracuse Northern at Woodard in Clay, crossed the Oneida River and entered Oswego County at Three Rivers Point. It passed through Phoenix and made a junction with the Midland at Fulton.

* * * * *

The Oswego area paid a high price for its railroads. In addition to individual subscriptions, the municipalities spent just over two million dollars for stock. At the most, but a few cents on the dollar were redeemed.

But railroads could not be written off simply in terms of their cost. A population of 75,000 in a region thirty-four miles square now had access to 190 miles of railroad, an impressive achievement. Five lines radiated from the Oswego waterfront, and the Town of Richland and the village of Fulton tapped three each. Few residents lived more than five miles from the nearest line, and dozens of whistle-stops served the country-side. Travelers could reach Buffalo, New York or Boston within the span of a single day, seasonal laborers might find work in the hop harvest in Madison County, and fruit and strawberry growers by the 1890's could supply markets in metropolitan New York and Philadelphia. The Midland and New York Central shops and the National Railway Spring Company offered employment to several hundred in Oswego, and as many more found work as firemen and engineers, brakemen and yardmen.

The railroads also attracted industries which utilized harbor and rail facilities. The malting industry has been mentioned previously; also the box shook plant of the Standard Oil Company. In 1893 the Diamond Match Company erected a plant with convenient rail and harbor frontage. The Ames Iron Works and the Fitzgibbons Boiler Company, manufacturers of stationary and marine engines and boilers, flourished for many years. The Vulcan Iron Works produced steam dredges used on the lakes. Henry S. Conde and his sons, Frederic and Swits, established extensive knitting establishments, and Neil Gray, with a genius for mechanics, initiated the manufacture of shade cloth by machines.

Railroads had arrived in time to supplement the declining commercial activity, and manufacturing was taking up the slack.

At the turn of the century a single shadow hovered over the otherwise brightening industrial horizon: the future of Kingsford Starch, the city's largest employer. After several reorganizations reports circulated that the company was about to be absorbed by the starch trust and liquidated. It became an issue in the election of 1900 when William Jennings Bryan, Democratic nominee for the Presidency, made the starch trust his principal target. He warned an Oswego audience that Kingsford was imperiled and about to succumb. It provoked a quick denial from the King-fords, and dwarfed all other questions until election day.

The consolidation was consummated two years later, and the management of the firm was shifted to the Corn Products Company of Chicago. But Bryan's grim prophesy remained unfulfilled for a time; the plant continued to operate, surviving two disastrous fires. At last, in 1923, the centripetal pull of the corn-belt proved irresistible, and the whistle blew the last time.[31]

15

EDWARD AUSTIN SHELDON
AND THE OSWEGO MOVEMENT

On a day in September of 1847 a young man stood on the deck of a canal packet as it was locked down into the basin at Oswego harbor gazing intently upon the changing panorama of the river front, the mills, warehouses and the cupola of the Presbyterian Church beyond. It was his first view of the village. Disembarking, he walked briskly up the slope of the east hill to the residence of his partner. The stranger was Edward Austin Sheldon. He was eager to get to work and to make his mark.

Sheldon was born on October 4, 1823, at Perry Center in Genesee County, New York, where his father and mother had settled a few years earlier, after a covered wagon journey from New England. Life was hard on the frontier, but Edward accepted the labors of the farm in good spirit, and came to love the land and its cultivation. It became his solace when his stamina bent beneath the relentless pressure of his work, and twice was his therapy for serious mental distress.

He found the district school a poor substitute for the out-of-doors, but persevered in his studies at the insistence of his father. A teacher in the local academy stimulated his intellect, and guided him towards college.

Meanwhile, he imbibed the Calvinism of his forebears. Every Sunday afternoon, he recalled years later, his father read one of Dr. Emmon's sermons to the assembled family. The sovereignty of God, His immutable decrees, and His election "formed the meat on which we were fed." He accepted the necessity for regeneration, and at length at seventeen experienced a conversion, and was received into the Congregational church.

To the end of his life he was a missionary of the Lord. Issues assumed moral overtones, and he resolved many problems in prayer.

On the day of his departure for Hamilton College his father asked the preacher to be present, and to read God's promise to Moses to guide him through the exodus. "After the final meal had been taken, all were gathered round the family altar; the minister read the chosen chapter, and led in prayer. It was an impressive ceremony, never to be forgotten."[1]

Edward was then driven to Cuylerville on the Genesee Canal, where he boarded a packet for Rochester, Syracuse and Oneida. At the latter he took a stage for Clinton and "College Hill." It appears to have been his first trip from home, and though twenty he was undoubtedly one of Hamilton's least sophisticated freshmen.

He entered college intending to prepare for law. He was a conscientious student and ranked near the top of his class. But in his second year, while engaged in strenuous preparation for the Junior Exhibition (an oratorical contest) he was stricken with a malady, diagnosed as pleurisy. He withdrew from college and convalesced at home. During his junior year his health remained delicate, and he sought relief in horticulture, finding employment with a professor of chemistry, who provided him with a garden plot, seeds and plants.

By the year's end he decided to discontinue his studies, and accept a position as a horticulturist in Newburgh. A few months later, with his health restored, he set out for Oswego, where he had purchased a share in a nursery.

He was soon disillusioned. His partner was hopelessly in

debt, and he had few opportunities to get his hands into the ground. He salvaged several building lots from his investment, and sold them piecemeal as he cast about for another situation. When it came, it was so completely unanticipated, that he could only believe it was Providential.

While marking time in the nursery he volunteered to assist in the Sabbath schools of the village. In so doing, he came into contact with Oswego's poor, their ranks multiplied by the influx of refugees from the famine in Ireland. He surveyed the community, and concluded that an appalling number, possibly 1500, were illiterate. He resolved to ease their plight, and though unacquainted with local leaders, spearheaded the organization of the Orphan and Free School.

His description of his conversion to the project affords a succinct record of its inception, and also an insight into the humanitarianism of its founder.

A few Sabbaths after I came here, I visited a mission Sabbath School recently started here. I was surprised to find a large number of them, children eight and ten years old, who could not read their *A, B, C!* As I passed through the streets that day and saw great numbers of ragged, profane children romping the streets, having no idea of the sacredness of the day, my heart was pained within me, and I went to my room reflecting what might be done for these poor children. I told my chum, if I had the means, I should not hesitate what to do. I would open a school into which I would gather these children and teach them free. He said he thought the means might be raised. We then formed a resolution to make an effort; laid a little plan; made some estimates. got upon our knees and implored the blessings of God to give it success.

We first introduced the subject in a public manner at a prayer meeting; there appointed committees to make further investigation. Since then we have had two or three meetings of the citizens generally. Christians are praying for it in private and public; our ministers are all urging it from the pulpit; several discourses have been based entirely on this subject. For the week past we have been circulating subscription lists; have got six hundred dollars subscribed, and shall probably get three hundred or four hundred more.

Next Tuesday night we meet to organize. We hope to be able to accommodate one hundred or one hundred and fifty scholars.

Clothing will have to be furnished these children more or less, as well as books. An effort will be made to get as many as possible into good families. They are to be taught moral as well as mental precepts. Benevolence must search them out, visit the families from time to time, extend to them the hand of sympathy and affection, and teach them that they may become worthy citizens as well as others . . . .

I sometimes tremble at the responsibility I am taking upon myself, for it is all new, *entirely* new business for me. I put my trust in God, who alone can give me wisdom to direct and strength to perform. It has opened a pretty effectual way for me to become acquainted with the people of Oswego, for old and young, high and low, rich and poor, have pretty well learned by this time who is the poor boy's friend. I wish I could take you with me a little while in my visitations among the poor, I could show you what you have only dreamed of before.[2]

Just one thing remained: a teacher. None stepped forth, and the committee turned to Sheldon. He at first refused, insisting that he had never taught, and knew not how to teach. But there was no other, and he had to accept or drop the plan. He consented, thereby scrapping tentative plans to enter the Auburn Theological Seminary. When he was asked to suggest a salary, he declared that he could live on $275 a year. The committee decided upon $300.

Thus it was settled that I was to take charge of the new "ragged school," as it was dubbed. Nothing could have been farther from my thoughts than the idea of teaching school; nothing for which I considered myself so poorly adapted. But the duty seemed to lie before me, and however much I might shrink from it, there seemed to me no alternative.[3]

Thus it was not the law or the ministry, but pedagogy which Sheldon chose; and while his role was undetermined, the path was charted, and he was taking his first step.

The school opened its doors on January 14, 1849, in the Tabernacle on West Second Street. If the local daguerreotypist had been present he might have recorded a scene unique in America: Seventy "scholars" ranging in age from small children to young adults, but nonetheless with much in common. They were ill-clad, ill-housed and illiterate. Two weeks later there were ninety; and thirty more were on the rolls.

Sheldon's diary affords not only a graphic picture of the school but perhaps the best surviving description of the plight of the indigent in the community.

> Two of the boys came today two miles; they cried piteously with cold. They have for pants ragged and very light and thin cloth. For a coat one has but ticking; and neither have vests . . . Have not had to punish a child today. They begin to show signs of improvement . . . Supplied a little boy by the name of Patrick Burke with shoes, has been to school nearly a fortnight, next thing to barefoot; his clothes are also very poor. His mother has run away; his father is a poor miserable drunk without money, or a home. They go from one poor shanty to another, living on the charities of these poor people. He is a smart active boy, and needs a home very much.
>
> . . . Joseph Perkins left school for want of pants and coat. He has two sisters[who] want dresses, petticoats, shawls and shoes . . . .
>
> Today have commenced a little on the Lancastrian plan; made my scholars assistants . . . I have my fears about the working of the thing; but it is impossible for me to do all the work. Tonight I was so tired I could hardly stand up or speak a loud word . . . .
>
> Called on a poor widow by the name of McGuire. [She] was but poorly clad hovering over a cold stove, industriously plying her needle. . . . There was not fire enough to make the least impression on the snow which had drifted in the night before. The widow has a boy and girl who have been at my school; bright, intelligent children. The boy had on one boot and one shoe, but the shoe was little better than none at all. The girl . . . was about the room with nothing on her feet and hardly enough clothing to cover her nakedness.
>
> The school has been unusually noisy today . . . This morning had some trouble in school . . . A great law-less boy after disobeying me laugh[ed] in [my] face. I struck him [and] he rose and showed fight. I plied the rod closer . . . Tonight went to see his mother, found her a widow with a large family . . . Went to see the poormaster but without success. For the boy I hope to be able to get a place. The poor widow to show her gratitude to me for the interest I

took in her, fitted me out with an umbrella, and asked me to take some punch or wine; upon which I gave her a short temperance lecture.

Sheldon seems to have left no evaluation of his almost hopeless struggle to educate and regenerate his raggamuffins, but his resolution wavered with the coming of summer. In his second quarterly report in July he noted continued progress, but acknowledged that regular attendance had dropped to fifty-two. Most of these were smaller children, the older ones having found places to live, or work to do. Contributions in clothing and offers of foster homes had decreased, and many pledges of money remained unpaid.

> It is a painful fact that while we are sending missionaries at a great expense half way around the globe to educate and reform a degraded heathen people, we make little or no provision for the thousands in our very midst . . . There is spread out here within the sight of our own eyes a broad field for doing good. Let us then one and all, as we value the credit and morals of our city, as we would avoid crime, misery and degradation, improve the opportunity afforded us. Let us do what we can to enlighten the ignorant, reform the immoral, reclaim the wanderer, feed the hungry, clothe the naked, and we shall at least be entitled to the blessing in store for him, who careth for the poor.

Sheldon's dedication failed to loosen the purse strings of his fellow citizens, and the school closed its doors.

Instead of admitting defeat, however, he simply transferred his activities to a broader stage, and initiated a campaign to organize a free school system in the newly created city of Oswego. His plan called for the consolidation of twelve districts, each having a one or two room school and its individual board of directors, into a single unit with grade schools at convenient points, a senior school (junior high school) on each side of the river, and a single high school.

The proposal at once ran into vested interests. Opponents labeled it a Protestant plan, thus arousing Catholic hostility, and the consolidation failed. Proponents next turned to Albany to obtain the unification by state legislation. After several postponements, it was won in 1853.

Meanwhile, Sheldon had found a wife.

Returning to Perry Center from college at the close of his second year, he had met a young teacher, Frances A. B. Stiles of Syracuse. "From the first, I felt irresistibly drawn to her," he noted. "I immediately courted her companionship. She consented to further acquaintance and correspondence." Frances returned to Syracuse and the shy suitor to college, but he found frequent opportunities to seé her during the months which followed. When her family disapproved, they exchanged secret missives. "This opposition rather gave edge to our love and courtship."[4]

They were married in the Globe Hotel in Syracuse in the presence of a few friends and relatives; their wedding trip was their journey to Oswego. "A new and most joyous life was now opened to me. Being in full sympathy with me in my work, Mrs. Sheldon aided me in many ways."[5]

With the "Ragged School" closed, the school unification delayed and a wife to support, Sheldon took charge of a private school, heretofore directed by a Miss Bloomfield in a wing of the former United States Hotel on West Seneca Street. The newlyweds occupied rooms in the building, and Frances taught in the school and sang in the Episcopal choir. During their residence here a daughter, Mary, was born, the first of five children.

After two years, Sheldon moved to Syracuse as superintendent of the public schools. He initiated an evening school and introduced classification and grading; but he had scarcely gotten his innovations underway when he was invited to return to Oswego where his supporters had secured the passage of legislation creating a city school system. "I accordingly decided to return to my first love. I resigned my position in Syracuse, and entered at once upon what proved to be my lifework in Oswego."[6]

Though his title was that of Secretary of the Board of Education, he was in truth the superintendent from the moment of his arrival.

Before beginning his first term he took two giant steps

forward. He reassigned the students to schools and grades appropriate to their achievement, thus eliminating at a stroke the numerous ungraded one and two room schools. He also insisted that the teachers qualify for appointment to the city system through written examinations, and despite a rumble of protests from both parents and teachers carried his point. He promoted outstanding instructors to positions of greater responsibility, and induced top-flight members of the Syracuse faculty to follow him to Oswego. He even found time to renovate some of the buildings and replace antiquated furnishings.

He then braced himself for the expected storm. "The first day of school under the 'new system' was the strangest one ever experienced by either parents or children connected with the public schools of Oswego. Families were separated, some members going one way to a primary school, others a different way to a junior school and still others to a senior or high school. As might well be imagined, the confusion was complete." Irate parents flooded the board with complaints and petitions. But Sheldon gave no quarter. He spent countless hours in the homes of the children, explaining and counseling. He also showed rare skill in handling the Board of Education. He worked to secure and retain members sympathetic to his philosophy, and when a critic gained admittance, he strove to convert and indoctrinate him. With but few exceptions, the board accepted his leadership and gave him his head.

The success of his reorganization could be read in part in the attendance. It almost doubled during the first year; and local private schools were soon withering on the vine.

Having placed himself in the driver's seat Sheldon turned to the improvement of instruction. He set up "arithmetic schools" for older boys whose attendance was confined to the winter months when they were unemployed, and an "unclassified school" for those with deficiencies in subject areas. He met with his teachers weekly to discuss educational methods, believing that continued consultation was essential to unity of thought and method. He once boasted that "By looking at my watch, I could tell exactly what every teacher in the city was doing."[7]

He was later to do an about-face, and seek to fit education to the changing needs of the child, but for the moment, he focused on a "strait jacket" system. He constructed a series of graded examinations, and required them as prerequisites to advancement at every rung of the educational ladder, the children moving successively from primary to junior, junior to senior, and senior to high school.

At the close of the first year, Sheldon showed his talent for public relations by inviting the State Teachers' Association to hold its Annual Meeting in Oswego. "We were better known after this meeting," Sheldon observed, "and the schools had grown into the confidence of the people."[8]

But after several years he lost confidence in his splendid educational machine. It now seemed too formal and wanted vitality. He began to grope for something which would "wake up the pupils, and set them to thinking, observing and reasoning."[9] He collected illustrative materials adapted to the ages and interests of the children, and in collaboration with others began to publish charts and manuals.

In the fall of 1859 he visited the schools of Toronto (regularly scheduled steamers then shuttled across Lake Ontario), and was astonished to find in use there extensive collections of objects, pictures, charts, and books for teachers giving full directions for the use of this material; in brief, the very teaching aids he had sought. Most of them, he discovered, were the products of the Home and Colonial Institute of London, a training school for teachers. He invested $300 in the materials, and incorporated them into a new course of study for the primary grades.

He also accepted the Pestalozzian philosophy of the Home and Colonial Institute: that education consisted, not in the amount which could be crammed into the mind from without, but in the growth of the mind through its own development and exercise; and that instruction should be adapted to the natural development of the mind.

Though he may never have heard of Pestalozzi, the Swiss innovator, until this trip to Toronto, he became a Pestalozzian overnight, and resolved to find an expert in the Pestalozzian philosophy and techniques to instruct his faculty and to train teachers as they were needed.

He located such a teacher in England: Miss Margaret E.M. Jones, for eighteen years a member of the staff of the Home and Colonial Institute; and when the Board of Education failed to find the funds to cover her salary, he raised them himself. He recalled years later that she was paid in part from contributions which he solicited from the teachers—sums up to half their yearly salaries "in view of the benefit that would come to them."[10]

The story has been repeated many times, but was refuted by I.B. Poucher, a teacher in the system, and later Sheldon's successor as head of the Oswego Normal School. The money, he insisted, was contributed by interested citizens, but not the teachers.[11]

Sheldon's first impression of Miss Jones was scarcely reassuring. At the train he found "an unpromising looking woman with a weather-stained face, and in a stooping position half covered with boxes. We could not entertain the thought that this was our importation and passed her by, but as there was no other person in the car, we could but inquire if this was Miss Jones. To our great chagrin she proved to be the veritable Miss Jones. [However, she] entered at once upon her duties, and as time went on it became very evident to all that we had the services of no ordinary woman. She proved herself to be all that was represented to us, and fully equal to the work she had undertaken."[12]

The first training class began in May of 1861, with thirty-nine students, and of course Sheldon, in attendance. During late afternoons and Saturday mornings Miss Jones instructed the teachers in the Oswego schools. Sheldon did not require attendance, but most of them accepted the challenge, and thus the object method took root.

When Miss Jones returned to London at the end of the year, Sheldon replaced her with another Pestalozzian, Hermann Krusi. Son of a co-worker with Pestalozzi, and a distinguished scholar in his own right; he remained for twenty-five years.

Sheldon now assumed the principalship of the little training school, the first of its kind in the United States. In order to publicize the school and the object method of instruction he invited educators from New York, New Jersey and Connecticut to observe the system in operation. They came, and were favorably impressed. A report prepared by a committee of the visitors was published and widely circulated. Hundreds of inquiries were soon pouring in, and Sheldon responded with a *Manual of Elementary Instruction,* and *Lessons on Objects,* prepared by Miss Jones and Krusi. The Oswego Normal and the Object Method were becoming familiar to a growing body of school men.

The irrepressible Pestalozzian next prepared to broaden the service of the training school. In return for accepting trainees from the various counties of the state, the New York Legislature voted an appropriation of $3,000 in 1863. Two years later it increased the grant to $6,000, with the stipulation that the City of Oswego furnish suitable buildings and grounds for the school.

Sheldon called upon the community for help; and got it. Civic leaders, headed by Gilbert Mollison, E.B. Talcott and Simeon Bates, serving without reference to politics, used the platform and press to sell the project to the citizenry. They reminded business men of the expenditures which students would make, and tax payers of the savings to be derived from the use of student-teachers in place of regularly hired staff. They also pointed to the elevation of quality in the schools which would result from the employment of master teachers in the normal school.[13]

Resolutions were adopted at a public rally calling upon the city to purchase the United States Hotel and convert it into a school; and the city fathers complied to the sum of $31,000. Thus the training school, now basically a state institution, and titled the Oswego State Normal and Training School, was assured. It moved to its new quarters on February 28, 1866.

Three years later Sheldon resigned as Secretary of the Board of Education to devote full time to the training of teachers. He attracted an outstanding faculty to supplement the offerings of Krusi and Poucher. His daughter Mary, Henry Straight, father of the brilliant engineer and international banker, Willard Straight, and Dr. Mary V. Lee, who combined teaching and medical practice with a crusade for dress reform, were among the most noteworthy.

Sheldon's insistence that the courses of study and methods of teaching be adapted to the nature and capacities of children, and that teachers be trained to teach in accordance with the natural laws of child development, was the beginning of a renaissance in elementary education. Many teachers had been dissatisfied with note learning, and like Sheldon had looked for something better. Now Sheldon seemed to offer a panacea through the object method.

Nothing prior to John Dewey and the Progressive Movement equaled its impact. Teachers from Oswego fanned out across the United States to ignite little Oswego Movements in dozens of colleges and universities. It eventually reached far off Japan, where an Oswego graduate, Hideo Takamine, reorganized teacher training in that kingdom.

Time and usage inevitably formalized the object method. Elaborate teaching manuals spelled out a succession of exercises for each subject in the curriculum. For unimaginative teachers, it became a substitute for thought, a routine stripped of both spontaneity and originality. But responsibility for this stultification fell upon the user, not the originator. Sheldon remained receptive to change. He accepted Froebel's revolutionary philosophy of learning through activity, and added the kindergarten to his model school. Later he subscribed to manual training, and made

Oswego a center of the Herbartian movement with its emphasis upon psychological bases for learning.

However, innovation did not dim the missionary impulse which had guided him into education. His remarks at morning exercises were apt to stretch into religious exhortations. And it was his character above all else which impressed his associates. Krusi, for example, had reservations regarding Sheldon's scholarship, "But whatever omissions there may have been in the supervision of the intellectual part of the school," he noted, "nobody will accuse him of neglecting the moral part, to which he attended in a conscientious, truly Christian spirit, and which seldom failed of its effect."[14]

While the Oswego Movement was spreading across the nation, Oswego townspeople had their reservations about the Normal. Possibly its humble origins as an adjunct of the public schools was a factor. Certainly its free tuition was a target of its critics, who labeled the students "state paupers." Krusi resented the slurs of the "mushroom gentility," and observed that they overlooked the fact that their sons and brothers also paid no tuition to West Point.

For a time students at the Normal had difficulty finding rooming and boarding houses. A solution was found for the young women by converting the Welland Hotel into a dormitory; but the men, who were always outnumbered by the women, continued to pull door knockers. Takamine and his brother, Saze, who otherwise might have faced housing problems, lodged with the Krusis.

Faculty members were especially grateful to the families of George B. Sloan and Judge Churchill for their help in breaking down local prejudice. They accepted the students as their social equals, and Helen Sloan, "a strong-minded, noble girl," had herself enlisted as one of the students of the school. Her example was followed by others, and the institution became more "respectable."[15]

The Normal celebrated the completion of a quarter-century in 1886 amid plaudits from educators far and near.

Six years earlier Sheldon had suffered a nervous break-down, and had offered his resignation. But his faculty induced the Board to refuse it, and give him a leave of absence. The aging educator again found solace and strength in his orchard and garden. Upon his recovery he resumed his duties with unabated vigor, and continued the pace year after year.

He lectured at Chicago when sixty-five, and in Min-neapolis a year later. At seventy he toured the eastern states in search of new ideas and methods, dispatching detailed accounts of his observations to the local papers. In 1895, when seventy-one, he and his wife visited their daughter Mary at Stanford University, where she and her husband were distinguished professors. A year later Mrs. Sheldon died, and Sheldon for the first time looked as old as the snow white Lincolnesque beard, which he had worn for many years. But he attended the Annual Convention of the National Education Association in Milwaukee the next summer, and tarried in Chicago to enroll in a short peda-gogical summer session. But after his return to Oswego in August he suffered a heart attack, and died at the age of seventy-three.

More than a century after Sheldon founded the Normal, graduates of the State University College at Oswego par-ticipate in an annual torchlight ceremony around a statue on the lawn. As the circle of light widens, spectators witness a life-sized, bearded figure with a child at his knee. The bearded one holds out a globe for the little one's inspection. It is Sheldon giving an object lesson.[16]

16

DR. MARY WALKER,
STORMY PETREL OF THE
WOMAN'S RIGHTS MOVEMENT

During World War I the Board of Medal Awards, undoubtedly stirred by the all-embracing patriotism of the moment, took a backward look at the list of Civil War recipients of the Congressional Medal of Honor, the nation's most cherished award. In the Board's judgment Civil War standards had been too low; and some might be reversed, even at this late date.

When their work was done, a host of aging veterans discovered that they were not entitled to the honor, though they had worn the coveted star for more than a half-century.

At least one of the victims of this purge did not take the action lying down. Eighty-five year old Dr. Mary Edwards Walker shot back a stirring defense of her award. The medal was for valor. Had she not earned it? She insisted that she would go right on wearing both medals (One was a replacement). And true to her word, she retained and wore them to her last breath, the official list in Washington notwithstanding.

Dr. Walker's counteroffensive was completely consistent with her life. She had been fighting for "lost causes" since girlhood, and she had gained a notoriety enroute, which had made both her name and outlandish appearance familiar to her countrymen from the Atlantic to the Pacific. Even today she is remembered by millions, who can reach back in memory to the early years of the century; though the myth is often more familiar than the actuality.

Dr. Mary Walker was not the first woman to practice medicine in the United States, but she was among the first generation of practitioners. Neither was she the first woman to wear a short skirt with protruding pantaloons. But again she was in the vanguard, and continued to wear this badge of emancipation long after the original Bloomerettes had gone back to conventional dress. However, she was the only Acting Assistant Surgeon of her sex in the Civil War, and the sole recipient of the above mentioned Congressional Medal.

She was also the Oswego Valley's most widely known personality of the nineteenth century, though Oswegonians were sometimes reluctant to admit their acquaintance with the bizarre little doctor. An Oswego physician recalled that on his first day at medical college in New York the registration of his name and home address elicited a flock of questions about Dr. Walker. He never forgot his embarrassment.

Mary Walker was born on a farm on the Bunker Hill Road in the Town of Oswego in 1832. Her parents, Alvah and Vesta Whitcomb Walker, had driven to New York State from Massachusetts on their wedding journey in a covered wagon. They lived for a time in Syracuse, where Alvah worked as a carpenter. Ill health, and the burden of four young daughters induced him to trade the house which he had built for a partially cleared farm. A fifth child, whom they named Mary, arrived shortly after the family's removal to their new home.

Lacking brothers(though one was born later) to do the chores on the farm, the girls often did boys' work; they loved the out-of-doors, and acquired a good deal of self-confidence and resourcefulness; and though the income from the little farm was limited, the girls managed to go to school, first attending the little one-room school adjacent to the farm, and later a few terms at Falley Seminary, a secondary academy, at Fulton. Each, in turn, became a teacher in one of the district schools in the neighborhood prior to marriage.

In the absence of modern medical science, it is difficult to analyze the causes of Mary's nonconformity. But it undoubtedly stemmed in part from her somewhat unorthodox parents. They objected to the consumption of tobacco and alcohol, and to corsets, stays and bustles in women's clothing, considering them unhealthful. They also believed that girls should be educated to enter the professions. Alvah accepted the innate goodness of man, and rejected original sin, damnation and hell; and Vesta once wrote a letter to the press objecting to the refusal of a Presbyterian minister to permit a woman to speak in a prayer meeting. Mary's sister Aurora became a devotee of Phrenology, and Alvah, Jr. was an agnostic. He was also a ventriloquist and did sleight of hand with a traveling show. During his long illness, Alvah purchased a number of medical treatises, seeking to cure himself, where doctors had failed. Mary read them, and they stimulated her appetite for more.

For these reasons, and possibly others, Mary gave up teaching after several years to enter the Syracuse Medical College, where she took the short and rather superficial course which then passed for a medical training in a host of small medical schools, and received a medical degree in 1855.

The profession was at once a challenge to pursue a way of life appropriate to it. She found the current fashions in women's clothing wholly out of place for work requiring freedom of motion, and she adopted the bloomer costume then enjoying a limited vogue among the less inhibited.

She opened an office in Columbus, Ohio, where she lived with relatives; but she did not find the public receptive. Like other practitioners, such as Elizabeth Blackwell and Lydia Sayer Hasbrouck, she soon had to find means to supplement her income or give up the profession entirely.

She returned to Oswego after five years, and married Dr. Albert Miller, a former classmate at medical college. The wedding ceremony in the Walker parlor was unorthodox in several respects. Mary wore a "reform-dress" with panta-loons, she abjured the traditional promise of the bride to obey her husband, and also retained her maiden name, conceding only the inclusion of "M." or "Miller" before Walker.

Despite her outlandish dress, Mary was not an unattrac-tive bride: Small, petite and vivacious, her long brown curls and lacy collar added a touch of glamour to her rather plain face.

The Millers (or Miller-Walkers) moved to Rome, New York, where they shared a medical practice in adjoining offices on Dominick Street. They became incompatible, however, and separated after about two years. Mary charged Albert with infidelity.

Mary remained in Rome, but her practice was small, and she found time to engage in feminist causes. She joined a reform-dress society in Syracuse, and lectured occasionally on the advantages of the mode. She also wrote columns for the *Sibyl*, a magazine dedicated to dress reform and wo-man's rights, published by Dr. Lydia Sayer Hasbrouck. Later, she spent a year in Iowa in an unsuccessful quest for a divorce. During her residence there she attended the Bowen Collegiate Institute for a time, where her noncon-formity precipitated a series of incidents which rocked the administration as well as the student body, and resulted in her expulsion.

Then the Civil War came as a godsend. She assumed that the army would need her services, and applied for an appointment as an acting surgeon; and unwilling to await an answer, parked herself at the door of the Surgeon General. She was rejected despite the vigor of her pursuit, the Surgeon General refusing to break precedent and appoint a female. She finally appealed directly to President Lincoln; and although he wrote a sympathetic reply, he refused to intervene or act against the wishes of the Department.[1]

Meanwhile, she volunteered to assist in an improvised hospital in the United States Patent Office. "Every soul in the hospital has to abide by my orders as much as though [the surgeon in charge] gave them," she noted with obvious pride. Her work was challenging and satisfying after the frustrations of her marriage and medical practice. During the months which followed she offered her services without stint; she was a hospital administrator, therapist, amanuensis and confessor.

She found that her unofficial position, though it left her without an income, enabled her to come and go as she liked, and to attend whatever caught her attention. When she discovered that mothers and wives of soldiers who came to Washington were sleeping on park benches, because they could not secure other accommodations, she helped found the Women's Relief Association. She also kept Oswego families in touch with the sick and wounded in the Washington hospitals, and returned to Oswego on several occasions to lecture on Washington and the war.

She directed the removal of the sick from field hospitals at General Burnside's headquarters at Warrenton, Virginia, to Washington; and worked in a tent hospital at Falmouth, just after the ghastly slaughter at Fredericksburg.

In the fall of 1863 she went to the Tennessee front near Chattanooga as the casualties from the battles at Chickamauga and Missionary Ridge poured in; and when a surgeon was unexpectedly needed for an Ohio regiment, she was ordered to fill the post temporarily. A newspaper clipping contains the following observation:

> The young lady is very pretty, and is said to thoroughly understand her profession. We imagine that the bitter pills which the sick of Col. McCook's Brigade take hereafter will be deprived of a great portion of their nausea by the fair hands which prescribed them.[2]

But the medical director of the Army of the Cumberland resolved that the sick should not be handled by such a "medical monstrosity," and had her removed.[3]

Still clad in a military cloak, a surgeon's green sash, and a feathered hat, Mary roamed the countryside ministering to southern families in need of medical attention. While on such a mission on April 10, 1864, she was captured, and subsequently imprisoned at Castle Thunder in Richmond, Virginia.

She seems to have left no stone unturned to secure a release and after four months' confinement through the heat of the summer, had the satisfaction of being exchanged for a Southern major; and as she recalled with pride, "one who was six feet tall."[4]

At last in September of 1864, with recommendations from General George H. Thomas and Colonel Dan McCook of the Ohio Fifty-Second Infantry, she was awarded a contract as Acting Assistant Surgeon with a salary of one hundred dollars a month, retroactive for six months. As a *female* surgeon she was unique in the American Army. She retained the rank until the war's close, and served for a time as surgeon of a Women's Prison Hospital at Louisville, Kentucky. Seven months after Appomattox she received the Congressional Medal of Honor for Meritorious Service from President Johnson. The citation read in part that she had devoted herself with "much patriotic zeal to the sick and wounded soldiers, both in the field and hospitals, to the detriment of her own health, and has endured hardships as a prisoner of war four months in a southern prison while acting as contract surgeon."[5] It was Mary's proudest moment, and she wore the medal always, until it was almost a part of her.

After Appomattox many veterans exchanged their muskets for the tools they had dropped in 1861. But for Mary the transition was more complicated. The public remained skeptical of female medics, and she was no exception. She opened an office in Washington, but spent more of her time in championing the claims of Civil War nurses for pensions, and incidentally, in gaining one for herself. She failed, but initiated a practice of going to Congress, the state legislatures and other agencies to promote woman's rights.

Through the years she made dozens of appearances, until she was identified on sight by thousands of Americans from the President down.

In 1867 she went to England to attend a social science convention. Her unusual appearance captured the imagination of her English hosts, and she remained to tell the story of her war service and captivity, experiences as a doctor, and the benefits of dress reform to audiences from London to Scotland. And though medical students came out to heckle and medical journals were critical, the public watched and listened, and the newspapers had a field day. In a few months Mary was better known in Great Britain than America. After a jaunt to the Paris Exposition, where she wore a sash of stars and stripes, and "extemporized a sensation" at an American dinner, she returned to the United States.[6]

At home Mary attempted to repeat her successes on the lecture platform, but audiences were sparse. She finally broke off her most ambitious tour in Texas, and returned to Washington.

Jumping into the Woman's Suffrage Movement, she shared platforms with Lucy Stone, Mary Livermore, Susan B. Anthony, Belva Lockwood and others, moving from convention to convention, and concentrating upon Washington when Congress was in session. However, the failure of a woman's suffrage amendment at this time convinced her that one was not really needed; that the privilege was inherent in the Declaration of Independence and the Federal Constitution; and that all that was required was the pressure of thousands of women at the polls.

When she saw her advice rejected she went her own way, fighting her own battles. She turned up at conventions, but was shunned by the leaders, and denied admittance to their councils. Ironically, her final testimony before a congressional committee in 1916 was in opposition to the Nineteenth Amendment. She was unwilling to concede to men the prerogative of deciding whether women might vote!

As the years went by, Mary became increasingly eccentric in appearance and manner. Her dress became almost completely masculine: men's pants and shoes, a starched front shirt, a cutaway coat and a tall silk hat. Only a mink cape worn over her coat in cold weather hinted that there was a woman under the male facade. She dreamed of converting her modest home on the Bunker Hill Road into a sanitarium for the treatment of consumption, or into an "Adamless Eden" for the training of young women for emancipation. Her odd appearance and dictatorial manner were obvious targets for caricature, and the Bill Nyes of that day made the most of their opportunities.

Finding speaking engagements fewer now, she consented to appear on the stage of Dime Museums in New York, Detroit, Toledo, and elsewhere, delivering a series of short lectures in rapid order. She was flanked by Mexico feather workers and a Punch and Judy show. She injected herself into the famous Worden murder trial in New Hampshire, only to be ordered to leave the state, and be sued for slander. She forced herself upon Oswego Democrats, and attended Presidential nominating conventions: Chicago in 1892, and St. Louis in 1904, as an unofficial delegate. In 1917, when eighty-five, she dispatched a cablegram to Kaiser William II of Germany calling upon him to stop the war, and to hold a peace conference on her farm.

Mary never retired from her strenuous pace; her momentum simply slowed down. Back at her country home she was ready to drop the mundane when duty called in Washington or Albany. In 1897 in the armory over the old Central Market in Washington, she addressed the First Congress of Mothers, later renamed the National Congress of Parents and Teachers. She spoke out against compulsory vaccination and in favor of a safe and sane Fourth of July. She pronounced as humbug the theory that germs caused tuberculosis, and insisted that it resulted from her life-long enemies, tobacco and nicotine. She advised the Czar regarding his search for a male heir, after he had been "blessed" with four daughters.

She also became absorbed in her place in history. She converted her home into a museum, and offered it to the New York State Historical Association. They refused it. Rejected locally for membership in the Daughters of the American Revolution, she won an election in St. Louis, and promptly added her membership to the list of affiliations on her calling cards.

During her last illness—it began with a fall on the Capitol steps in Washington—she was taken to the post hospital at Fort Ontario. It was unprecedented, but setting precedents was an old custom of hers. She died at eighty-six. The service was simple; only the male attire and the American flag draped over the casket indicating that they were burying an unusual American.

Incidentally, her longevity had enabled her to follow women's suffrage to its fruition. And by World War I women were wearing slacks in the war plants and donning pajamas at night!

History, despite Mary's sense of it, has not been kind to her. Her early withdrawal from the leadership of the Woman's Suffrage movement dulled her lustre as a suffragist, and the public's absorption in two World Wars eclipsed for a time interest in the "Great War." Even her acquaintances at the time of her death knew little of her early achievements, and remembered only her eccentricities. With no children to bear the Walker name she dropped out of sight. Her old homestead burned to the ground, but fortunately most of her furnishings, including her papers and medals, were saved.

Nevertheless, she keeps popping up when least expected. She was remembered in New York State's Freedom Train after World War II. The Congress of Parents and Teachers in 1960 recalled her services on its sixty-third anniversary. Just a few years ago a portrait of Mary in her Civil War uniform was uncovered in the old Army Medical Museum in Washington. And the Centennial of the Civil War kept rediscovering her—in a Washington hospital, on her way to the western front, a prisoner in Castle Thunder, or on a Matthew Brady photograph in her petite surgeon's costume. But it is rather ironic that as her name appears again, the inaccuracies are told anew. A recent work on the feminist movement repeats an old falsehood that she obtained permission to wear men's clothes through an act of Congress. In actuality she was arrested on several occasions for wearing male attire, and when the myth was mentioned in her presence at a congressional hearing, she categorically denied it. She could think of nothing more repugnant than seeking permission from an all-male body to wear men's clothes!

17

SOCIAL TRANSITIONS

Ensign James Fenimore Cooper might be excused for his condescension as he viewed Oswego's rough and tumble social milieu during his short residence in the village in 1808; but scarcely a decade was to pass before the raw frontier began to yield to the refinements of civilization. More substantial edifices framed with timber or stone replaced the heterogeneous shelters of the first generation, and their occupants more frequently reflected the tastes and fashions of the older communities.

As more distinct social classes emerged the apex of the social pyramid was occupied by the McWhorters and Bunners, both of whom were set off from their fellow townsmen by their heritage.

George H. McWhorter and Margaret Laurance McWhorter settled in Oswego in 1819. Margaret, a daughter of Senator John Laurance, inherited her father's extensive land tract in the Hamilton Gore, which he had held in partnership with Alexander Hamilton and John B. Church. The McWhorters erected a spacious stone residence on the hill on the east side surrounded by primeval oaks and commanding a broad outlook upon the lake.[1] Built in the Georgian style of the previous century, the stately mansion had an elegance reminiscent of the well-born back east. A student of classical literature, McWhorter and his scholarly sons, John Laurance and George C., were identified in the early directories simply as "gentlemen."

The Bunners were also drawn to Oswego by their invest-

246

ments; and again, the original holding was a wife's heritage. Elizabeth Bunner was a daughter of John B. Church, Commissary-General of George Washington, and Angelica Schuyler Church, and a granddaughter of General Philip Schuyler of Revolutionary War fame. Thus her social position in New York or Oswego was impeccable.

Her husband, Rudolph Bunner, was a graduate of Columbia College and a classical scholar. His letters reveal an earthy sense of humor and a zest for the cup and bowl. Like McWhorter he was freed from the daily struggle for a living, and could look with some detachment upon his adopted abode and its citizens. He and his family lived in the grand manner in an imposing stone edifice on the heights overlooking the lake just west of the harbor, its gardens reaching down to the water's edge.[2]

Following severe losses in the Panic of 1837 and the death of her husband a short time later, Elizabeth Bunner sold the family home, and moved into a more modest cottage at the edge of the grounds. To supplement her limited income she turned to the translation of French literature, trusting that it might be used in the schools. Several of her publications are still to be found among the rarer items in the Library of Congress.

A son, Rudolph II, also attended Columbia College, and edited a newspaper in Oswego; and a grandson, Henry Cuyler Bunner, was a distinguished author and editor of the famous comic weekly *Puck*.

McWhorter and Bunner, who had entered the political arena as Federalists, survived that party's demise by espousing Jacksonianism. According to a local tradition Bunner wrote Jackson's first inaugural address.[3] He also advised Van Buren on local politics. Mc Whorter was a friend of both Van Buren and Governor William Marcy, and was collector of the port at Oswego and a federal marshal.

Both families were Episcopalian, and were instrumental in founding Christ Church. Their affiliation helped to give it a social preeminence which endured for a century.

Scarcely to be compared with descendants of the Hudson River gentry at the outset were members of the expanding commercial community, but they were soon moving up the social ladder. Matthew McNair discarded his pedlar's pack to become a merchant and shipbuilder. Captain Edward O'Connor had little in worldly goods to bequeath his daughters. Yet Mary married Alvin Bronson, the community's most eligible bachelor, and settled down in a massive stone residence built in the federal tradition of New England a few blocks west of the harbor. Its handsome stairway curving upward for three stories remains a showplace more than a century after its erection.[4]

The commercial growth of the village and its designation as a county seat in 1816 provided opportunities for the legal profession. True, it was touch and go for some of the early members. One barrister taught singing lessons; another tutored his landlord's son in grammar in return for his office rent; a third pawned his watch to hold on to his office. John Grant, Jr., however, shared in the promotion of the Oswego Canal, and served simultaneously as first Judge of the Common Pleas and as postmaster and collector of the port. His virtual monopoly of the local offices was inevitably challenged by other arrivals. Joel Turrill, a graduate of Middlebury College, hung out his shingle in 1819, and was soon active in business and politics. His junior partner, in turn, David P. Brewster, succeeded Turrill as county judge, and later served in Congress.

Abraham P. Grant opened a law practice in 1828. A native of New Lebanon and a graduate of Hamilton College, he was a leader of the Democratic Party for several decades and a member of Congress. He was also prominent in business and railroading.

Perhaps the most distinguished member of the Oswego bar was William Fitch Allen, who came to the village in 1829 from Windham, Connecticut, after attending Union College. Prominent in Democratic councils, he was an Assemblyman, and United States Attorney for the Northern District of New York during the presidency of James K.

Polk. He was also a justice of the State Supreme Court and
frequently mentioned as a nominee for Governor. After
removing to New York City in 1864 he was twice elected
State Comptroller, and declined a third nomination in order
to accept a place on the Court of Appeals.

William Duer's arrival in Oswego lengthened the list of
notables. His aristocratic lineage was matched by that of his
wife Lucy, the daughter of Beverly Chew, collector of the
port of New Orleans, cashier of the New Orleans branch of
the Bank of the United States, and a descendant of an
illustrious Philadelphia family.

If law was the likeliest path to political eminence, milling
was the most direct approach to affluence. Opportunity
knocked in the 1830's, when the Welland, Oswego and
Erie canals opened the flow of grain from the West, and the
damming of the Oswego River provided the power to process it. A half-century later railroads were usurping much of
the grain traffic, and mills were moving west in search of
grain, but during the intervening years Oswego was *El
Dorado*. Two devastating. fires, it is true, and two severe
panics, kept the millers on a tight rope, and some fell off,
but others survived to reap the golden reward.

The first generation of millers included Henry Fitzhugh,
Frederick T. Carrington and Myron Pardee; and each left a
stone mansion as a testimonial of his affluence.

Fitzhugh's forefathers were planters on the Virginia and
Maryland tidewater. Low tobacco prices and western New
York's potential induced Henry's father to migrate to the
Valley of the Genesee, where his family and their cousins,
the Carrolls, became identified with the gentry of the region.
Henry settled in Oswego about 1830, and entered the milling
business. His sister Ann became the wife of Gerrit Smith,
whose liberal credit to Fitzhugh eased his plight during
several financial crises. Another sister, Elizabeth, married
the noted abolitionist, James G. Birney.

The Fitzhughs reared a niece, Alida Tabbs, a descendant
of Charles Carroll, a signer of the Declaration of Inde-

pendence. Alida came to the Fitzhughs in the care of a Negress of the Carrolls, and when she married DeWitt C. Littlejohn, the young partner of her uncle, she brought the servant to her new home.

A small slab at the corner of the Littlejohn plot in the Riverside Cemetery marks her resting place:

ANN DALY
BORN A SLAVE IN THE CARROLL FAMILY
IN MARYAND, AND FOR MANY YEARS A
FAITHFUL SERVANT IN THE FAMILY
OF D.C. LITTLEJOHN.
DIED AT OSWEGO
JAN. 2, 1875
AGED 90

As the wife of Oswego's most magnetic political figure, Alida Littlejohn moved with her husband to Albany and Washington, and resided for a few months at his headquarters with the One Hundred Tenth Regiment in Baltimore during the Civil War. She is remembered as a vivacious hostess and an indefatigable worker for local charities. She was a founder of the Home for the Homeless, and earned the tribute offered by the Board at her death. "Hers was not only the brain to plan, but the hand to execute."

Carrington and Pardee were business partners. The former, as senior member, tended the office, while the latter covered markets as distant as Montreal, New York and Chicago. In 1847 Pardee brought home a bride from Maine, and shortly thereafter constructed "Lakeside" for her. It stood on the west hill just east of the Bunner property, its walled gardens extending to the lake shore. A divided "hanging" stairway was the most magnificent in the area. Late in life Carrington undertook the erection of a "medieval castle" on the west hill, said to have been dubbed "Carrington's Folly" by his wife. Unfortunately, he died before he had time to enjoy its luxury, and his widow preferred a more modest dwelling. The castle was eventually converted into a public school and identified as the "Castle School" for many years.[5]

By mid-century Theodore Irwin and George B. Sloan, two young millers, were well on the way to becoming the city's wealthiest residents. Each built an ornate Italian Gothic villa; Sloan on the west hill and Irwin on the east.[6] Sloan's tastes led him to an avocation in politics, where he was a power in Republican caucuses, whereas Irwin was attracted to the fine arts, finding pleasure in surrounding himself with rare books, engravings, paintings and ceramic treasures. He specialized in first editions of the great masters of English literature, and his collection eventually included Chaucer's quarto, more than fifty volumes of Dibdin's editions of the Classics, Caxton's Aeneid and Shakespeare's first folios. He also collected illuminated manuscripts from the middle ages, a Gutenburg Bible, engravings by Albert Durer and Rembrandt, and paintings of modern artists, foreign and domestic.

After his death many of his treasures went to the J.P. Morgan Library in New York, and others to the Huntington Library in Pasadena. The Oswego Historical Society was the recipient of his Louis XV commemorative medal and massive portraits of Irwin and his wife, Louisa Braman Irwin.

Other millers to accumulate fortunes included Samuel B. Johnson, Joel B. Penfield and John E. Lyon. They and their families, like the Sloans and Irwins, were social leaders for two generations.

Bankers also occupied prominent positions in the Oswego community. Luther Wright gave his name to one bank and was involved in the founding of several others. His stately residence, facing Montcalm Park, was worthy of his position.[7] Delos De Wolf was an eminent banker, and, if the Civil War income tax returns in 1865 can be relied upon, he had an annual income of $50,000, the highest in the area. The De Wolf home was later incorporated into a section of the Oswego Hospital.

A third Oswego family to furnish leaders in banking circles was that of Thomas S. Mott. Mott was a grocer, a wholesaler of grain, a ship builder, a director of Kingsford Starch and a founder and President of the First National Bank of Oswego. His sons, John T. and Elliott B., were bankers and yachting enthusiasts; yachting having become popular in the 1880's. John married Alice J. Wright, daughter of Luther Wright, thus uniting two banking families. Their son, Luther Wright Mott, continued the traditions, and also served in Congress.

Manufacturers in Oswego, who could not have bid against the lawyers and millers for the choice pews in the local churches in the early years, were second to none in prestige before the century's close.

Pre-eminent as manufacturers were Thomas Kingsford and his son Thompson. The Kingsfords built their homes near their mills, but of course on the right side of the tracks, and they redeveloped farms on the periphery of the community into well manicured country estates.[8] They subsidized a brass band and a fire company, and contributed liberally to the West Baptist Church and to charity. They were loath to dismiss workers during slack seasons, and tided them over by employing them in the fields. Democrats were prone to complain that the Kingsfords subtly promoted the Republican ticket among their employees. But by and large they were treated with deference.

The Thomas P. Kingsfords (the third generation) scored one of the social triumphs of the century, when on June 16, 1887, they entertained in honor of their house guest, Frances Folsom Cleveland, the young (aged twenty-three) and beautiful bride of a year of President Cleveland.

The sixty-four guests, privileged to be present at their "drive-whist" party, found the grounds of the Kingsford residence on West First Street ornamented and lighted, and the drawing and reception rooms decorated with a profusion of flowers. The ladies' toilettes were elegant; but the focus of attention from first to last was Mrs. Cleveland. Edgar

Dole Johnson drew the coveted card to be the first partner of the charming guest, and the game began. The Kingsford band played "softly and beautifully" throughout the evening.

The local press advised that there was but one impression about Mrs. Cleveland. "Her beauty, simplicity, intelligence and cordiality won all hearts."[9]

Second only to the Kingsfords as industrialists were the Condes, Henry S., and his sons, Swits and Frederic. The Condes moved to Oswego from Central Square in 1855 after Henry had been elected County Clerk. He entered into the manufacture of knit goods, and was immediately successful. His investments eventually included oil in Pennsylvania and cotton and sugar in the South. Swits joined his father in the knitting business; Frederic established his own plant.

The Condes traced their lineage to the French aristocracy of the twelfth century and took an obvious delight in emulating it. Swits held memberships in the Union League, the Huguenot Society of New York and yacht clubs in both New York and Oswego. He also maintained a winter home in New York, and at thirty-eight erected a fifteenth century style English manor house in Oswego at the northeast corner of West Fifth and Seneca streets. Designed by Oscar S. Teale, a noted New York architect, it was reported to have cost $150,000. Allowing for exaggeration it was undoubtedly the city's most costly residence.

Two years in construction, it was elegant from its "sanitary appointments" to the ornamental vane and finial surmounting its three story oriel. And it was only appropriate that its opening should be the most elaborate and costly (reputed to be $10,000) in the area's history. The three hundred guests, a few of whom were borne by private railroad coach from New York, entered "Mon Repos" under a canopy erected to shield them from the throng of spectators, which swarmed over West Park. The guests could have had only a brief glance at its broad, sweeping gables, bold, projecting eaves, and spacious balcony with its curving arches. But they could not overlook the massive Santo Domingan mahogany doors, profusely ornamented with mouldings and carvings, or the arch of graystone bearing the Condé coat-of-arms.

And though they could not have observed it, the newspapers had already informed the public that the hall as well as the rooms on the first floor might be lighted from the second story by simply "touching an electric button." In fact a similar button might illuminate both the gas lights and fireplaces. The same source revealed that electric bells signaled the servants and could be employed as a burglar alarm; also that every discharge pipe was iron enameled on the inside, and that every trap used in the plumbing had separate ventilation pipes on the roof.

More obvious to the guests were the costly drapes and portieres, the tinted flock walls, and the flowers, grown in the Condé conservatory, and arranged by a New York florist.

The Oswego three hundred were met by their host and hostess, the latter resplendent in "imported black satin with Catharine de Medice Collar, black kid gloves to shoulder, pout lace and diamonds." They received dancing programs served from trays by two Negro youths in livery of the fifteenth century, and described in the press as "diminutive sons of Ham." Music for the dances, a combination of lanciers, quadrilles, galops, racquets and waltzes was furnished by the Utica Symphony Orchestra. The catering staff of the Brunswick Hotel of New York served the supper; a contract with Delmonico's having been canceled by the host, when he learned that they could provide only a buffet service. The menu, in French, offered four *entres* classifed as *Chaud,* including *Consomme a la Conde*! There were eleven choices of *Froid,* and six *Sucres,* in addition to desserts and beverages.

For Oswego's elite it was an evening to remember, and even today a dance program, carefully preserved these eighty years, turns up among old family papers.[10]

Swits Conde lived to enjoy the splendid appointments for twenty years, but a decade after his death the mansion was dismantled, and the spacious grounds carved into building lots. Only the "children's cottage," a two and one-half story dwelling, large enough to house a college fraternity, remains on the block.

Oswego's real estate through the years has been a source of both profits and losses, and while there was a gradual appreciation of values, the losses were often more spectacular than the gains. Excepting Gerrit Smith, who had gotten in on the ground floor, the most successful purveyors of land and buildings appear to have been the Richardsons.

Jacob Richardson, the founder of the family in Oswego, was trained in the law, but preferred real estate. In time he owned a great deal of the business property on the east side.

Jacob was survived by his widow, Naomi Bennett Richardson, and three children, Maxwell, Laurence and Harriet. Max stepped into his father's shoes, and expanded the family investments. He was also a community leader, and served two terms as Mayor.

In the 1880's he rebuilt the family home on East Third Street, and converted it into an elegant Victorian mansion in the Tuscan manner of the day. Its sixteen-foot ceilings offered an ideal setting for the moulded plaster of the drawing room, the cherry of the library and the oak paneling of the dining room. A magnificent skylight flooded the hallway with color.[11]

Financially independent, Max traveled widely over Europe and Asia, and adorned his home with works of art. A patron of the theatre, he brought Broadway to Oswego by erecting a splended theatre with appointments comparable to show places in the larger cities.[12] Seats were auctioned for its grand opening on January 24, 1895, and Oswego's Brahmins paid up to fifty dollars each for the choice boxes. The first audience was treated to a performance of *Robin Hood* by Barnabee and MacDonald's Opera Company. Through 5,360 performances the ornate playhouse ran the

gamut from Shakespeare to burlesque, and at last in 1931
succumbed to the movies.

Neither Max nor Laurence married, and they sometimes
flaunted Victorian conventions. Elder residents recall that
they elicited a good deal of conversation; often in whispers.

Harriet married Byron Bates, but shortly after the birth
of a son, Norman, Byron disappeared leaving no forwarding address.

Little Norman grew up in the big house, the pride and joy
of his mother and uncles. A teen-aged companion, who
became a distinguished architect and theatrical producer,
remembered more than thirty years later that Norman had
been a handsome and dashing figure living in "a great
house set in a great yard, with a rich uncle [Max], who
indulged him to the utmost. Norm always had the first of
everything: the first tennis set, the first Columbia bicycle,
the first tight pants, the first flat derby. I used to hang
around for hours in the hope of being asked to try my hand
at tennis, or of being permitted to mount to the seat perilous
above the great nickel-plated wheel, and my patience was
usually rewarded for Norm was both generous and kind,
and we had a great affection for each other.[13]

Young Norman's charm did not wear off with manhood,
and like his uncle Max he was a civic leader as well as an
excellent judge of property. He married Florence Morley
and reared four children.

Upon the death of Florence Morley Bates, the old edifice,
with many of its furnishings intact, was presented to the
Oswego County Historical Society by the heirs. It remains
in the 1960's one of the finest memorials to the massive and
gaudy ornamentation of the Victorian age.

* * * * *

While Max Richardson and Swits Conde were consulting
their architects, John B. Edwards, enroute to the water
front properties of his employer on the east side, stopped at
Seneca Street to observe a gang of juveniles, "both male and
female, black and white, together with all the intermediate

shades of color, representing all quarters of the globe."
They had surrounded a farmer's wagon loaded with apples;
and seeing the children "gazing with longing upon the
contents,[he] at once comprehended the situation; and
being prompted by all the generosity and magnanimity of
his nature, purchased the apples of the farmer, and with
pleasure depicted on his countenance, dealt them out to the
delighted children, who were greatly rejoiced at being so
suddenly placed in possession of that which only a moment
before they had considered it impossible for them to pos-
sess. Few indeed are the cities that can boast of a City
Father [Alderman] who is so kind to all his children."[14]

Neither the reporter of Edwards' charity nor Edwards
himself needed to be told that there were, in reality, two
Oswegos—that of the propertied and that of the poor.

The village had attracted the latter from the outset.
Laborers had arrived with the salt trade and the canals, and
a variety of lodging houses had soon lined the water front.
The identity of these hotels, taverns and lodgings in many
cases has been lost, but one who has the patience to scan the
early newspapers comes upon the Eagle Tavern, the United
States Hotel, the Franklin House, the Rideau Hotel, the
Frontier House, the Welland Hotel, the Fitzhugh House and
others. Early directories also reveal a host of roomers and
boarders.

The arrival of the Irish, often with families, multiplied
the number seeking lodgings. And unable to find anything
better, they squatted on back lots and waste patches. Such a
section near the canal initially occupied by French laborers,
was appropriately labeled "Pea Soup Flats." There was also
"Pious Hollow" (East Tenth Street), the "Flats" (the foot
of West Seneca Street), and "Corkey Hollow"(lake shore
east of Fort Ontario).

Village and city officials briefly focused their attention
upon these blighted areas when there were threats of
cholera, and sometimes went so far as to order a liberal
application of lime upon drains, stagnant water and back-

houses. But with the crisis passed, the jerry-built sections returned to their usual disarray.

When J.B. Edwards reported that a crate-box colony was rising on Vinegar Hill adjacent to the Cove Property, Gerrit Smith replied that they should not be disturbed until the land could be sold. But the squatters were not always treated with such consideration. On an April day in 1855 the police and Board of Health, assisted by firemen, demolished twenty or thirty tenements which had sprung up in the Pea Soup Flats area, with the explanation that they had been condemned as detrimental to the health of the city. The occupants had been notified, but had not heeded. The work went on swiftly, for the "frail fabrics" were not difficult to destroy. The residents made a hasty retreat, clutching their belongings. One woman was reported to have guarded her mudsill with a "doublebarreled gun," but she reconsidered and moved away without discharging it. By night the work was done. The huts were destroyed and the odds and ends of furniture were scattered along the streets. The "poor tenants" were gathered in knots, most of them without a spot to call home.[15]

Further evidence relating to the plight of the lowly, and more particularly of the Irish, is suggested in reports upon the community's first hospital in 1861-1862. It occupied a "somewhat dilapidated" house in Corkey Hollow, but everything was represented as neat and orderly, and the infirm and diseased paupers were declared to be comfortable and well fed, excepting one who complained of a lack of tobacco. Among the twenty males and seventeen females were five children and three young women, "victims of the wiles of seducers." Twenty-four were confined because of intemperance. Three were insane and two were blind. Twenty-six were born in Ireland, three in England, and four in the United States.[16]

Fortunately, low cost Canadian timber and an abundance of building lots in the 1850's and 1860's permitted many of the poor, whether Irish, French-Canadian, German or native stock, to rent or purchase small houses on the periphery of the community. Streets west of the starch factory, and others adjacent to the harbor on both sides of the river were gradually lined with small, rectangular one and one-half storied houses. It is interesting to note that many of these blocks remain almost intact a century later, their narrow lots affording space for porches, front and back, but precluding lateral extensions and garages.

The Irish spread across substantial sections of the eight wards. Catholicism became the largest denomination in the city, and Irish votes on election day made them a potent force in politics. Irish volunteers filled gaps in the local regiments in the Civil War, and a goodly number came out of the war with commissions. Those who remained at home found opportunities in the tight labor market. By the century's end the Irish were moving into the more fashionable blocks, and emigrants from Italy began to occupy their old homes. If the Irish had not yet "arrived" they were arriving!

Meanwhile, smaller colonies of German laborers settled in the Pious Hollow area and the Seventh Ward. Coming in smaller numbers, and often possessing skills sought by employers, their adjustment was less conspicuous than that of the Irish. Their reputation for hard work is suggested by a small item in the local press. After a heavy snow had halted traffic, the Germans of the Munn Street section were observed, shovels in hand, opening a swath down Murray Street to its outlet on Ellen Street. The newspaper complimented them for their industry, and added with a touch of humor, that the Irish would have never done it![17]

The plight of the children was not entirely unattended during this time of stress. Community leaders founded the Oswego Orphan Asylum in 1852, and built a home on Ellen Street in 1856. The socially prominent made it one of their principal charities, and competed to serve on its board of directors.

The Home for the Homeless (Old Ladies' Home), incorporated in 1872, offered a refuge for elderly women, and the Oswego Hospital, which opened its doors in 1881 depended largely upon the largess of the affluent and the gratuitous services of the medical profession. The Home for the Homeless and the hospital were also directed by the elite, the combined boards providing a key to the social register.

A glance at this list as the century closed reveals a significant transformation. The Bunners and McWhorters were gone; also the Fitzhughs and Littlejohns, the Duers, Turrills, Edwards, Allens and Churchills; and they would soon be joined by the Irwins, the Sloans and Condes.

But as the old names disappeared, new ones took their places: the Downeys, Emericks and Culkins, and Mackins, Bulgers, Morrisons and Fitzgibbons filled the gaps, and mingled with the Motts, Pages, Johnsons, Penfields, Bates, Posts and Kingsfords as leaders of the community. They found their way to the boards of the hospital and the Home for the Homeless, became devotees of yachting and members of the Fortnightly and the country clubs.

The twentieth century has continued to shuffle the names, and to lift up new ones to cope with changing times.

18

FLOWING INTO THE TWENTIETH CENTURY

Just over three centuries have passed since Father Le-Moyne glided down the Oswego River in an Indian canoe. If he could repeat the trip today he would find few land marks to guide him. The river is now a placid stream; dams at Phoenix, Fulton, Minetto and Oswego having subdued its boisterous rapids; and its awesome power appears only at the spillways of the dams.

On the other hand, there is much to remind the observer of the three intervening centuries. A boatman with a sense of history notes evidence of it as he approaches Three Rivers Point, whether his passage is from Oneida Lake or Seneca River. If his entree is from the former, he passes the Brewerton shoals, a fisherman's paradise since Archaic times, and on his left, Smith or Denman Island, with its countless Indian burials.

Ten miles further as he nears Three Rivers Point, he observes to starboard the Schroepel mansion. Its classic columns and charm reveal Old World ambitions to recreate beauty and culture on the New York frontier. Its magnificent nine-foot clock, the work of skilled craftsmen from Schroepel's native Germany, has been removed to Phoenix, but it has been preserved, and puts on a revue each hour on the hour, as it did a century ago, for its owner, J.C. Birdlebough.

The traveler, who comes down the Seneca branch, en-

counters Oswego history as he approaches the bridge at
Belgium, two miles above Three Rivers Point. Set back
from the left bank is the Willett House, erected by the
Reverend William M. Willett about 1827. Colonel Marinus
Willett, his father, received title to a six hundred acre lot
here as a part of the twenty-four hundred acre land bounty
paid to one of his rank for service in the Revolution. Willett's civic and business responsibilities kept him in New
York, but his son, a Methodist minister, occupied it in his
place.

It was truly a pretentious house for a Methodist Circuit
Rider—or for that matter for any frontier family. Rectangular in form, with four great chimneys, it had a broad
central hall, and a majestic stairway reaching to the third
floor. Ten fireplaces once provided warmth through the
long winters. With many of its original appointments intact
it stands today, a monument to the leader of the snow
march of 1783.

At Three Rivers Point the past yields to the present, and
by contrast, the river bank is bathed in the garish lights of a
night club, steak house and motel!

At the first rift, Phoenix comes into view. The power site
spawned a village, and required a lock on the canal.
Phoenix was the home of Thaddeus C. Sweet, paper manu-
facturer, Speaker of the New York State Assembly, and
Congressman. An air enthusiast during the early stages of
air travel, his promising career was cut short by the crash of
his plane while commuting to Washington in 1928. The old
Sweet paper mill now stands empty. A spotty business block
along the river bears witness to the village's most destructive fire. It occurred in 1916, and wiped out the entire
business section. A block eastward towering elms and
maples mark the residential area, which retains much of its
nineteenth century charm.

At Hinmansville a lock on the original canal is almost
intact; its gates have rotted away, but the heavy stone walls
remain in place. Well decayed sheds line the bank—
hangovers from the days of the canallers.

Several miles down stream the silhouette of Fulton takes form. On the right the brick superstructure of Nestle's looms above lesser buildings around it. And if the breeze is out of the northeast the aroma of roasting cacao beans identifies it. Fultonians still refer to the plant as the Peter Kahler Company, which was founded in 1907 by Swiss investors, who discovered that Americans had a sweet tooth for their chocolate products. They selected Fulton, an early press release emphasized, because the local milk supply was as good in quality as any in Switzerland. A colony of Swiss soon arrived to operate the plant, and their descendants can still be identified in the community.

On the right bank at the falls the Sealright Company spreads over many acres. As early as 1840 paper was manufactured here from straw. Then, just after the Civil War, Forrest G. Weeks, a resourceful young Englishman, working his way through Falley Seminary as a blacksmith, began to experiment with wood fiber for paper making. He acquired power rights at the falls and erected a pulp mill; and, in association with H. Lester Paddock, subsequently established the Oswego Falls Pulp and Paper Company. They initiated the manufacture of "Fulton Board" for the packaging of liquids, and became one of the principal producers of paper containers in the United States. Today, the Sealright Oswego Falls Company's markets span the globe. It is the largest employer in the area.

On the opposite side of the falls aging factory buildings recall the once preeminent woolens industry. Almost single-handedly this manufactory built the west side of Fulton and gave it its ethnic pattern.

A small mill was erected here just in time to obtain orders in the Civil War. But demand slackened at its close, and the business passed through a confusing succession of reorganizations, succumbing in both the panics of 1873 and 1893. But it rebounded under the direction of Charles Fletcher, a former English butcher boy, who made "Oswego Worsted" a trade-mark of quality. Expansion proceeded at such a rapid pace that it outran the local labor market, and a swarm of emigrants from Poland and the Ukraine filled the vacuum. Fletcher erected row upon row of factory houses, but, unlike some other builders of company towns in this era, sold them to thrifty tenants, accepting small payments and offering long term credit. Employment passed one thousand at the turn of the century, and eventually reached 2,400. Its woolens clothed armed forces of the Spanish-American (though they were scarcely needed in tropical Cuba) and the First and Second World Wars.

The Company provided the community with Recreation Park on the shore of Lake Neahtawanta, featuring a dance pavilion, auditorium, amusements for the children, and athletic fields. On Sundays there were free movies, and on week days a schedule of "Name Bands". A dance marathon initiated here in the 1930's created a national fad.

Then came the great Depression; and to make matters worse, woolens began to lose favor, and were often replaced in the wardrobe by synthetics, The industry—now a unit of the American Woolens—revived briefly during World War II, but came to a sickening halt in 1952. Five hundred thousand square feet of brick buildings with an assessment tag of $510,000, a mere fraction of its value just a few years before, were auctioned off for $35,000. The plant never reopened. Fortunately, Sealright and Nestle took up much of the slack.

The business section of Fulton grew up between the locks of the canal, and took much of its nourishment from the raceway of the lower dam. Lumber and flour mills, machine shops and paper plants concentrated on its banks, and at the turn of the century electricity generated here afforded Fultonians with their first opportunity to enjoy electric lighting.

One of the users of water power in 1867 was Frank Dilts, who had a general shop and small foundry. As paper manufacturers came to the river they looked to Dilts for repairs upon their machinery. He soon went a step further, and began to produce wood pulp grinders and pulp wet machines. Dilts' machines found markets beyond the valley, and his company later merged with Black and Clawson as the Dilts Division, Paper and Plastics Converting Systems.

Below Fulton the channel curves past Pathfinder Island, in horse and buggy days, Fulton's principal recreation area. Only a clearing remains. Beyond it on the right bank is Van Valkenburgh's Point, where his tavern once added gaiety to the somber frontier. Further downstream the Armstrong Cork Felt Mill marks a power site now covered by the deepened stream, and just below it two of the Van Buren homesteads reaching back to the early canal era face the river. The first was once a tavern with a spacious ballroom; the second remains an elegant Grecian temple with massive white columns.

Just ahead, the river sweeps to the left and passes a small wooded island, remembered after 1756 as Bradstreet's, and later simply as Battle Island. It was here that Bradstreet was ambushed, and gathered his defenders. To the left the traveler spots rolling hills of a variegated green, which he soon identifies as clumps of pines and corridors of grass leading to emerald green ovals: the Battle Island Golf Course and State Park.

Two more miles brings Minetto into view. Once a company town adjacent to the Columbia Mills, manufacturers of window shades, it provides a rural setting for a growing tide of commuters to Oswego, Fulton and Syracuse.

Beyond Minetto the river straightens for its final descent to Oswego. Here the wooded banks have changed little since young James Fenimore Cooper observed them in 1808—only the water is different. The roaring flood of pre-canal times moves sluggishly behind the breast of the Oswego "High Dam." Its crystal-like irridescence is now lackluster and emulsified!

Oswego, a mingling of the old and new, comes into view. A hydroelectric plant stands on the west bank where once the Varick Canal left the river; and just below it, the weather-beaten ruins of Kingsford Starch tells the story of its decadence after its absorption by the starch trust in 1902 and closure in 1923. On the east bank there are also gaunt survivals in brick and stone of nineteenth century enterprise: a tannery, cotton mill, weighlock of the old Oswego Canal, and a boat yard; and below the Utica Street bridge the foundations of the Perot and Pardee malt houses.

A final lock lowers the observer to the level of Lake Ontario, and opens a passage into the lake. The panorama of the early and recent continues. On the left a radio station occupies a section of the century-old village hall and market house. The remainder of the stained old structure has been abandoned to the pigeons, but a trace of its early grandeur is suggested by the graceful arch over its doorway.

On the right bank open spaces mark the site of grain mills and elevators, which burned in 1892, and coal elevators, dismantled a half-century ago, and above them rise the modern lines of an urban renewal project. Still advancing with the current the viewer notes a broad expanse of warehouses operated by the Oswego Port Authority and a crowded marina occupying the Cove Property of Gerrit Smith.

Just back of it on a low bluff stands old Fort Ontario, the fourth bastion on this spot. It was garrisoned until World War II, and then abandoned as obsolete. For some months it was a refugee center for a thousand of Europe's misplaced, and for several years thereafter a housing center for students and faculty of the college. Then its gates were closed. Fortunately, the state intervened, and restored it to its Civil War proportions. Today it has become a show place, viewed by more than one hundred thousand visitors annually.

To the left elevators housing grain and cement almost obscure a boulder marking the site of Fort Oswego. A mile beyond them, but clearly visible are the lofty stacks of the Niagara Mohawk Power Plant. Less distinct along the lake shore, but taking shape as the observer reaches the harbor's mouth, is a complex of tan brick structures, the State University College, once Sheldon's Normal, on a site adjoining his old home on the lake. In the late 1960's more than four thousand students hurry to and from its class rooms seeking to maintain schedules on a campus which has expanded tenfold in twenty years.

A sweep of 180 degrees reveals the shining exterior of a new aluminum plant across several miles of water, and nine miles beyond it, where only a wooded shore is visible, workmen are completing a nuclear power plant.

Could Father LeMoyne have made this excursion his second voyage down the Oswego River after the passage of three centuries, he could have identified few of the old landmarks. The slow-flowing stream, the open countryside, the villages and cities lining its banks would have seemed strange and out of place. But once the craft had moved out of Oswego harbor, the clear and sparkling water of Lake Ontario, the curving, tree-lined shoreline off to starboard pointing toward the St. Lawrence River and Canada would have restored old memories, and he would have set out for Quebec reassured.

NOTES AND REFERENCES

INTRODUCTION

1 Notable exceptions to this generalization include A. M. Schlesinger's *Rise of the American City 1878-1898* (A History of American Life, X), New York, 1933; Richard C. Wade's "Urban Life in Western America," *American Historical Review*, LXIV (1958), 14-30; and Constance McLaughlin Green's *Rise of Urban America*, New York, 1965. Rochester has been favored with Blake McKelvey's three volumes: *Rochester, the Water-Power City, 1812-1854*, Cambridge, 1945; *Rochester, the Flower City 1855-1890*, Cambridge, 1949, *and Rochester: The Quest for Quality 1890-1925*, Cambridge, 1956. He has also written *Urbanization of America 1860-1915*, New Brunswick, 1963. Mention should be made, also, of Catherine E. Riser's *Pittsburgh's Commercial Development 1800-1850*, Harrisburg, 1951.
2 Charles Evans Hughes spent several years of his boyhood in Oswego, where his father was a Baptist minister.

CHAPTER 1

WHERE EMPIRES CLASHED IN THE WILDERNESS

1 See William A. Ritchie, *Indian History of New York State,* Part II, *The Iroquois Tribes*, Albany, 1953, 3.
2 W. L. Grant, ed., *Voyages of Samuel de Champlain, 1567-1635*, New York, 1907, 289-290.
3 Champlain's biographer, Morris Bishop, concludes that the village was on the site of Syracuse, and that a pond mentioned by Champlain was Onondaga Lake. However, Madison County historians identify the village at Nichols Pond, 40 miles east of Onondaga Lake. See Bishop's *Champlain, The Life of Fortitude*, New York, 1948, Appendix F, 355-359. A recent archaeological study casts further doubt upon the Nichols Pond site. See Peter P. Pratt, "Archaeology of the Oneida Iroquois as Related to Early Acculturation and to the Location of the Champlain-Iroquois Battle of 1615;" (doctoral dissertation, University of Michigan, Ann Arbor, 1966).
4 Reuben G. Thwaites, ed., *Jesuit Relations*, Cleveland, Ohio, 1896-1901, XLI, 97-125.
5 *Ibid.*, XLIV, 159-161.
6 E. B. O'Callaghan, ed., *Documentary History of New York*, Albany, 1849, I, 437.
7 John Bartram, *Observations . . . in His Travels from Pennsylvania to Onondaga, Oswego and Lake Ontario . . .*, London, 1751, 48-49.
8 Cadwallader Colden Papers, New York Historical Society *Publications*, IX, 103-104.
9 E. B. O'Callaghan, ed., *Documents Relating to the Colonial History of New York*, 1853-1861, VI, 105.
10 *Ibid.*, VI, 177.
11 *Ibid.*, VI, 538.
12 *Ibid.* I, 459.
13 Bartram, *op. cit.*, 48.
14 See John A. Schutz, *William Shirley*, Chapel Hill, 1961, 213-247; Lawrence H. Gipson, *The British Empire Before the American Revolution*, VII, *The Great War for the*

Empire, New York, 1949, 162-211. A recent reappraisal by a Johnson scholar may be found in ilton W. Hamilton, "Hero of Lake George: Johnson or Lyman?" *New England Quarterly*, XXXVI (Sept. 1963), 371-382; See also Johnson Cooper, "Oswego in the French-English Struggle in North America," (doctoral dissertation, Syracuse University, Syracuse, 1959).

15 To Gov. Robert Hunter Morris, Penna. *Archives*, 1st ser., II, 424-425.
16 Stanley Pargellis, ed., *Military Affairs in North America*, 1748-1765, New York, 1936, 287.
17 Mercer to Shirley, Feb. 22, 1756, Lord Loudoun Papers, Huntington Library.
18 Mercer to Capt. William Williams, Mar. 14, 1756, Loudoun Papers.
19 *Ibid.*, March 23, 1756.
20 Pargellis, *op cit.*, 187-192.
21 Robert Macdonald, ed., "The Diary of Stephen Cross," *Yearbook*, Oswego County Historical Soc., 1941, 15.
22 Captain Alfred T. Mahan, *The Influence of Sea Power Upon History, 1660-1763*, Boston 1895, 291.
23 Pargellis, *op cit.*, 210.
24 Robert Macdonald, *op. cit.*, 18.
25 *Ibid.*
26 *Montcalm and Wolfe*, Boston, 1895, I, 475.
27 See John A. Schutz, *op. cit.*, 213-247; also Gipson, *op. cit.*, 162-211.
28 Parkman, *op. cit.*, quoting Bougainville's *Journal*. See Edward P. Hamilton, ed., *Adventure in the Wilderness, The American Journals of Louis Antoine de Bougainville*, Norman, Oklahoma, 1964, 115.
29 The Oswego County Historical Society has one of these rare coins; there is another in the Louvre, Paris.
30 *An Impartial Account of Lieutenant Colonel Bradstreet's Expedition to Fort Frontenac*, London, 1759.
31 H. Beckles Wilson, *Life and Letters of James Wolfe*, London, 1909, 369-397.
32 Captain Francois Pouchot, *Memoirs*, Roxbury, Mass., 1866, I, 208-9.
33 J. Clarence Webster, ed., *Journal of Jeffrey Amherst*, Chicago, 1931, 222.
34 *Ibid.*, 239; See also A. G. Doughty, ed., *Journal of the Campaigns in North America, 1757-1760*, by Captain J. Knox, Toronto, 1914, Volumes II and III.
35 Milton W. Hamilton, "Sir William Johnson's Five Visits to Oswego." *Yearbook*, Oswego County Historical Society, 1955, 42; See also Howard H. Peckman, *Pontiac and the Indian Uprising*, Princeton, N. J., 1947, 288, 297.

CHAPTER 2

WAR AND PEACE AT THE MOUTH OF THE OSWEGO RIVER

1 Sally Smith Davis told the story to her grandson, George A. Davis; Martin Kellogg in conversations with his son. Lewis Kellogg, corroborated much of the Davis reminiscence. George H. Goodwin interviewed others who remembered Town. These accounts appeared in issues of the *Mexico Independent* in 1871. See also Elizabeth Simpson, *Mixico Mother of Towns*, Buffalo, 1949, 137-155.
2 Washington to Willett, Dec. 18, 1782, John C. Fitzpatrick, ed., *The Writings of George Washington*, Washington, 1938, XXV, 449-451; See also Edwin M. Waterbury, "Colonel Historical Society, 1939, 5-25.
3 George Washington to Marinus Willett, Feb. 2, 1783, Fitzpatrick, *op. cit.*, XXVI, 90-93.
4 Marinus Willett to Governor George Clinton, Feb. 20, 1783, quoted in Waterbury, *op. cit.*, 17.
5 William M. Willett, *A Narrative of the Military Actions of Colonel Marinus Willett*, New York, 1831, 93.
6 Immanuel Drake of Rhode Island; Edwin M. Waterbury, *op. cit.*, 24.
7 *Oswego Palladium*, June 19, 1824.
8 John C. Fitzpatrick, *op. cit.* XXXVI, 165-166.
9 Jeptha Simms, *The Frontiersmen of New York*, Albany, N. Y. 1883, II, 647-656, quoting from Alexander Thompson, "Journal of a Tour from the American Garrison at Fort Rennsselaer (Fort Plain) in Canajoharie on the Mohawk River to the British Garrison of Oswego, As a Flag, to Announce a Cessation of Hostilities on the Frontiers of New York."
10 Schoedde to E. B. Littlehales, August 15, 1793, Correspondence of *Lt. Governor John G. Simcoe*, Toronto, 1924, II, 23.
11 From remarks by Helen Osborne delivered on the centennial of John Van Buren's arrival in Fulton; *Oswego Times*, Feb. 7, 1896.
12 John C. Churchill, *Landmarks of Oswego County*, Syracuse, 1895, 119.
13 Simcoe Correspondence, II, 204.
14 *Ibid.*, Sept. 25, 1793.
15 Crisfield Johnson *History of Oswego County*, Philadelphia, 1877, 50.

16 *Simcoe Correspondence,* IV, 104.
17 Diary of Henry Glen, New York State Historical Association, Cooperstown, N. Y.
18 E. M. Waterbury, "Oswego County Simultaneously Under Two Flags from 1783 to 1796," *Yearbook,* Oswego County Historical Society, 1949, 42.
19 *Simcoe Correspondence,* II, 204-205.
20 Duke de la Rochefoucauld-Liancourt, *Travels Through The United States . . . 1795, 1796, 1797,* London, 1800, II, 4-7.
21 Frederick K. Zercher, "The Economic Development of the Port of Oswego," unpublished doctoral dissertation, Syracuse University, 1935, Chapter V. Zercher's study includes many statistics illustrative of the harbor's growth.
22 Quoted by Anthony Slosek in "Oswego, 1796-1828, Fragments of Local History," *Yearbook,* Oswego County Historical Society, 1959, 39.
23 From an address delivered Feb. 24, 1852; quoted by F. Hosmer Culkin in "Alvin Bronson, A First Citizen of Oswego," *Yearbook,* Oswego County Historical Society, 1951, 69.
24 Newton, Pennsylvania, 1805.
25 James Fenimore Cooper, *Lives of Distinguished American Naval Officers,* Philadelphia, 1846, II, 126-129.
26 Susan Fenimore Cooper, *Pages and Pictures,* New York, 1865, 309.
27 William W. Campbell, ed., *Life and Writings of DeWitt Clinton,* New York, 1849, 77-81.

CHAPTER 3

GEORGE SCRIBA'S DREAM AND NIGHTMARE

1 Many years after the Selkirk name had virtually disappeared from the area, the State constructed a well-shaded camp grounds on the lake shore a few miles south of Port Ontario. It seemed appropriate in Albany to name it Selkirk Shores State Park. Local historians were on the alert, however, and were soon protesting that the Scottish Earl had never owned the land south of the Salmon River, and that Selkirk was not suited. But it sounded proper enough to catch on with thousands of campers; and Selkirk it remains.
2 Description based upon a portrait in the Oneida County (New York) Historical Society.
3 Francis Adrian Van der Kemp, *Letters on a Tour of the Western District of New York 1792,* Utica, 1877. See also Harry F. Jackson, *Francis Adrian Van der Kemp,* Syracuse, 1963, 122-136.
4 Scriba mss., State Library, Albany, Jan. 12, 1795.
5 *Ibid.,* Oct. 11, 1796.
6 *Ibid.,* Nov. 24, 1796.
7 *Ibid.,* Dec. 31, 1796.
8 *Ibid.,* Feb. 27, 1797.
9 See Elizabeth Simpson's *Mexico Mother of Towns* for details on Scriba's land promotion in the Town of Mexico, 29-83.
10 Scriba mss., Feb. 9, 1798.
11 Simpson, *op. cit.,* 94. The story was told to Silas Davis, son of Sally Smith Davis.
12 David S. Bates to Scriba, Jan. 30, 1801, Scriba mss.
13 One of these handbills is in the possession of the Oswego County Historical Society.

CHAPTER 4

PIONEERS: THE WAY THEY REMEMBERED IT

1 Joshua V. Clark, *Onondaga or Reminiscences of Earlier and Later Times; and Oswego,* Syracuse, 1849, II, 183-185. See also Simpson, *op. cit.,* 17. Miss Simpson points out that Pulaski was not in the town of Mexico at this time.
2 Joshua V. Clark, op. cit., II, 185-186.
3 *Ibid.,* See also J. Elet Milton, 'Oliver Stevens, First Permanent Settler in Oswego County," *Yearbook,* Oswego County Historical Society, 1950, 47-61.
4 Duke de la Rochefoucauld Liancourt, *Travels Through the United States . . . 1795, 1796, 1797,* London, 1800, II, 19-27.
5 *Oswego Commercial Times,* March 19, 1859.
6 *Yearbook,* Oswego County Historical Society, 1954, 29-34.
7 Elizabeth Simpson, *op. cit.,* 161-162, taken from the files of the *Mexico Independent.*
8 *Ibid.,* 162.
9 Ibid., 168-169.
10 *Ibid.,* 163-165.

CHAPTER 5

THE WAR OF 1812, AND A STRAND OF CABLE

1 Johnson. History of Oswego County, 66.
2 *Ibid.*, 66-67.
3 *Ibid.*, 67.
4 Edwin W. Clarke, "Cemetery Register Book," Oswego Co. Hist. Soc.
5 "Reminiscences of Hamilton Colton," *Oswego Palladium*, 1876.
6 T. S. Morgan to Samuel F. Hooker, May 11, 1814, Morgan Letterbook New York Historical Society
7 Johnson, *op cit.*, 67.
8 Diary of Orrin Stone of Scriba Corners, Mrs. George M. Penney, Oswego, N. Y.
9 Johnson, *op. cit.*, 68.

CHAPTER 6

THE OSWEGO CANAL

1 Utica, New York, 1819.
2 Crisfield Johnson, *History of Oswego County*, 72.
3 Churchill, *opp. cit.*, 347
4 *Ibid.*
5 *Palladium*, June 2, 1830.
6 Feb. 16, 1831.
7 Aug. 11, 1830.
8 *Ibid.*
9 *Ibid.*, July 22, 1835.
10 *Ibid.*, July 29, 1835.
11 See J. Elet Milton, "Oneida Lake Navigation," *Yearbook*, Oswego County Historical Society, 1953. 30-45; See also Oneida Lake and River Steamboat Company papers, J. Elet Milton. Brewerton. N. Y.
12 *Oswego Palladium Times*, Centennial edition, Nov. 20, 1945, Sec. 2.
13 *Oswego Palladium*, May 11, 1847.
14 *Ibid.*, Feb. 2, 1842.

CHAPTER 7

BOOM TIMES AND MOUNTAINS OF STARCH

1 Edwards to Smith, July 21, 1865, Gerrit Smith mss., Syracuse University; see also Charles M. Snyder, "The Business Activities of Gerrit Smith," *Yearbook*, Oswego County Historical Society, 1952, 1-17.
2 *Oswego Palladium*, July 7, 1830.
3 *Oswego Commercial Herald*, Feb. 14, 1838.
4 Crisfield Johnson, *History of Oswego County*, 150.
5 Ibid.
6 Edwards to Smith, March 15, 1836, Smith mss.
7 Ulysses G. White to Joel Turrill, March 15, 21, 1836, Turrill mss., Oswego County Historical Society.
8 Robert Martin to Joel Turrill, April 19, 1836, Turrill mss., Oswego County Historical Society.
9 James Porter to Joel Turrill, Feb. 19, 1836, Turrill mss., Oswego County Historical Society.
10 McWhorter to Turrill, n.d. Aca. April, 1836), Turrill mss., Oswego County Historical Society.
11 Crisfield Johnson, *op. cit.*, 150.
12 Ralph V. Harlow, *Gerrit Smith*, New York, 1939, 27-32.
13 Edwards to Smith, April 18, 1836, Smith mss.
14 Edwards to Smith, May 16, 22, 29, 1837, Smith mss.
15 Ralph V. Harlow, *Gerrit Smith*, 326.
16 March 20. 1855.
17 *Oswego Palladium Times*, Centennial Edition, Aug. 31, 1948, III, 1.
18 *Oswego Palladium*, March 23, 1847.
19 Charles Wells. "T. Kingsford and Son, and the Oswego Starch Factory," *Yearbook*, Oswego County Historical Society. 1951, 4
20 Anthony M. Slosek, "George N. Bernard," *Yearbook*, Oswego County Civil War Centennial Committee, 1964, 39-45.

CHAPTER 8

DEMOCRATS AND WHIGS

1 Rudolph Bunner to Gulian C. Verplanck, Nov. 4, 1826, Verplanck mss., New York Historical Society.
2 Oct. 27, 1830.
3 *Oswego Free Press*, March 31, July 7, Sept. 1, 1830.
4 Oct. 24, 1830.
5 *Oswego Commercial* Herald, Nov. 21, 1838.
6 Turrill to Silas Wright, Dec. 23, 1838, Van Buren mss., Library of Congress.
7 Wright to Van Buren, March 17, 1839, Van Buren mss.
8 *Oswego Palladium*, 1846 and 1848.
9 *Congressional Globe*, 30th Congress, 1st session. XIX, Washington, 1848, 313-316, 1046.
10 *Ibid.*, 1010. The death of a young daughter also contributed to his absence from the House.
11 Robert J. Rayback, "Oswego County's Contributions to the 'Silver Grey' Movement," *Yearbook*, Oswego County Historical Society, 1949, 66. See also Rayback's *Millard Fillmore*, Buffalo, 1959, 259. Duer's dispatch is in the Fillmore Collection, Buffalo Historical Society.
12 D. S. Alexander, *A Political History of the State of New York*, 1906, II, 207.
13 March 6, 1855.
14 Littlejohn to Weed, Nov. 16, 1856, Weed mss., University of Rochester.
15 March 16, 1858, Seward mss., University of Rochester.
16 G. G. Van Deusen, *Horace Greeley*, Philadelphia, 1953, 251.
17 Littlejohn to Weed, Oct. 9, 1860, Weed mss.; Littlejohn to Morgan, Oct. 1, 1860, Morgan mss., State Library, Albany; Littlejohn to Seward, Oct. 20, 1860, Seward mss.
18 *New York Herald*, Jan. 3, 1861; quoted in H. J. Carman and R. H. Luthin, *Lincoln and the Patronage*, New York, 1943, 60.
19 New York, 1887, 218.

CHAPTER 9

RELIGION IN THE VALLEY

1 E. B. O'Callaghan, ed., *Documentary History of New York,* III, 1120; Leon N. Brown, "Pioneer Oswego County Preachers and Their Churches," *Yearbook,* Oswego County Historical Society, 1940, 16.
2 *Ibid.,* 17.
3 *Mexico Independent,* quoted in Elizabeth Simpson's *Mexico Mother of Towns,* 468.
4 Leon N. Brown, *loc., cit.,* 17.
5 John B. McLean, *A Brief History of the First Presbyterian Church of Oswego,* Oswego, 1890. The passage is taken from an address delivered in 1852.
6 Leon N. Brown, *loc. cit.,* 18-19.
7 Elizabeth Simpson, *op. cit.,* 479.
8 Churchill, *op. cit.,* 432.
9 Edwin W. Clarke mss., Oswego County Historical Society.
10 Clarke mss.
11 *Oswego Times,* Aug. 1, 1890.
12 John B. Edwards to Gerrit Smith, Aug. 15, 1844, Feb. 17, 1845, Smith mss.
13 Roger H. Ferris, "History of the Seventh Day Adventists in Oswego County," *Yearbook,* Oswego County Historical Society, 1959, 55-63.
14 Elizabeth Simpson, *op. cit.,* 332-333.
15 Smith to Mills, Smith mss., Sept. 5, 1839, Mar. 14, April 2, 1840.
16 Edwards to Smith, Jan. 19, 1848, Smith mss.
17 *Yearbook,* Oswego County Historical Society, 1943, 26.

CHAPTER 10

THE ANTISLAVERY CRUSADE

1 Elizabeth Simpson, "Two Famous Abolitionists of Oswego County," *Yearbook,* Oswego County Historical Socety, 1940, 90.
2 Elizabeth Simpson, *Mexico Mother of Towns,* 348.
3 Oswego Palladium, Sept. 30, 1835.
4 Edwards to Smith, Oct. 14, 1844, Smith mss.

5   *Ibid.*, Nov. 4, 1844.
6   *Ibid.*, Nov. 11, 1848.
7   *Ibid.*, June 13, 1860.
8   *Ibid.*, Sept. 20, 1847.
9   *Ibid.*, Feb. 1, 1851.
10 *Ibid.*, April 29, 1847.
11 *Ibid.*, April 19, 1860.
12 *Ibid.*, March 19, 1860.
13 Clarke mss., Oswego County Historical Society.
14 Jerry McHenry was forcibly removed from a Syracuse jail and released on October 1, 1851 by Abolitionists, who were attending an Abolitionist convention. Details are shrouded by folklore. See Joseph H. May, *Some Recollections of Our Anti-slavery Conflict,* Boston, 1869, 375-383; see also Harlow, *Gerrit Smith,* 297-303.
15 Frieda Schuelke, "Activities in the Underground Railroad in Oswego County," *Yearbook,* Oswego County Historical Society, 1940, 10-11.
16 Grove A. Gilbert, "The Annual Pilgrimage of the Oswego County Historical Society, Remarks at Gilbert's Mills," *Yearbook,* Oswego County Historical Society, 1960, 63-64.
17 Edwards to Smith, Dec. 17, 1846, Smith mss.
18 *Ibid.*, Oct. 16, 1850.
19 *Oswego Times,* Oct. 8, 1850.
20 Gallagher to Smith, Dec. 8, 1856, Smith mss.
21 *Oswego Times,* Oct. 18, 20, 1856.
22 *Ibid.*, Feb. 6, 1861.
23 *Oswego Palladium,* Mar. 5, 1866. For further details regarding Antislavery in Oswego County, see Charles M. Snyder, "Antislavery in the Oswego Area," *Yearbook,* Oswego County Historical Society, 1955, 2-12; Charles M. Snyder, "Oswego's Abolitionists and Their Tunnels," *New York Folklore Quarterly,* Summer 1961, XVII, 95-103.

CHAPTER 11

OSWEGO IN THE CIVIL WAR

1   April 13, 1861.
2   *Pulaski Democrat,* May 2, 1861.
3   Sept. 20, 1862.
4   Crisfield Johnson, *History of Oswego County,* 83.
5   *Oswego Times,* July 30, 1863.
6   *Ibid.*, Aug. 1, 1863
7   *Ibid.*, July 31, 1863
8   *Ibid.*, Aug. 5, 1863
9   *Ibid.*, Aug. 22, 1863
10 *Oswego Palladium,* April 8, 1898.
11 *Pulaski Democrat,* May 2, 1861.
12 *Oswego Times,* March 2, 3, 1863.
13 Ibid., June 5, 1863.
14 *Ibid.*
15 L. P. Brockett and Mary C. Vaughan, *Women's Work in the Civil War,* Philadelphia, 1867, 404-415; see also Fred P. Wright, "Elmina Spencer, Heroine of the Civil War," *Yearbook,* Oswego County Historical Society, 1954, 39-46.
16 John B. McLean, *A Brief History of the First Presbyterian Church of Oswego,* Oswego, 1890.
17 April 15, 1865.
18 *Mexico Independent,* April 21, 1865.
19 Edwards to Smith, May 31, 1865.
20 Edwards to Smith, Oct. 25, 1865.

CHAPTER 12

REPUBLICANS AND DEMOCRATS

1   March 25, 1862; Nov. 8, 1861.
2   Oct. 23, 1862.
3   Oct. 25, 1862.
4   April 21, 1863.
5   Sept. 2, 1864; see also issues between Nov. 1863 and Nov. 1864, Littlejohn had resigned from his command in February 1863 and had returned to Oswego from Louisiana. Since there was no special session of Congress his duties did not require his retirement until

December. In personal correspondence he explained that he was marking time in Louisiana and was impatient to withdraw. In an interview he attributed his resignation to pressing business responsibilities.

6   Sept. 2, 1864. Littlejohn's illness may have been a form of Malaria contracted in Louisiana.
7   Sept. 8, 1864. Ira Brown, who had been the editor of the *Times,* had recently retired.
8   *Oswego Palladium,* Sept. 1, 1864.
9   *Ibid.,* July 19, 1872.
10 *Ibid.,* Nov. 1, 1872.
11 *Ibid.,* July 22, 1873.
12 *Ibid.,* Nov. 6, 1872.
13 Edwards to Gerrit Smith, March 6, 1873, Smith mss.
14 Sept. 16, 1874.
15 *Oswego Times,* June 29, 1876.
16 June 23 and 25, 1877.
17 *Oswego Times,* May 25, 1881.
18 See Chapter XIV.
19 Oct. 6, 17, 1882.
20 *Oswego Times,* Oct. 27, 1883.
21 *Ibid.*
22 *Ibid.,* Dec. 31, 1883.
23 *Ibid.,* Dec. 20, 1883.
24 Elting E. Morison, ed., *The Letters of Theodore Roosevelt,* Cambridge, 1951, I, 63; *New York Tribune,* Dec. 10, 21, 31, 1883.

CHAPTER 13

FROM MAIN STREAM TO TRIBUTARY

1   Littlejohn to Smith, May 30, 1864, Smith mss.
2   *Ibid.,* Dec. 15, 1864.
3   June 23, 1890.
4   July 14, 1890.
5   Oct. 10, 1890.
6   *Oswego Times,* Oct. 6, 1890.
7   *Ibid.,* Sept. 15, 1891.
8   *Ibid.,* Dec. 30, 1893.
9   July 16, 1891, Smith mss.

CHAPTER 14

THE MIDLAND AND A RASH OF LESSER RAILROADS

1   *Oswego* Times, April 3, 8, 1863. The Rome and Watertown had been incorporated into the Rome, Watertown and Ogdenburgh Railroad in 1860.
2   *Mexico Independent,* Dec. 14, 1865.
3   *Ibid.,* Nov. 16, Dec. 14, 1865.
4   *Ibid.,* Jan. 4, 1866.
5   *Ibid.*
6   *Ibid.,* Jan. 10, May 2, 1867.
7   *New York Laws,* Ch. 398 (1866); cited in Harry H. Pierce, *Railroads of New York,* Cambridge, Mass. 1953, 18. For a history of the railroad see William F. Helmer, *Ontario and Western,* Berkeley, Calif., 1959.
8   *New York Laws,* Ch. 917 (1867)
9   Smith to Littlejohn, Oct. 12, 1866, Smith mss.
10 Common Council Proceedings, City of Oswego, March 10, 1868.
11 Smith to Bronson, Sept. 18, 1867, Smith mss.
12 Edwards to Smith, Oct. 5, 1867; Jan. 31, 1868; Feb. 27, 1868, Smith mss.
13 Common Council Proceedings, City of Oswego, Aug. 11, 1866, Sept. 4, 1866.
14 Clipping from a Skaneateles newspaper (otherwise unidentified), Aug. 11, 1872, Oswego Co. Hist. Soc. The tracks did not reach Skaneateles, and the town was not bonded.
15 *New York Laws.* Ch. 917 (1867)
16 *Assembly Journal* (1870), 874-875, 1775; *Assembly Journal* (1871), 1395-1396; *Senate Journal* (1871), 1196.
17 *Oswego Times,* Nov. 2, 1869; *American Railroad Journal,* Nov. 6, 1869; See also Pierce, *op. cit.,* also George W. Pratt, "History of the New York Ontario and Western Railroad," (Master's Thesis, Cornell University, 1942).

18 Minutes of the Board of Directors, New York and Oswego Midland Railroad, Cornell University.
19 Pierce, *op. cit.*, 57.
20 *Oswego Times*, Oct. 27, 1869.
21 *Ibid.*, Oct. 22, 1869; *Oswego Republican*, Oct. 23, 1869.
22 *Oswego Palladium*, July 11, 12, 1873.
23 *Ibid.*, Nov. 15, 1873.
24 Quoted in Edward Hungerford's *Story of the Rome, Watertown and Ogdensburgh Railroad, New York*, 1922, 124.
25 Edwards to Smith, July 1, 1864, Smith mss. The Secretary's record of early stock sales in the Oswego Co. Hist. Society.
26 Oswego Co. Hist. Society.
27 Oswego Times, Jan. 22, 1870.
28 *Oswego Palladium*, July 22, Oct. 8, 1872.
29 *Oswego Times*, May 12, 1874. See also Hungerford, *op. cit.* for its purchase by the Rome, Watertown and Ogdensburgh, and its subsequent financial reverses, 124-127.
30 Pierce, *op. cit.*, Table 1, 187; see also Hungerford, *op. cit.*, 105-109, for additional details.
31 Charles Wells, *op. cit.*, 10-22.

CHAPTER 15

EDWARD AUSTIN SHELDON AND THE "OSWEGO MOVEMENT"

1 Mary Sheldon Barnes, ed., *Autobiography of Edward Austin Sheldon*, New York, 1911, 47.
2 *Ibid.*, 76-77
3 *Ibid.*, 78.
4 *Ibid.*, 87.
5 *Ibid.*, 88
6 *Ibid.*, 94.
7 *Ibid.*, 115.
8 *Ibid.*, 115.
9 *Ibid.*, 116.
10 *Ibid.*, 135.
11 Donald Snygg, "Significance of the Oswego Movement in Education," *Yearbook*, Oswego County Historical Society, 1945, 60.
12 Mary Sheldon Barnes, *op. cit.*, 136-137.
13 *Oswego Palladium*, March 26, 1864, June 5, 15, 1865.
14 Herman Krusi, *Recollections of My Life*, Elizabeth Sheldon Alling, ed., New York, 1907, 223. For a comprehensive analysis of Sheldon's contributions see Dorothy Rogers, *Oswego: Fountainhead of Teacher Education*, New York, 1961, 3-57.
15 Herman Krusi, *op. cit.*, 243-244.
16 The statue of Sheldon and the child was sculptured by John Francis Brines, and financed by gifts of pennies by several hundred thousand school children. It was dedicated by Governor Theodore Roosevelt at Albany in 1900, but it was soon relegated to one of the darker recesses of the Capitol. It was removed to Oswego in 1922 and rededicated Finding that it crowded the lobby of the college it was shifted to the lawn. The colorful ceremony was instituted in 1936 on the seventy-fifth anniversary of the founding of the college. Lida Penfield, a professor of English and descendant of one of the area's "first" families (milling) wrote the script. See Dorothy Rogers, *op. cit.*, 40, 93, 139.

CHAPTER 16

DR. MARY WALKER, STORMY PETREL OF THE WOMAN'S RIGHTS MOVEMENT

1 Charles M. Snyder, *Dr. Mary Walker The Little Lady in Pants*, New York, 1962, 49. There is a copy of the letter in the Poynter mss. in the Woman's Medical College of Pennsylvania. Lincoln's reply reads:

> The Medical Department of the Army is an organized system in the hands of men supposed to be learned in that profession, and I am sure it would injure the service for me with strong hand to thrust among them anyone, male or female, against their consent. If they are willing for Dr. Mary Walker to have charge of a female ward, if there be one, I also am willing, but I am sure controversy on the subject will not subserve the public interest.
>
> A. Lincoln
> Jan. 16, 1864

2 Snyder, *op. cit.*, 41.

3 Quoted in Helen B. Woodward, *The Bold Women,* New York, 1953, 292. The unfavorable report was commented upon also by a member of the army board in *New York Medical Journal,* V (1867), No. 2, 167-170.
4 Mrs. Charles Sivers papers, Oswego, New York.
5 Original in the Walker mss., Oswego County Historical Society.
6 Moncure Daniel Conway, *Autobiography,* Boston, 1905, II, 174.

CHAPTER 17

SOCIAL TRANSITIONS

1 Except for a wooden extension this building remains almost unchanged at 69 East Mohawk Street.
2 Substantially remodeled, this house is at 15 Bronson Street.
3 The biographers of Jackson have not corroborated this claim.
4 At 60 West Cayuga Street.
5 A medical center has replaced the "castle" at 42 Montcalm Place.
6 Sloan's villa, its exterior almost unchanged, is at 107 West Van Buren Street. Irwin's mansion at 158 East Sixth Street was razed and its garden carved into building lots.
7 At 40 West Sixth Street.
8 The Kingsford home stood at 270 West First Street. It was removed to make room for Oswego High School.
9 *Oswego Palladium,* June 16, 17, 1887; see also the *Oswego Times,* June 16, 17, 1887.
10 *Oswego Palladium,* June 2, 8, 1883; see also issues of the *Oswego Times.*
11 The building is now the Headquarters (Bates-Richardson) House of the Oswego County Historical Society. Its interior retains its Victorian appointments.
12 It stood on East First Street at the foot of Oneida Street.
13 Claude Bragdon, *More Lives Than One,* New York, 1938, 26.
14 *Oswego Times,* Oct. 22, 1866.
15 *Oswego Palladium,* April 24, 1855.
16 *Oswego Times,* Dec. 9, 1861, June 16, 1862.
17 *Oswego Times,* n.d.

INDEX

279